T0354901

DIGGING UP GRANDPA

Elizabeth Poss Colebrook

Order this book online at www.trafford.com
or email orders@trafford.com

Most Trafford titles are also available at major online book retailers.

© Copyright 2011 Elizabeth Poss Colebrook.
All rights reserved. No part of this publication may be reproduced, stored in a retrieval
system, or transmitted, in any form or by any means, electronic, mechanical, photocopying,
recording, or otherwise, without the written prior permission of the author.

Printed in the United States of America.

ISBN: 978-1-4251-7993-9 (sc)
ISBN: 978-1-4251-7994-6 (e)

Trafford rev. 08/10/2011

 www.trafford.com

North America & International
toll-free: 1 888 232 4444 (USA & Canada)
phone: 250 383 6864 ♦ fax: 812 355 4082

Betts, you have been a joy and inspiration, a teacher and friend for many years. Your courage, wit, wisdom, intelligence, madcap *joie de vivre* and vulnerability shine through every story and poem in this wonderful memoir. Your stories encompass the Zeitgeist of the 20th century. Thank you for your honesty as you share your journey with all of us and thank you for letting me be a part of it.

Rev. Marilyn Johnson

"A delightful read! Wise, Witty and Wonderful. Ms. Colebrook's *memoire* reveals a life well-lived....to the hilt!"

Arden Fowler, Author: "ITALY, My Beautiful Obsession. An American Italophile Falls In Love."

Dedication

My heartfelt thanks to all the dear people who believed I could create this book:

To my father, Louis Poss, my lifetime inspiration and the center of my life, eternal devotion for being my architect.

To my mother, Flora Poss, who was always my staunch supporter whose real spark I didn't appreciate enough until I wrote this book.

Arden Folwer, gifted writer, who insisted I could do it and nurtured me to go for it.

Ronni Miller my first editor.

Phyllis Grumney who plowed through the whole manuscript.

Marilyn Johnson who read through the book with no sleep and checked every word: comma, period, colon, semi-colon.

To Connie Buchler-Gill for her fanciful painting to create the cover design.

And first and foremost to Kim Pease, my loyal and loving typist who struggled through six editing's.

Also to my four children who gave me the stuff to write about and encouraged me throughout the process saying this book will be a memorabilia through the generations to come.

What would I do without devoted friends like this? My love to you all dear friends and family.

Contents

Jess Arouses My Slumbering Muse

Jess Arouses My Slumbering Muse

For many years my muse lay nascent buried in a dark hole under a concrete slab. Then Jessica called to interview me for a fifth grade assignment to write about the life of a grandparent. She chose me and her maternal grandmother. We were so different. The other grandma grew up in a tiny hill town in Italy. She came to the United States when she was sixteen, knowing no English, little education. Admirable and brave. I was a privileged child with the best education available, a premiere girls preparatory school Hathaway Brown and then I went to Vassar, one of the prestigious "seven sisters" private female colleges in New England. We both have become remarkable women.

I was proud that Jess chose me too. I baked cookies, served tea. She brought her tape recorder, her carefully framed questions. We sat cozily in the living room. Our feet on the coffee table. Gradually the decades between us blurred.

Shared secrets poured out.

Like being with a colleague friend I told her about our secret elopement during college. I waxed verbal. Her book "The Life of Elizabeth Poss Colebrook" was done when she was twelve. She typed it on her computer, laminated the paper and put a picture of me as a child in my mother's rose arbor with my child's butter churn on the front cover. "About the Author" she wrote about herself. Her teacher was so impressed she had Jess read it to the school board in our little town. Many parents were there about some big concern. Then she was asked to read it to the County School Board.

The littlest child will get you in the end! Jack had bought a building for me. I, the resident family psychologist, trusted family therapist, having established my practice and named it "Center for Better Living" and working with adolescent groups in the church, I was found out. No clothes on.

I hoped she wouldn't have her interview sent to the state school board next. I had clients who came from all over Ohio. It didn't matter, apparently; clients kept appointments. My workload increased. But the huge pay-off was to me. My daunted muse emerged from the dark hole, pushed up the concrete slab and starting pouring forth her stories.

"If she can do it, why can't I?" I decided I could write a book. I've been writing since I was six years old.

Thank you Jessica. I write to release my soul. The process of writing each story has allowed fresh revelations about family members and about myself. I owe this to the daughter of my son and Rosie, children of my heart.

Jess ready to travel to Europe with the Aurora Band

Jess as a toddler with scant hair

Some years later Jessica wrote:

<u>Slow Down</u>

Slow down
Don't let life go so fast
Or before you know it
Your life will be past
With no fond memories
Or recollection
Of times gone by
A funny selection
Always rushing, always running
Whether physically
Or just in your mind
You speed and rally
Time slips away
And it shouldn't be taken for granted
Or later you'll regret
What may have been presented
Minute by minute
Day by day
Time flutters by
And slips away
Watch how you are perceived
Be wary what you say
You may end up
Regretting it someday
So no matter what your obstacle
Go ahead and climb

Jessica Colebrook 2003

They married by the lake on our property.
The most glorious bride I ever saw

Jack and Jess, before he died, sadly
missing the wedding

Foreword

I will try to write bits and pieces so that you will know the progenitors as well as I can describe them. I will try to let you know me as well as I can. I would like to live long enough to make my scribbling into a fulsome account of the important shaping of my life so that you, my descendants will then know more about yourselves. I know how many questions I wish I had asked all those interesting ancestors.

Every family has secrets--- some, I think most secrets, cripple people- making their lives like fighting out of a paper bag with their eyes closed. As far as I know there aren't any deep, dark secrets- but yes, perhaps a few that may shed some light on your vague unconscious awareness. Some will always remain hidden from all of us.

So I shall begin my saga and hope to finish. I am relishing this introspective search. I hope you will too. I write mainly out of love, I write for those of you who are living and I know: I love those who will come along after I am gone. Oh, to live forever.

Always, always know that I couldn't love each of you more. You are beautiful people inside and out. My greatest treasures- what I would save if my house were on fire are the portraits you had done for me on my seventieth birthday. Sometimes I just stand for a long time absorbing each of you. Your eyes, (your souls), your body language pierces my heart and then puts warm mittens around it. I think of your rosy cheeks in the winter in red snow suits stamping your snowy feet as you burst into the house after coasting at the country club. Hot chocolate and marshmallows.

Ah, times were simpler then; simpler to ease your pains, tend your needs. I wish I could nurture each of you these days as simply, lovingly as I did then. I knew what you needed then and I fulfilled it as best I could.

A Loving Will To My Family

"In memory, we never tire of reflecting on the same events. I spent many summers in my childhood on a farm with an Uncle who told stories endlessly. This, I now see, was his method of working the raw material of his life, his way of turning his experience round and round in the rotation that stories provide. Out of the incessant storytelling I know he found added depths of meaning. Storytelling is an excellent way of caring for the soul. It helps us see the themes that circle our lives, the deep themes that tell the myths we live. It would take only a slight shift in emphasis in therapy to focus on the storytelling itself rather that on its interpretation."[1]

"Care of the Soul"
Thomas Moore

My Husband

What Should I Call Him?

I call him "Jack" in this book and sometimes nostalgically – "Cope." I truly hated the name "Jack". His mother had named him after her dead dog in her usual unpredictably strange way. When he was a toddler he remembered neighbors coming to call. Lying on the old fashioned register in the living room with his bottle, he remembered hearing them ask "How is Jack?"

Mom answered "Jack is dead!" Isn't it amazing that he turned out to be reasonably normal?

In later years after college and marines he was referred to as "Jack." But, in my heart I call him "Cope."

What should I call him?

Here's to you!   *The kindly philosopher*

Prologue

At eighty-seven I find it hard to put those years, experiences, and changes between two covers of a book. My life has been filled with joy, survival, depression, crippling illnesses – mine and my husband's. So many deaths. I was saved from several aborted suicides by family and friends. Desperate times when I could find no hope for the future.

* * * * * *

Poignant Ambiguity

Yes, I always wanted a happy ending. I couldn't envision anything else. Reality set in after we were married and with babies. Then came the drudgery of everyday living after a passionate love affair full of adventure and daring. We settled down to abject poverty in our married life and had two babies. Jack had a swing shift from 3pm to 11pm. There was no life. Living in suburbia we all followed the yellow brick road. Women had no careers. I was desolate, loving my babies, but a deep sense of "Is this all there is," labored within me every day. I was taught at college to go out and "become". But, at Vassar and at Wellesley in the 40's, another message was insistent "find a man, get married." I saw no other future beckoning, but, eventually I made it happen.

* * * * * *

After many intervening years I find I am full of curiosity about the people whose genes, values, and idiosyncrasies I inherited. What was I really like as a child? It didn't occur to me when I was consumed with the gigantic task of becoming myself to think beyond my own skin, to ask the myriad questions that pester me now about those whose cells and visions I came from. What was their childhood like? Why did Grandpa really leave his family in Germany to come to the U.S. when he was fourteen? How did my parents meet and how come they fell in love? Why did they marry? What was life all about for them?

I wonder if it's possible for me to put into words my unformulated spiritual sense of what I think life is about? Digging back in dusty files I find that I started writing when I was six.

My prize came at the end of all those years of struggle during which I survived deadening suburbian life. I had contracted and survived cancer, lived through the convulsions of academia, graduated the oldest person on the platform to receive her doctorate at fifty-eight, lived with the fear that our only son Michael would be sent to Nam to die while he was in the Army, suffered the alienation and death of my much loved father and the contusions of our children's' rebellion and evolution. Through those turbulent years, old values and mores were over-turned and we wondered whether any values would survive – or if our children, like Humpty Dumpty, would never be put back together again.

Now I see my children as strong, questing, loving, creative, family oriented people of whom I am deeply proud. Their devoted love cheers me on.

Moi

As Thomas Moore says, we learn by telling stories. In the process of writing these memoirs I have learned something new about each person in my extended family and myself, as I leaned back in my chair after the last period, letting the knowledge seep into my soul. Writing from the interior gives a new view of our family, our lives, like turning a kaleidoscope of jewels.

Life is a continuous process
of living,
and learning,
and losing,
and laughing
to fill the gaps in between
recovering the
joyous times.

One of my flings

Reminiscing

Each chapter I have written has led to astonishing discoveries. My perception about my family of origin - displacing negatives for positives - such valuable treasures.

I realize how many extreme changes I have lived through, from only radio news and programs, a party telephone, no thought of space travel or other planets, no internet, no real connection with countries outside of the U.S.

Mother and I; unearthed from the dusty storage room

Dad and I

In Mother's garden

Here I am with my
little butter churn

I Was Born And Lived!

The first turning point, and probably the most important one, occurred when I was born: I LIVED. Two of my siblings had died shortly after their births. Maybe I was charmed into life by my ten-year-old sister's prayers for a baby in the family. Then she took one long look at my squalling red face and prayed that I would go back to wherever I came from; however, I was safely taking nourishment.

The first born, a boy, died of infant diarrhea. Hospitals in those early times were not very sanitary. So, Sis was a home birth and lived. Dad had hired a live-in-nurse a month before the due date. The third birth, a little girl was what they called a "blue baby." She died while my father was giving a direct transfusion lying on the gurney next to her. My mother was so distressed; Dad dragged my eight year old sister, Kathryn, in to visit Mother, against all the rules. So I was born at home. My parents never, ever talked about those babies and their desolation. I only know about them through my sister. I have no idea where they were buried or if they had names.

When I was born Dad was forty-three and Mother forty. So, I was "Custer's last stand" and became Dad's "boy."

My first memory is of Mother pulling me on a little sled through deep snow when I was two. We were moving to Aurora for good: renting while my parents had their summer home remodeled for winter living. My life, of course, was forever shaped by growing up in the small town where I put down my roots. I fell in love with my husband-to-be when I was fifteen. Years later, we married and our children grew up in the same little town of five hundred people.

Grandma and Grandpa lived next door. Grandma was my role model. Grandpa was my playmate and best friend. He and I loved all our animals; I rode my pony soon after I learned to walk.

I played with neighboring boys, exploring the countryside, shooting snakes, climbing trees from which I sometimes couldn't crawl down. I loved my tomboy life. Everyone was friendly; it was a safe magical time and my children had the same experience.

My older cousins, Ken and Les, with their parents, Aunt Lottie and Uncle Ernest, occasionally came from Detroit to visit. I adored Les who became a physician. He was a beacon in my life.

Aunt Lillian and Uncle Reuben, Dad's youngest brother, and their son, John, visited from Chardon. My father said Aunt Lillian was strange; so we all thought that way too. It was an innocent childhood. Dad went to work early every day, didn't talk about the depression and the labor strikes against his Worsted Mill in the thirties or his struggles to build his own empire. He washed the dishes at night, rarely complemented Mother on her marvelous meals, but said, "I'd remark if the food wasn't good." Mother responded to his silence by saying, "Nice dinner, Flora." They led separate lives.

Mother was a schoolteacher, but when she married she retired, as was the custom. She kept house, gardened vigorously and started most of the organizations in Aurora. A wonder woman, she was a great organizer, and had a way of getting people together and activated. Mother didn't drive, but always found people to drive her wherever she needed to go.

My only problem was that she left me behind – alone. In the thunderstorms I got scared. It was lonely. But I don't remember complaining.

I knew the days when she was baking bread and came straight home from school to fresh warm bread and butter and homemade strawberry jam. No kitchen ever smelled sweeter.

Mother was rather stern, although kindly. Dad was the humorist from whom I developed a sense of humor and whimsy.

I didn't know until years later how complicated life really was.

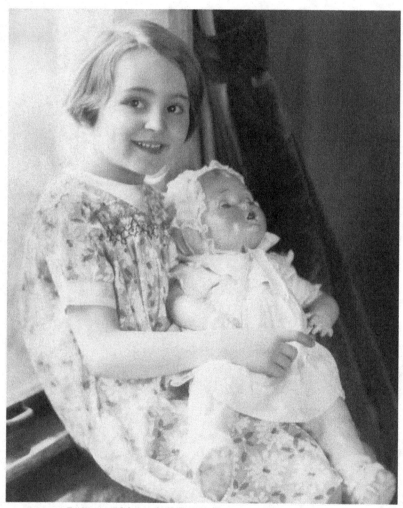

Betts and her doll "Dolly" I loved her most when her eyes fell in

Abandoned

My parents abandoned me when I was five. One day I spied a strange looking big black thing in their bedroom. They had started putting their clothes in it. So I did too. I put my pantywaists, panties and a Teddy bear in it. Every day they were removed. So it went on for days. One day Mother and Dad told me to go over to my Grandparents' house next door.

When I came back my parents were gone and so was my sister, who was fifteen. So was the big black thing. In their place was a woman who turned out to be mean and nasty. I thought they would never come back. They were gone for three weeks or three years. I don't know. I only remember that I was disconsolate and scared. I hid in corners and closets. One day Aunt Addie arrived on the train with a pint of melted chocolate ice cream. Saved by her caring! Yet, no one told me what was happening. This was the first time they left me and took my sister.

They finally came home. I was delivered from such desolation. I have never been able to pack for a trip to this day without intense separation anxiety. Turns out they didn't tell because they couldn't bear to see me cry. They had taken the Canadian Pacific Railroad to Banff, Lake Louise and Vancouver, the new rage of travel.

Betts on Jenny and my proud dad

Our Home
Grandpa's and grandma's
next door to the left

They Gave Me Wings

Recently I drew a picture of my house; it gave me a telescope into my childhood. It was located on Garfield Road in Aurora, Ohio. No address needed then. The house had been a summer cottage thirty miles from Cleveland and from Akron. My father had butcher shops in both cities.

As a boy Dad drove a horse and wagon from Cleveland, where he grew up, to Aurora through uncharted territory to collect the animals for slaughter from farms in the countryside for Grandpa and Grandmother's butcher stall in the Old Central Market. Those thirty miles took him all day and when a wheel broke he had to cut a limb from a tree to repair it. So he knew the Aurora countryside well. He made friends wherever he went and often stayed at Ebenezer Sheldon's home, the first resident of Aurora.

When his parents, my Grandpa and Grandmother Poss, retired and moved to the country, so did we. I was two years old, it was 1925. Aurora remained a small town all the time I was growing up. There were fewer than five hundred people living there including a large community of Mennonite farmers in the countryside. Mother never learned how to drive. She tried but Dad said she had a heavy foot on the gas pedal. I'm still amazed that she gave up because she was feisty. Of course, his was twice as heavy. He drove only one speed: fast. When he had me drive on our motor trips to visit Aunt Addie in St. Petersburg, Florida if there was a speed limit sign he would say "Betts, see that sign, double it." I grew up to have lots of speeding tickets. I walked all over town and knew everybody's name and the names of all their dogs, cats and horses. It was an intimate, friendly feeling and I've loved small towns ever since. I grew up with a sense of rootedness and connectedness and identity. Little did I know that this kindly town would years later turn against us and make pariahs of Cope and me. But more of that later.

Mother and Dad had the summerhouse next to Grandpa and Grandmother enlarged and converted for full-time living. The house sprawled across the ground in its one-floorness with a huge attic and basement the full size of the house. These, along with Grandpa's barn next door, were my favorite play areas. My father, never one to do things in a small way, had a commercial size furnace installed. It filled a whole room.

He brought a commercial size mangle for ironing clothes. When it was put up it almost filled the kitchen. One day it disappeared. The kitchen was clearly Mother's domain.

In the basement I was the teacher and queen of the stove. My parents gave me one of the large basement rooms for my own playroom. The walls were made of big building blocks. I painted them yellow and black, one yellow, one black, etc... as high as I could reach. The combination must have made everyone but me dizzy.

I had a real electric miniature stove. It was black cast iron with nickel-plating and four burners and an oven, just like Grandmother's. Children today have to pretend they're cooking on plastic make believe stoves, not I! I made horrible concoctions on that stove. I had watched and helped my mother cook and bake wonderful things without recipes ever since I could walk, why couldn't I?

My favorite food production was whipped egg white and flour baked in my oven. I suppose I thought I was making an angel food cake. I made my playmates, the neighborhood boys, eat those shoe leather creations. When they wouldn't, as invariably happened, I would lock them in our huge clothes chute with the dirty clothes. There were wood slats on the front of the chute and my buddies looked like animals in a zoo as they crouched among the clothes, holding on to the slats. They must have bought into the rules of the game because I couldn't have lifted them up to the clothes chute by myself; it was four feet off the floor. Of course, one of the boy's nickname was Dumbbell, so who knows? We had some sort of ritual forgiveness, allowing them out of the chute, that I have forgotten.

I think I invented Snow White and the Seven Dwarfs. I fed the little boys and set up a little school with workbooks and lesson plans that I prepared ahead of time. Later in life I founded and taught the first nursery school and kindergarten in Aurora when my children were those ages. I had majored in Child Study at Vassar, my preparation for family and early career as it turns out.

I loved my playroom and I have loved decorating our homes and cooking ever since. I cook to nurture people I care about and I take my cookbooks with me wherever I live, even temporarily, for security, but I rarely use them. A recipe is just a diving board for me to allow all kinds of fanciful additions on the way to the plunge. I make up recipes in my head - and so do my daughters. But I haven't had to lock anyone in a clothes chute lately. I've become a pretty good cook and I haven't seen a clothes chute in a long time.

In the large hay mow of the barn among the bales of hay and straw I was the Queen. My playmates were my courtiers. We were bandits, Indians, cowboys. The possibilities were endless. We moved bales around to construct a palace and a throne, courtyards and caves. We liked to sit around and smoke, "lady cigars," catalpa pods from one of Grandpa's trees. One time I thought it would be even better to smoke one of Dad's Havana Havana's to act as a punk to keep the catalpas lit. I stumbled out of the barn pretty green and sick. William, our gardener and my buddy, carried me into my bedroom past Mother in the living room giving a paper on India to her study club. She looked up as we passed by, but never dropped a word. I am horrified at this distance to think of how dangerous this was to us, the barn and the vulnerable animals I loved so much in the stalls below.

Our attic was a treasure trove. Mother never threw anything away, so the attic was full of stuff we children could use for props for an infinite variety of games and dramas. Two big cedar closets of clothes to dress up in and boxes of photographs of ancestors to laugh at and make up stories about. The attic had a sloping ceiling and a pull-down stairway that we kids could pull up and be snug in our haven. It was a magical place, like a big elves house.

There were no end of things to be discovered. I found one sock that Mother had knitted for a Finnish soldier during World War I. She apparently had never started the second one. I don't know why this seems so poignant to me. But when I think of it lying in her knitting bag, I get a catch in my throat.

The sock inspired us to set up a field hospital. I made beds for the wounded soldiers and gave them medicine. I became Florence Nightingale... Sometimes we just invented stories. Often we wondered to each other what our parents were really like. When we were a little older, we assured each other that our parents never had sex, but wondered how we got here. Or even what "having sex" was like. One boy said they did it standing up in the bathroom.

Years later, I watched with amusement and understanding as my children and their cousins ran for the pull-down stairway to the attic as soon as we got to Grandpa's house - and pulled it up behind them. That old magic! My attic has been many things to me and my children and their cousins.

I had painted an old wooden trunk that I found in the attic bright red with yellow trim. It weighed a ton, but I took it to camp when I was twelve. I must have looked like I just got off the circus train. Later my children loved to dig into my old battered red trunk to explore its musty contents, my old letters from camp, old toys and my camp clothes, every time they went to the attic. I wondered what dramas were unfolding in the nether regions. As I write I appreciate the incredible gift Mother and Dad gave me in letting me express myself, even though sometimes in outrageous ways. For such task-oriented, hardworking Germanic people, it was truly a miracle that they valued my playtime and encouraged me to be fearless. I tried to pass on to my children opportunities like the playroom, the attic and the haymow provided for me, to grow into confident, imaginative adults through child's play.

I realize now that these arenas were the stages where I could explore parts of me and develop my fantasies. They were the embryonic launching pads of my abiding love of the theater. Years later my husband and I started the Aurora Community Theater and I had several leading roles. I evolved from the *ingénue* in *Tender Trap* to the lead rolls in *Pillow Talk* and *Third Best Sport* to Ethel in *On Golden Pond* just a few years ago. My swan song.

Grandad with pipe

Grandpa with Sis and me in his sleigh and Dolly his faithful horse

Digging Up Grandpa

Grandpa knew the Easter Bunny,
I begged him to let me talk to him.

Grandpa said I couldn't
because the bunny only spoke German.

I wanted to be sure
that my red Easter Egg
would be in its annual nest
on our terrace.

It always was
faithfully there until Grandpa died.

I still know the woods
where the Easter Bunny lives.

Cause Grandpa showed me
when we drove
through the county side
in his buggy in the summer and sleigh in the winter.

* * * * * * *

Grandpa taught me German rhymes like this:

A B C dur capte Lieben sche
Vebsurealascum ven sir zeedbrosthzom
Hat sie weibe hosenon

The cat jumped in the snow
And when she came out again
She had no pants on
Our morning ritual was a child's delight
Grandpa came every morning
to pick me up

with his faithful horse, Dolly, with his buggy in summers and sleigh
winters.
Mother wouldn't let me go
till I swallowed my orange juice
and the deadly cod liver oil
I would have taken arsenic
to go with Grandpa

We drove through the countryside
heavy blankets tucked around us
in winter snow in our faces.
Home to Grandpa's down to the wine cellar
where we sampled every keg.
I never asked why
it was a ritual
and a lot of fun.
Grandma would call down
"Put a little sugar and water
in Betty Lou's"
Grandpa just winked at me
"One leetle glass"
hold it up to the light
till he was satisfied.

There were a lot of huge oak kegs
elderberry, dandelion, grape
apricot brandy.

Then Grandpa would seat me on a pile
of books.
We played cribbage
he read to me in German.
One morning on our escape to the countryside
we saw a little boy with a baby goat
a rope and heavy stone
around its neck
the little boy crying
he had been told to drown it.
It was a male and no use
on the farm where they sold goat's milk.

Grandpa and I looked at each other
with complete accord.
No words needed
we jumped out of the buggy
took the goat, hugged the boy
and drove the kid goat home.

Grandpa, ever fanciful,
and I hid the goat in the basement
of my house.
I made my version of gruel
got a small baby bottle
and fed him regularly.
When the kid began to bleat
and try to crawl up
the basement stairs
our secret was out.
My baby had to go to the barn.

We made a stall for Billy
christened by now
in the barn with the two horses,
my pony, the pig and the sheep.
Hens clucked appreciatively
in their coop.
Billy was now an
accepted member of the clan.
Billy followed me everywhere.
Trouble reared its ugly head
when he followed me to school one day.
The principal was not amused.
He ordered me to take him home straight away
and he was never allowed to
come to school again.

Grandpa had bought a cow
named Bessie
when I was a baby
so that I would always

have sweet fresh milk.
One fateful day
the county inspector came
he pronounced Bessie "tubercular"
and took her away
to be slaughtered.
Luckily I did not have tuberculosis.
Grandpa sat on his back porch
Tears creasing down his checks.
I moved my little rocking chair
next to his
we rocked together
I, so anxious to console him
brought over my old saved
valentines
held his hand and
read them to him.

I was five when grandpa's pet white rooster had unexpectedly attacked me
With his sharp angry bill
headlong running at me
I screamed "Grandpa, help"
the hens squealing in the coop.

Grandpa roared out of the barn with his axe

cut off his white rooster's head with one blow

my kind, gentle Grandpa

Angry red cockscomb still lying in the grass,
headless body staggering around:
didn't know he was dead.

Grandpa ended its life with the axe

I was frozen

I knew how much Grandpa loved his white rooster

Knowing for certain how much he loved me.
I hated it when my parents
had to boil me out
and send me to kindergarten.
Playing with beads
could never compare
to mornings with Grandpa.

There came a time
When some of Grandpa's hens died.

Christmas Eve my father drove out to the country
to a Mennonite farm
he brought four bewildered
Rhode Island Reds
into the living room
one settled on the couch

one perched on the lampshade wings fluttering

two at Grandpa's feet

patience, Mother

Dad couldn't stand
to see his father disappointed

later when the hens stopped laying
my father told me to get up

promptly at six o'clock every morning before school
To slip an egg under each hen

he couldn't bear to see him disappointed

I wonder what Grandpa thought
when he reached under
the warm hens
and collected cold eggs

Grandpa died when I was ten
holding his hand at his bedside

the grown ups were
talking grown up talk
In grandma's living room
I just kept holding his hand

never saw a human death before
no, not Grandpa
the joy and nurturer of my life
The rest is a blur

I had another death that summer
so I became a practiced mourner

I was trying to raise a tiny orphan bunny

so small, shivering
when it died

Even after I gave it a
smithering
of Grandpa's homemade apricot brandy
from one of his illegal kegs in his cellar
(Prohibition time)

I buried my bunny silently

The only mourner

everyday as soon as I woke
I dug up my bunny

Still dead

I thought if I could revive my bunny. I could dig up Grandpa
And bring him back to life

He was the center of my childhood

I spent that summer
with a cross of ashes on my forehead
and became a practiced mourner.

Kristina loving her bunny! She carried the bunny torch.

Great Grandpa's Industrial Revolution

Cope's grandfather Edwin worked on an assembly line in a paint factory. The process of filling cans and capping them was slow and laborious. He invented the assembly line and received a raise of five dollars a month! That was the beginning of the industrial revolution.

The company was patriarchal if niggardly. When Great Grandfather's seven sons each developed different diseases with seven different quarantine placards on the front of the house, the company sent men every night to care for the children so the parents could sleep.

That's the way it was back then.

My mother, Flora Amelia Augusta Gedecke Poss

A Theme In The Family –
Bonding Through Gardening

Mother was a gardener! In the winter she poured over catalogues and at the hint of spring, the orders went in. Her name was Flora. She was a beauty. I never knew her before her hair was white, except when it got a little blue or yellow at the old fashioned beauty parlor in Aurora where a permanent would take all day.

Mother had a stolid figure, but a sweet face when she smiled with her dark brown eyes. She was feisty and I thought a little cold, but then, I was a pesky kid. Reading her letters, looking at pictures of Mother now make me realize how deeply loving she was. I mostly remembered her sternness. Excerpts from her letters to my sister at Wheaton College in the '30's show what a complex, totally loving person she was. She even kept track of sis's B.M.'s – she held her as though she were still in her womb. Luckily for me, she let go. She was a dutiful, disciplined woman who worked from dawn to dusk in her home and in the community. She was very involved in community organizations and church activities, describing them thoroughly in her letters. At the age of fifty she started singing in the church choir. I see now how much of an influence she had on my sister and me - we followed right in her footsteps.

Mother was altogether kind. She sent her cleaning lady to Sis's and my house weekly and sent William to do the heavy work. She was loving in so many ways, but never huggy or said "I Love You" though we knew it. I guess that was the Germanic way and the culture of our time.

Mother didn't have canisters for flour and sugar on her counters as we often do today. She had huge bins that opened under a shelf. They each held twenty-five or more pounds of flour and sugar. She was a serious baker.

In her carefully annotated diary she notes "I paid Mrs. Huff two dollars and fifty cents for twelve dozen eggs." Our milk man delivered two quarts of milk: cream on the top so thick one could not easily pour it and two bottles of thick cream everyday.

I remember that we had an ice man who delivered ice daily for our refrigerator.

Mother baked for the community, church functions and friends. I remember hearing her on the telephone one morning while I was still in bed inviting people to a party that day because there were so many leftovers from the day before due to parties celebrating my sister's forthcoming wedding - all seven bridesmaids were visiting.

Not until just now writing my book have I realized all that my mother was. After her mother died at fifty-two, she helped raise younger brothers including Otto, who was blind, and through whom she met Helen Keller and other famous blind women. She managed to complete high school with honors and went on to what was euphemistly called "Normal School" for women. Which meant that it was abnormal at that time for women to go on to higher education.

Mother became a teacher of German for several years before she married my father, her life long companion. Mother was bright, highly intellectual, yet somehow these qualities never shone through to me. Was that my father's attitude?

Mother delivered many lectures on diverse subjects at the clubs she attended. Many of them she founded.

So much of her was buried.

Much of Mother's true creativity and inner satisfaction came out in her gardening. Her gardens were veritable artistic creations. She had large formal English gardens with grass paths, rose arbors and rustic bridges over the stream between our yard and Grandma and Grandpa's. Each variety of flower had its own bed. There were beds of anchusa, larkspur, zinnias, canterbury bells, marigolds, petunias, pansies, flowering nicotina and a tall stand of spectacular delphinium. There was a stone walled garden planted with wildflowers and verdant ferns. A round bed of oriental grass was in front with a gazing pool in back for goldfish. Her strawberry patch was bountiful. During season I had to pick all the ripe strawberries before I could go out and play. Often there were eight quarts.

A path with beds of roses went down the middle of the garden through two arbors covered with climbing roses. Another bed of roses wound along the creek. I helped Mother in the garden and she taught me all the Latin names of the flowers as well as the popular ones. Perhaps her early seeding gave me the impetus to study Latin. I took four years of Latin in prep school and loved it, and achieved high honors on my College Boards. At that time, four years of Latin and four years of another foreign language were the requirements for the female, "Seven Sisters," Colleges of the Eastern Seaboard, where I was destined (by my father) to go. I got honors in the math board too. Hard to believe since it all went in the diaper pails.

My three daughters gardened with me and love their gardens now. Kristina is planting in her desert home in Arizona, but when she visits in our northern and southern homes we plant together in a kind of loving harmony, connecting with our early mother-child bond. My daughter Deborah, who lives with her husband Peter, and two sons, Christopher and Nathan, in North Conway, New Hampshire, financed her green thumb by working part-time in a nursery in exchange for plants. Her gardens are expanding with beauty. She plants in my northern and southern homes and they are the show places of the neighborhoods.

My eldest daughter Susan has become a creative outdoor and indoor gardener, an incredibly creative homemaker and cook. Beside all that she is an outstanding businesswoman.

Our son, Michael, married a gardener. Rosie grew up gardening with her grandfather who was a devoted Italian gardener. Rosie and Michael's children Jessica and Maxwell, are both gardeners. Rosie says at age five Max had the soul of a true gardener. Rosie's gardens wouldn't dare have weeds- so carefully does she tend them. Continuity! And now Max has been working for me during his summers off from College (where he receives honors) hallelujah! It has become a treasureful bonding.

My most successful child garden was the one I planted on top of Grandpa's manure pile. I grew, "Love Over the Fence," that was about ten feet tall. I felt like Jack and the Beanstalk. The animals provided plenty of manure and compost to nurture the gardens. I can't remember a weed or a disease in Mother's gardens - there were acres of beauty.

I went into business when I was four. I combined my budding culinary arts with my love of flowers and baked mud pies in the sun - pressing a flower on top of each for decoration. When I got bored with the flower motif, I found a box of keys to the house and pressed a key on top of each mud pie. Soon the keys were all gone. I had a little red wagon and sold those pies all over the neighborhood for two cents each. It didn't seem to matter to my parents - we never locked our doors anyway. My father even seemed to think it funny. A neighbor, Mrs. Johns, kept one of my mud pies in her safe all the years until I was married and gave it to my husband at our wedding. He lost it in twenty minutes. I don't think he was interested in my mud pies.

The back of our property was lined with fragrant mock orange bushes tumbling down a small hill and hiding the railroad tracks that ran behind. I drifted into sleep with the lulling sound of long freight trains. I can still hear the staccato rachety-ratch theme over the heaving rumble of the trains. During the Great Depression hobos jumped off the freight trains where they had hidden in boxcars or in hammocks slung underneath and came to our house, to our mother for food and clothes. I think they had marked a spot behind our house because they knew Mother would never turn them away. Nor did she - but in her Germanic way, she always had some sort of job for them to do in return. She probably invented the W.P.A. (Works Progress Administration) and the C.C.C. (Civilian Conservation Corps)

Mother had a large vegetable garden across the creek on our grandparents' property and an acre more of vegetables across the street. They were bountiful and the canning that went on was awesome. Mother made sweet and sour red cabbage for a church dinner once and apparently not many people ate it. She canned what was left. Dad and I would look at each other and grimace every time it made yet another appearance at the dinner table. That was known as the, "winter of red cabbage."

Mother had a full-time hired man to help in this big gardening enterprise. He was Finnish. His name was William Anderson. William was of medium height, lean and spare with a sweet leathery face. Typically, he showed no emotion but he loved my mother and I think he loved me.

William was a binge drinker. Sometimes when he was a bit sloshed he would come to see my Mother and pull his pictures of his Finnish family out of his pocket to show her and cry with loneliness and yearning. I never knew why he left home or even how old he was. When he reappeared sober after a toot he was a wreck. He would ask Mother for some money, "to taper off," and she would give it to him as though she understood in spite of the fact that she never had a drink in her life except once and she thought it was fruit juice. Then, presiding over the elite Shaker Study Club, she kept putting her hat on backwards when she was fixing her appearance in the Ladies Room.

Once when we took a motor trip to Washington D.C. for a few days, Dad sternly admonished William (as was his wont) to take good care of the horses and the other animals. "Don't desert your post," said Dad. And William didn't. When we got home and drove the car into the barn there was William sprawled at the feet of Dad's horse, dead drunk - but as Mother and I said, "He didn't desert his post!"

William was so good to me while I trailed around watching him work. His English was not bad but he could never manage the "Js." He used to say, "I did a nice-a yob on yenny," after he had curried and combed my pony Jenny.

He liked to chew tobacco. I used to practice being William and sit under the huge carved walnut dining room table chewing coconut while I tried to teach Mother's cleaning lady, Mrs. Huff, how to speak the German I learned from Grandpa. I wrote all the phrases and poems phonetically in my little lesson book. Poor Mrs. Huff, bad enough having to put up with this kid around, then the kid tries to be her teacher. Mrs. Huff, a thorough-going Yankee, had to work at saying, "eech," instead of, "ik," over and over again while I chewed coconut under the table.

William went on a colossal binge after Mother died and tearfully told my father that he couldn't come to work on our yard anymore without my mother. To my agony my father let everything go to weeds. The garden had been the pride of the county and Dad loved walking people around it, telling the names of dozens of varieties of roses. But after Mother died, he didn't care about it. Whether the heart went out of it for him as it had for William or whether he resented Mother's preoccupation with gardening, I will never know, but the day after the funeral, he charged out and cut down Mother's favorite cherry tree behind the house - the only physical labor I ever saw him do around the yard. Perhaps it was a rite of exorcism.

I was inescapably aware of my parents' complicated relationship. I grew up playing the role of the "cheerful little mascot" to keep my parents happy. It occurs to me that I have been triangulated all my life.

My father lived for many years surrounded by his weeds, his children and grandchildren to whom he gave a great deal. He was outstandingly successful in business. He and my mother were the impetus to my strivings. As I write my memoirs I am more profoundly aware than ever of my parents' caring gifts to me for my happy, full childhood.

Post- Script:
William died a pauper and an alcoholic. My sister and I were the only mourners at his graveside.

Deborah dug into the musty storage room and unearthed a priceless photograph book of my babyhood: full of Mother holding me – loving me.

I am filled with joy and peacefulness.

Deborah devoted to her garden

Mother prunning her rose bush

William our faithful gardner

Mother with me in the wheelbarrow

My Dad

My Father, A Masai Warrior

This is the hardest chapter I have written because I was so close to my father; I couldn't gather myself to write about him – so painful because of our close relationship and subsequent, unforgettable alienation.

Dad was my hero. He was my architect, my inspirer, my sweetheart. I wanted to be everything he wanted me to be. Except a Republican, the party he had stood for all his life against all Democratic programs. When he heard at the dinner table that I had voted for F.D.R. and I passionately defended my view, he had apoplexy. We never discussed politics again. However, he would mutter "those pinko professors" when he visited the once so coveted Vassar Campus.

Stories about Dad's boyhood abound in family lore. When he was young, one of his jobs was to deliver meat to peoples' homes. He stopped at the servants' entrance and waited while the cooks inspected each piece of meat suspiciously. One of the largest estates was the Hodgson's – there he experienced the worst of indignities, being treated like a servant boy.

A definitive event recorded in family memory took place when he was reading a book one day during his fifth or seventh grade class (I don't know which because the story of which grade has become apocryphal during the years). His teacher said "Louis, put down that book and listen to me or you will never learn anything!" He promptly said, "Well, I will never learn anything listening to you": emptied his desk, walked out of the room and thus ended his formal education. He was so bright and so shrewd he carved out his own empire, though his teacher probably thought he would never amount to any good.

He started his own business when he was twelve with a small kiosk in his neighborhood selling meat. For generations the Poss family had been butchers. But it appears that my father didn't want to do that forever. He decided to rent a stall downtown in the new central market, his Uncle John counseled him, "Lou you will never make it downtown. This is a man's world." Dad said, "Just watch me!"

Of course, he became very successful and moved on to establish seven meat stores in Cleveland and Akron. There seemed to be no

Mother wrote this!

Dad as a young man on a weekend trip in Aurora,
he is on the right

obstacle Dad couldn't breach, except controlling me and the Unions; they finally beat him many years and battles later.

His second grade Sunday school teacher, Mr. Stafford, was so impressed with the workings of my father's mind that he followed his career and enlarged his opportunities. He selected him to be on the Boards of the Union Trust Company, and the Sheriff Cold Storage Company, where Dad eventually was voted president.

Then O.M. (as Dad referred to him) arranged an interview for Dad at the Board meeting of the Cleveland Worsted Mill, which was facing bankruptcy.

Dad didn't know one thing about a worsted mill. The mills were located all over New England with the main mill in Cleveland. The board considered Dad because of his reputation as a shrewd business man. It was during the Great Depression and businesses were folding right and left.

The auspicious meeting was scheduled for nine o'clock in the morning. Dad arrived at seven-thirty through a rear entrance and toured the progress of the raw wool through its winding fourteen buildings processes to finished cloth. When Dad walked into the meeting, he simply said "Gentlemen, I'll tell you what's wrong with your operation." Open jawed, they hired him to be President, when the subject of salary came up my father said, "I don't want any salary for my first year; we'll see what happens. After that I will name my own salary."

Dad's pride was regained when many years later the Board of the failing Cleveland Worsted Mill named him president, superseding then president, Mr. Hodgson.

Thence, one week-end Dad had Mr. Hodgson's mahogany office walls torn down, all accoutrements removed, nothing left but his desk and brass spittoon. Head bowed, he left.

He closed all the mills in New England, leaving the towns destitute but resolving the wasteful process of rail transport weaving around the country. He consolidated all the processors into the fourteen building

Cleveland plant; with a dye works in Ravenna where the mill owned lakes and water was plentiful.

Just before World War II broke out, Father bought a million dollars of wool still on the sheep's backs in Uruguay – a dangerous risk representing billions of dollars today and the question of the farmers honoring the agreement and of safe delivery through mined seas.

The wool was stacked in huge mounds, covered with canvas all over the mill parking lots. His was the only mill able to supply all the needs of the war to come: uniforms, upholstery for planes and trains, etc. When one of the workers, who were mainly displaced people from central Europe, complained to my father about his meager salary, Dad replied "how much are you making? That's that much more than I am."

He replaced antiquated looms and other hand operated machinery with the latest technology from Warner and Swasey Company.

My father fought off all the efforts of unions to take over the mill. One time we drove to Florida. He discovered that the mill had struck as soon as he left so he turned right around and drove non-stop twenty-four hours in a Ford car of the thirties: broke through the union lines and held his fort in the mill. He suffered from pepper spray, but miraculously was otherwise unscathed.

He organized the faithful workers and my sister, age sixteen, to break through the union lines in a stream of cars. Headlines in the Cleveland newspapers called him "The White Haired Tyrannical Union Hater." They got that right!

When he suffered his first stroke, we took him to Cleveland Clinic. I went to see him early the next day fearing I would not find him alive. He was lying flat in bed, sheet up to his neck, sides of his bed up. He pulled the sheet down and there he was: completely dressed, suit, vest, white shirt, tie and shoes. "Young lady you are taking me to the Worsted Mill Annual Meeting." "Daddy I can't. You haven't had tests for a diagnosis and treatment plan and no release has been signed." He jumped out of bed and said in his commanding voice, "Young lady, we are going now."

The meeting only lasted ten minutes, but he foiled the plan for a takeover and home we went. Father triumph! A true Masai warrior without a spear, just guts.

After he could no longer defend the Worsted Mill from unionization, he closed the mill. He declared, "This will be no fire sale," my father sat at his desk alone in his fourteen buildings until the last piece of machinery was sold.

There came a time when he grew angry at my husband when Jack retired from his presidency at the storage company and recommended selling it, as it was too antiquated to compete with modern ones. A world known financier offered Dad a job. My father said, "I have never worn another man's horse collar and I am not going to start now." Dad stopped every afternoon at our house and screamed at me in unforgettable rage. He was furious with Jack for wanting to sell; though that is what he would have done when younger. I guess he couldn't face closing another company.

He would not hear any of my responses. It grew so painful and intolerable I stopped being home or visiting him. I was thus triangulated between the two men I loved most.

When he had his final stroke he was paralyzed on his right side, unable to speak or write. The last time I saw him alive a tear trickled down his cheek. Mine were awash with longing tears.

That day as I was weeding in my garden, I had a sudden flash that I needed to be somewhere. I jumped into my car and went to the university believing it was the day I had to register for classes. Standing in line my intuition told me I should be at the hospital. I drove about one hundred miles an hour. At the third floor I knew he had just died. The nurse paled when she saw me get off the elevator. She said "you can't go in there, your father just died." "I know it, that's why I'm here."

There he lay stripped of his old lion's robe, pale and vulnerable. Only from this distance do I realize I couldn't have changed things. He was no doubt in the beginning stage of dementia or Alzheimer's. It helps a little bit.

Writings Saved By Dad

After my father died, these early writings of mine were discovered in his office safe with some of his important papers. I was so touched I sank to the floor and wept. Some tears were of devoted love. Some bitter, realizing that I hadn't been able to heal the alienation he died with and I lived with forever.

What I Saw

(Written In 1931 When I Was 8 Years Old)
From My Father's Office Safe After All These Years.

One night when the Moon was hidden behind a cloud.
I saw, what do you think I saw?
I saw a little grasshopper pulling a hickory nut.
And inside, what do you think?
There were twelve little fairies.
They were having the best time.
There was a little fairy in front riding on a butterfly.
She had a little firefly on a stick.
So she could have some light.
They hopped far and wide.
I followed them.
After a while we came to a little grass tunnel
we went in it.
After awhile we came to a secret beautiful dining
room.
It was lighted with diamonds.
After they ate they went to a secret door.
They opened it.
And where do you think it led to?
Why it led right into our house.
The house was all messed up.
They got busy and cleaned it all up.

Betts leaning on a war canoe

Letter From Camp
Innocent Enough To Drive Parents Crazy
Age Thirteen
(Unearthed From My Father's Safe In His Office)

Dearest Dad,

It certainly is a good thing I came to this camp, I certainly have had an experience I couldn't have had at many other camps! We had a nice service yesterday morning. Very simple, four hymns and a prayer then scripture reading. They take a collection for girls who are too poor to go to camp, and they help them to go out into nice families! Last night we had counsel fire, but since it was raining we had it in assembly with a grate fire. We all put on our pajamas and stretched out on the floor. They read the first issue of "Arey 'Appenings" it was very good – Louise Morley, Christopher Morley's daughter is editor and she is swell. You know one night at dinner we were all talking about the girls who are daughters of famous men and they said that about Christopher Morley and I said who is he? And Lou said, "don't you know who he is" so I said – "no, you see I came from Ohio." So the kids always tease me and say – oh, you know she comes from Ohio. Oh dear, to get on with the story – we stayed in assembly until about 11:30 o'clock last night because it was just pouring and thundering – it was terrible – so we all sang songs to keep from going to sleep. We finally went to our tents and to sleep! At about 2 o'clock I woke up and there was a small gale blowing up in our tent there was about an inch of water there so I fastened down the sides and tried to wake Bimley, my tent mate – but no sale. So I piled everybody's suitcases, tennis rackets, etc, etc, from off the floor on my bed and tried to sleep. I was sopped by that time and tried to squeeze between things. So pretty soon we were waked up and told that the flood had one tent to go and it would hit on us. We looked out and saw rushing water through the tents in Junior Row, beds, bureaus, trees, trunks, everything flowing along – some kids lost clothes – the "admiral" one of our war canoes sunk. Whole tents being pulled apart and people just sopped carrying the little kids in. We ate breakfast thinking of all our things floating down, but our tent didn't even get very wet except the floor!! One of the kids got bitten by a chipmunk and another by a snake – while pulling a bed or something out of the lake. So we all have to get tetanus shots tomorrow.
Love Betts

Aurora Train Station and old steam engine

Our first 4th of July parade

Written About 1936 While I Was Thirteen
Years Old
And Just Unearthed From A Box Of
Mementoes In 1996

AURORA

There's nothing quite like a small hometown to create, to mold, and to form in all ways its citizens from birth until death with infinite care. And such a town is Aurora. According to original plans, Aurora was destined to be a thriving metropolis. In fact, according to these same plans, it was to vie with Cleveland in importance and population. A wide thoroughfare was built by some person with questionable foresight in order to join these two large cities. Aurora's present total population, however, is five hundred people, counting, of course, the farmers!

This whole sad tale can be explained all too briefly; Cleveland happened to be located on one of the Great Lakes, and Aurora had the Chagrin River flowing to Lake Erie. Cleveland's giant factories and magnificent stores expanded and businesses abounded.

Even though these two towns were founded at the same time, about one hundred fifty years ago, there is a distinct difference in their present appearance. Two grocery stores, two post offices, two gas stations, two garages, a depot, a telephone exchange, a hardware store and lumber and coal yard make up the commercial center of Aurora. We have an up-to-date fire department with two vehicles. One of them is my father's old 1920 Cadillac converted to a red hook-and-ladder truck. On the amusement side we find a country club and pool, one church, a town hall, a community hall, a school, two beer parlors, and the far-famed Aurora Inn. Quite enough diversion. I don't think I need to go into Cleveland's figures on similar buildings, and besides, who likes blunt contrasts?

Our river was destroyed by a flood in 1913. It was choked with debris, fallen trees and boulders piled up by the force of the waters. Aurora's cheese factories were swept away. Her maple sugar camps suffered severe setbacks since the Chagrin River was the vehicle of transit to the Great Lakes and then across the country.

During the twelve years of its incorporation, this busy little town of ours can boast of the fact that it has had the same Mayor, the same Marshall, and the same deputy Marshall, which all shows that on the whole, we are pretty satisfied customers and life runs along rather smoothly. There are, of course, our biennial elections when rival parties rise up and a great deal of antagonism is in full sway. These flare-ups are inevitably short-lived, however, and our ever-faithful and habitual office holders are again reinstalled.

This morning in church, our minister, who has held his post for ten years, announced an open-house and reception at the church for an old couple who will be celebrating their fiftieth wedding anniversary in a week. The church bells will be rung and the wedding march will be played. The happy man in this case is none other than the church janitor who has taken care of this job for many years.

One of the most inimitable of our modern conveniences is our unique telephone operator. Almost any night of the week, and especially on the weekend, she can tell when you ask for a certain number "They're up at Colebrook's this evening. Quite a party I guess." Or "the littlest one, Jeannie, is down with the flu, the doctor is there now. I don't think you ought to bother them" or "Gert Colebrook just went by with her hat on. She's probably going to Cleveland." In her way this rare and gifted woman reigns in all the affairs of Aurora.

Such is the genial intimacy and fine community spirit in our town that last Saturday, when I visited the grocery store in my search for the daily quota of flies for my chameleon, I received the whole-hearted cooperation of all present. Step ladders went up, fly swatters were pulled out of the traditional moth balls, and everyone joined me in the hunt. The number of flies available in a grocery store is positively amazing!!

It is just such insignificant little details as these that make Aurora what it is – a place loved by all who have ever lived in it and have become a part of it. To the young people it extends its embracing and protective old arms, and our roots become firmly attached. I never realized how deeply this affected my life.

(This was written with so many emulations of my father's expressions imbued in me; I see what a huge influence he had on me – always.)

Mother and Aunt Addie, Aurora ladies lawn party

Heart Song

"My dearest darling Aunt Addie," I wrote when I was eight: "I miss you so much. I want you to come back from Florida. I don't like it when you go away. Mother had a birthday party for me yesterday. We had seven girls and I got seven handkerchiefs. I ate so much cake and ice cream, I had to stay home from school today." The handkerchiefs wouldn't do for an eight year old today! They are not electronic.

It's possible some people would have thought Aunt Addie homely. But I loved her every wrinkle, pug nose, milky blue eyes. To me, her face was a lovely sunbeam, and she walked in grace. Aunt Addie told me a lot of little ditties. I learned which ones I could say in front of grownups. Not this one, I discovered!

> "Dimity, Damity Dust
> I hate like the devil to cuss
> But damn-it to hell
> I like it so well
> I have to do it or bust."

When I asked her what her real name was she would always say, "Adelaide Safira Jones Melissa Annaceaser." She was my mothers' best friend, and I loved her completely. I was thankful I wasn't named after her.

Auntie had endless patience with the probably demanding child that I was. She often walked with me to the little creek, nearly dried-up Chagrin River that crossed Route 82, our street, at the foot of John Gould's Hill. I skipped pebbles into the water and watched them bounce along the water, spreading ripples on and on. I never wanted to stop while there was another pebble in sight. Auntie taught me another favorite I learned not to sing for Mother's friends at her missionary committee meetings.

Jesus loves me this I know
Cause the Bible tells me so
I am Jesus' little lamb
Oh, goddamn-it, Yes I am!

She took me to the Euclid Beach Park in Cleveland; the amusement park was full of delights for a small child. More than the roller coasters and all the other rides, I was fascinated with driving the electric cars around the track. Endlessly I begged to go again. When Auntie said, "Now this really is the last time," I wanted it to last forever. I drove so slowly that I stalled out. All the kids behind me were stuck in a line, and the operator had to come and push red-faced me to the exit.

Her health was not good, but she never complained. She had severe arthritis that she took mysterious "gold pills" for. She and most of her family had tuberculosis while she was growing up. Her father and some of her siblings died. Nevertheless, when I asked, "Auntie, how come you're always so happy?" she replied, "I had a wonderful childhood." She went on to tell me that although they didn't have money, the children played all kinds of games and their parents often joined in. They made popcorn and strung it with cranberries to festoon the Christmas tree their father brought in from the nearby woods. "We were a happy family," she always said.

Aunt Addie had been a seamstress, making clothes, curtains and slipcovers in the various wealthy homes where she was employed. She married Dr. Hill late in his life. All I remember of him was he was a small man, with a gray mustache and a Van Dyke beard. He smoked a tiny pipe my father liked to poke fun at.

They had a cottage in St. Petersburg, Florida, for wintering, and an apartment in East Cleveland for summers.

When Dr. Hill died, Aunt Addie gave up the apartment and lived with us in the summers. She slept in the front bedroom. That was the best time of the year for me. Probably not for Dad: Auntie and Mother were best friends. Dad worked long hours building his business empire, sometimes getting up at 3:30 a.m. to make the rounds of his butcher shops, storage company and the Worsted Mill. His only avocation was riding horses with Sis and me. So mother cherished Aunt Addie's companionship.

When I was a teenager Auntie would wait until I got home from a date and invite me into her room. With a wink, she'd open a drawer in her bedside table; hidden there were a few precious cigarettes. We smoked together as I told her all about my evenings. When I would come home red-eyed from crying after a date with the man I would eventually marry, she would ask "Why do you go out with him if he makes you cry?" "I guess I love him but we get into fights," I'd whimper.

Years later, Aunt Addie shared a light, airy apartment in Cleveland with two friends, Mary and Eda, who although they were elderly (as was Aunt Addie) still held nursing jobs. When my first two children were young we'd visit her as often as we could. Then when my second two children arrived. I would take them. They too have fond memories of being with Auntie.

Auntie had the same patience with Michael and Suzie as she had had with me as a child. She let them throw sofa cushions down to the ground from the big porch, run down the three flights of stairs, bring them back up and throw them down again. She let Suzie play the antique organ, never minding the discord as her hands ran up and down the keys while she pumped away. "The organ will be yours someday," she said to Suzie. Today it stands in Suzie's living room, a poignant memory of the woman who loved her dearly.

One day, I dropped in to visit Auntie at lunchtime. Though surprised and delighted, she was distressed that there was nothing "good to eat." We had crackers with blue cheese and orange marmalade. To this day when I feel nostalgic about Auntie I haul out the blue cheese, marmalade, and crackers, and I am back there with her, feeling loved through and through.

When Eda and Mary decided to retire from their nursing jobs, Aunt Addie was not included in their plans. She was devastated to be thus abandoned. She had outlived her other friends, as well as her inheritance from Dr. Hill. I felt I had to find a way to care for her.

Luckily I found a room in Aurora, near our home, in a big old house that had been a hotel during the stagecoach days. Now owned by Mrs. Wolfe, who had an antiquated hairdressing salon in the front, and rooms for several boarders on the second floor. The third floor, once a ballroom, she kept all to herself. Mrs. Wolfe cooked all the meals for her boarders and when necessary tucked them in bed at night.

One day Auntie looked ruefully at her once lithe, graceful hands saying "look at these hands. They look like chicken feet." I could do nothing but kiss them. I said, "I love you, Auntie." Now I look at my hands – "chicken feet." I don't kiss them. And I don't love them.

Auntie often came to dinner at our house. I tried to do as much as I could for her but with four children and a busy life, I always felt guilty that I couldn't do more. I remembered the countless hours she had given me as a child.

Then the time came when Mrs. Wolfe became a menace on the roads. The finale, after many unreported accidents, was backing into a police car and almost demolishing it. Since she had become incompetent in performing her other tasks too, her daughter put her in a nursing home and put the house up for sale. We had to find a retirement center for Aunt Addie.

We found a marvelous place. It was attractive and the care giving abundant. Auntie was happy there but she was becoming progressively blind. She remained sightless and silent for her remaining years, but her helplessness bred anger. She gave up on life for the first time. We tried to help. The Braille watch we gave her infuriated her. She threw the box in a drawer and spent heartbreaking hours in darkness.

Aunt Addie's funeral was dreadful. She lay still and silent in a casket. Yet I knew no casket was large enough to contain her essence. I was certain her soul had flown away to some place I could not reach, but the nurturing, playful part of her would find immortality in my family through generations.

No one was at the funeral except a minister who didn't know her, two nieces who had never paid attention to her, and my husband and I. There was no one to stand up and say what a remarkable, loving, loyal woman she was. No one to weep and bemoan the loss, the bitter end of a proud woman. No one but me, and I was frozen in grief. My husband put his solid arms around me and that was good. Best of all, though, would have been to hear her voice just once more, chanting,

> "Dimity, Damity Dust
> I hate like the devil to cuss

But damn-it to hell
I like it so well
I have to do it or bust."

Grandma Revisited

When I was thirteen I saved my Grandma's life. It was a cold winter Thursday night; the one night my mother and father went out together. I was never allowed out on school nights, so when they went out on Thursday nights, I did too. Aunt Addie was living with us at the time and she never ratted on me. She knew I would get my schoolwork done, and that I was always on the honor roll. Usually, I went to the Browns' house to visit my friends Betsy and Jeannie. Nobody studied there, and all the kids who could get out went. The Brown girls both failed at school.

But that particular Thursday night I said to Auntie, "You know I was going to visit my friends, but somehow I don't feel like going out tonight." About twenty minutes later, the phone rang. I heard a kind of gurgling and then the phone went dead. Those were the days when we had party lines and a telephone operator who knew all about us. Bessie Hickox was ours. Bessie, listening as always, said, "Betty Lou, I think that call came from your Grandma's house." I threw on my coat and rushed next door to Grandma's.

I saw a huge flash of light through the kitchen windows. The rest of the house was coal dark. When I opened the kitchen door, I was blinded by stinging smoke and flames. I screamed, "Grandma, where are you?" There were sounds coming from her pantry, and I groped my way in. Grandma was disoriented, fumbling in the dark. I said, "We have to get out of here fast." The smoke was dense and the flames were shooting out all over, moving closer to us. Grandma said, "I am not leaving. This is Father's house!" For a moment I hesitated – she was the adult and I was the kid. I said, "Then I'll stay here with you." All of a sudden I became an adult. Such is the strength of love and the survival instinct; the adrenaline rush in crisis. I metamorphosed into the adult and lifted Grandma up and deposited her over my shoulder like a sack of flour and raced out of the burning house. Looking back I saw the flames consuming the kitchen where we had been standing. Running on the path under mother's rose arbor toward our house, I saw flames licking the roof, and there was a loud blast as the fire blew off part of the roof. I called Auntie who was standing by our sunroom door, "Call the Fire Department."

I set Grandma down in my father's big easy chair. She looked so tiny, singed black and blue.

Just then Dad and Mother burst through the door. They had seen our policeman, Art Hall, at the top of the hill and the fire engine below in our driveway. "Where's the fire?" Dad had asked Art.

"I'm afraid it's your mother's house, Lou," Art said.

I had never seen my father terrified before. He was always in control, but now his face was ashen as he took in the fiery scene and the sight of his indomitable little mother so bruised. He brought a shot glass of whiskey to Grandma from the bottle in the refrigerator. He, who never touched the stuff except for "medicinal" purposes. Grandma straightened up as best she could and with dignity coined this immortal phrase; "I'll take this without the whiskey, Boy."

Tossing in the night I thought of what would have happened if I had gone along with my usual Thursday night schedule. Grandma burned to death in her house and I laughing with my friends. A guilt I would live with forever. How tainted life would have been.

As soon as she was able, Grandma told us what had happened. Ready for bed, she had opened the cellar door to check on the coal furnace. The furnace door had sprung open. Flames flew out from the old coal furnace and ignited all of Grandpa's huge wooden casks of wine. When she opened the door, the rush of air made the furnace explode. The wine kegs blew up, and the force of the explosion upward knocked Grandma off her feet. Her shoulder was broken in the fall. All of Grandpa's specially made wine covered the cellar floor. Looking back now, I notice that nobody remarked at my bravery or sudden strength in emergency. In our house it was expected that everyone perform his or her duty.

While my father had her house rebuilt, Grandma lived with Aunt Julia and Uncle Carl, about a mile away. It was 1936, and Grandma was eighty years old when this happened. They had used an outhouse behind Grandpa's vineyard. In the rebuilding process, Dad had the house modernized, with two bathrooms and other conveniences. I often wonder now how those months of living with her fussy youngest daughter were for Grandma, used to being the queen of her domain.

I thought Grandpa was IT because he was my playmate, teacher, and nurturer. I always recall Grandpa making wine in the cellar all through prohibition. But just as I rediscovered my mother in the process of writing memoirs, I am rediscovering Grandmother. Grandma was the stalwart one. She "held the fort," as my father said. She had borne four children: my father, Louis, the eldest, Lottie, Julia, and Reuben. Grandma and Dad idolized each other. "Louis," she said, "no one will ever love you as much as I do." That effectively dealt with my mother. She worked with Grandpa in the meat stand, in the Old Central Market in Cleveland, and although poor, the two daughters went to college – Aunt Lottie to the Oberlin Conservatory of Music and Aunt Julia to Hiram College. It is interesting to me that a college education was provided to the girls. I think my father paid for them with his youthful hard-earned money. Fascinating that dad with virtually no formal education; valued it all through his life. He also sent his younger brother to college, and many other young people.

By the time I was born, Grandma was sixty-six. I thought she was very old. She was not quite five feet tall; she wore her white hair brushed back into a twist, and wore tiny spectacles. The upper part of her body had slipped down to her hips, so her figure was sort of squat. Her nose looked like a mushroom that had been squashed. We all privately hoped we wouldn't inherit Grandma's nose.

Grandma had a ready laugh. I never saw her frown or get angry or be less than positive. A wood stove and kerosene stove were in the kitchen. I remember her clothesline filled with sweet-smelling washing. Grandma used a hand washboard and irons that she heated on the coal stove when she ironed her beautifully snow white starched clothes and bedding. Until the day she died, Grandma made delicious bread and kuchens for all of our households on Saturdays. Our daughter, Deborah, has Grandma's kuchen recipe and is carrying on our tradition-making six or seven at a time with a small child in one arm and another tugging at her skirt.

When I was growing up I could smell the *hasenpfeffer* Grandma was cooking, I would just sort of show up at dinnertime. I didn't know it was rabbit until I was an adult or I probably wouldn't have eaten it. I'm glad I didn't know; it was so good.

I must have had a little nasty streak in me when I was a kid. I was only allowed in the immediate neighborhood on Halloween. So what to do with that restless bar of soap in my pocket? I soaped Grandma's windows! The next day I watched with consummate guilt as she patiently scrubbed away at those windows, never a word of complaint or accusation.

Weddings and funerals were big events in our small town of five hundred people. No invitations were issued, so anyone who wanted to could come to the services. Grandmother never missed one. She always wore her long purple *moiré* dress with a black hat and white gloves. Inevitably there was a man handy at the church steps, and she would say, "Give me your hand, Boy." Every man up through his eighties was a "Boy" to her.

One day when I visited Grandmother, I caught a glimpse of a white cloth wrapped around one knee. I said, "Grandma, what is the cloth for?" "Oh nothing," she replied. I insisted that she let me take the cloth off to see what had happened. Grandmother's daughter, Julia and son, Reuben, were Christian Scientists. I don't know if Grandma was too! She had a huge ulcerated sore on her knee. "Grandma, I have to call the doctor," I said. She firmly remonstrated, but I did it anyway. Our old country doctor took one look at that badly infected knee and said, "You have to go to the hospital." Grandma had never even walked inside a hospital. She said, "No, Boy, I'm not going to do that!" Dr. Chamberlain said, "You leave me no choice but to cut it out right here." Whereupon he did - no anesthetic, no sterile gloves, no antiseptic. It was very deep, but she never let out a cry or a complaint, while I almost fainted. With repeated house calls, the ulcerated hole cleared up.

Grandma made her life happen rather than letting life happen to her.

Grandma changed to an afternoon dress every day after lunch and went into the living room to listen to the radio and receive company. I don't think anyone ever came, but that didn't daunt her. Grandma kept up with all the current events and was a great conversationalist. She was up very early in the mornings to wave good-bye to Dad from her kitchen window and then to me when I was old enough to drive to Shaker Heights to school. I can still see her face smiling at the kitchen window and her vigorous good-bye wave.

I feel dreadful guilt pangs now when I realize how little I visited her after I got married and had children and made my life too busy. She never complained. When I drove in the common driveway to see my father, she was always at the window waving and smiling. I remember one time when Jack and I were dating and arrived home at dawn after a prom. He was in white tie, tails and I in a long formal. Grandma was laughing her head off at the window. My father, however, did not laugh! He met us at the door in his striped pajamas and ushered us into the bright lights of the living room. "No more barnyard scenes," he said with ominous authority. (We had been necking in the car and waved to Grandma.) Jack shrank under his powerful glare. I, who had a foot long crepe paper bow from the decorations in my hair, protested (ire meeting ire), "You old goat." Jack said later that he wanted to crawl out of the house and become invisible. Something in Dad liked it when I stood up to him. I was the only person in his life who ever did.

Grandmother died the way she had lived – calmly, acceptingly, with dignity, in 1947 at the age of ninety-one. I still see her sitting up as straight as she could, her face framed against the huge Victorian carved headboard of her bed. She held court there for three days in her starched crocheted white nightie and little bed cap. Her pillows and sheets were pure white-also starched, ironed and crocheted. She was surrounded with her dedicated life's work -housewifefulness. All of her children and grandchildren and great-grandchildren were in attendance. When she was ready, she quietly passed away. I had more of a feeling of celebration of her life than of deep grief. I will always carry the picture of her thus imprinted in my soul to inspire me. Grandma never had any question about what she was here for. She was here to caretake others and live her life to the fullest in a seemly way. She was a whole yard of cloth - a model for all of us.

Grandma in her famous purple moire long dress at our wedding with her ubiquitous smile

*Grandpa and grandma dressed for church
Grandpa makes a rare appearance*

Dad on Beansoup

Betts on Jenny

Dad & I

I remember the day Dad and I galloped our horses through wide-open meadows. Freedom. The getting away from it all – galloping hell bent on our beautiful chestnut mares, Dad's Beansoup and my Belle. Sensual, ecstasy! Wind blowing in my hair – green meadows stretching forever. Being one with my Dad. Sun in our faces. The feeling of being one with the powerful horse beneath me. Feeling her haunches working hard – Belle's feeling of freedom and joy of living.

Suddenly, Belle's foot stepped into a hole. She stumbled and I went pell mell over her head and she stepped on me. She hated doing that and looked down on me with sorrowful repentence.

Dad was panicked. I was lying on the grass inert with a huge bloody wound on my chest and a broken collarbone. He took one last mournful look at me and mounted Beansoup and took Belle's reins to follow him. He drove back for me in his car. Searching the meadow for me. I couldn't speak. I raised my other arm as high as I could and will never forget the relieved, loving look on his face when he found me. Somehow, he managed to pick me up and carry me the long walk to his car.

I had to wear a brace from shoulders to waist. None of my clothes would fit over it. Aunt Addie made me three dresses to wear for the next six weeks. They snapped at the shoulders so I could wear them over the brace: unforgettable dresses. One was peach linen, another flowered, the third pink. I was not allowed to move much. But, of course, my rebel spirit carried me to the slide, the swings and the jungle gym. I still sport the knot of broken collarbone never quite fused.

It was worth the exultant experience with my Father.

How I learned to drive a car

How I Learned To Drive A Car

My father was paranoid about the dangers of riding a two-wheel bicycle. So he got me a car when I was thirteen. Till then I had the world's largest tricycle and I was so embarrassed riding it that I made it as dangerous as I could. I learned to race full steam up to turns in sidewalks and dump the tricycle and me in every creative way.

All I got out of my stunts were bruised arms, skinned knees and grass stains on my clothes. I didn't want to go biking with the other kids, I was so ashamed. Today, I see people, grown-up people, riding even bigger three-wheel tricycles, mammoth ones, on the sidewalks of Longboat Key, Florida, smiling, seeming quite proud of themselves. I marvel at their happy faces. I well remember how shamefaced and downright stupid I felt.

Unbelievably, when I was thirteen, my father got me a car and a falsified driver's license; obtained through political connections. He never taught me to drive; I was supposed "to know things." Father was an administrator, never a teacher. Trying to master the stick shift, I ripped out the clutch a couple of times. Barely able to see over the steering wheel, I was a little armored tank.

I drove my friends around town and countryside. Since we didn't have any traffic lights in Aurora, Ohio, it was a rather challenging, homicidal situation at crossroads. We kids yelled and sang as the radio blared "Hut-Sut Rawlson on the rillerah and a brawla, brawla sooit" and other unforgettable classic favorites.

Years later I didn't remember how to spell it, so I called the reference library in downtown Sarasota and talked to a nice guy named Lenny. He said he would look it up and call me back.

The next day I was out and about. When I got home Jack said a guy named Lenny called for me. Jack said he would take a message but Lenny said he had to speak to me personally. Jack said, "Who is this guy Lenny who wants to talk to you?" An affair perhaps?

When I called Lenny back he gave me the correct spelling. He said "we had so much fun looking it up we also looked up," "Mares eat oats and does eat oats and little lambs eat ivy,' too." Something out of the ordinary expanding the horizons of the Selby Library.

One day I got a letter from the Attorney General of Ohio, from Ohio driver's license bureau ordering me to turn in my illegal driver's license immediately. I showed it to my father. "What do I do with this, Daddy?"

"File it in the wastebasket," he answered, his customary reply about anything that got in his way. Later, it would be the Office of Price Administration, the War Product Control, Union officials, whatever bureaucracy tried to control him.

In a month or so, another letter came. "What should I do now, Daddy?"

"File it in the wastebasket."

Then came the letter ordering me to prison if I didn't return my lovely, illegal license.

"What should I do now, Daddy?"

"LET ME SEE THAT."

And so, I lost my carefree motoring days. I had to find a solution. I saved eight dollars and bought a cast-off two-wheel bicycle from a friend. On my first ride in a meadow, with friends helping me shouting instructions, I drove smack into a cow, the only thing in the meadow. The more I tried to steer away from it, the closer I got.

When I got more confidence, I was riding down the road on the hill from the General Store when the front wheel fell off. I toppled into the ditch with the bike on top of me just as Dad was driving alongside on his way home from work.

His solution: he let me drive the car without a license. He was right; two-wheel bicycles were dangerous.

Hathaway Brown School

A weekend at kriders

Hathaway Brown Prep School:
Non Scholae Sed Vitae Discimus!
(We Study Not For School But For Life!)

I entered eighth grade in Aurora schools. My father took one look at our class picture, a misbegotten lot. He enrolled me in Hathaway Brown Prep School in Shaker Heights, the best girl's school in the country. He had sent my ten-year-older sister there too.

I felt like a country bumpkin, although it helped that we had to wear uniforms. The school was full of daughters from a privileged class of old aristocracy of Cleveland, who had studied French and literature since kindergarten.

Strong cliques separated us. To my surprise I was the only one on the scholarship and citizenship honor roll first semester. A kindly red haired girl befriended me, thank goodness. Then one of the snootiest girls took me aside and said, "you know Connie is a Jewess" with a sneer. I was befuddled. I didn't know what "Jewess" meant. There was no prejudice voiced in my family, nor in my town. No need to. It was a WASP community.

H.B. was so segregated that when a father brought his daughter to register, our head mistress, frowned, and said.... "Well, she's Catholic". This was in 19836. Today in the new century I revel in pictures of the H.B. girls of every color and country of the world!

To my surprise I was selected to play a part in a French play by Molière, *The Imaginary Invalid*. So naïve and loyal was I, that I couldn't let my hockey team down for the big game. I skipped the meeting when the play was translated into English.

When I got back to rehearsal, I didn't know what was going on in the play, nor how I was supposed to act - surprised, angry, funny etc. So I memorized the whole play in French and went on stage. No mean feat!

Recently I was invited to the play at one of our theatres. Seventy years later I found out what it was all about!

I had five wonderful years at H.B., learning in the best way from the best teachers I will always be indebted to.

One teacher, Miss Blake, was my teacher for four years of Latin which I loved in spite of her hounding me. "How is the bright star of our class today?" She was both a tyrant and an excellent teacher, I guess.

I had high honors in Latin and math on my college boards, a great achievement. Then, Miss Blake invited me to her home for tea and treated me like a human being. She was overjoyed that I was accepted at Vassar, her alma mater.

Miss Simons my math teacher was a joy. I grew under her tutelage and loved math.

I was easily accepted at Vasser the college of my choice with my H.B. credentials. It was then one of the finest of the elite "Seven Sisters" on the Eastern seaboard.

*Betts at fifteen ready to embark
on the Scottish liner Caledonia*

The Scottish Experience

When I was fourteen and then when I was fifteen I made two life-changing decisions. The first was at Camp Arey on Lake Keuka, the camp I had loved so much since I was twelve. At mail call when we gathered expectantly, Impy Lee, who was my model, got her official acceptance at Vassar and Smith, two of the top women's colleges. I asked her which one she would choose, "Vassar of course."

My fate was sealed. I decided to go to Vassar, of course. Three years later, fortunately I was accepted. The second turning point was when I was fifteen and expected to go to camp again, my father gave me a choice: camp or a seven-week student trip to England and Scotland that he had read about. I told him I would have to sleep on it. The wonder of it all was that he gave me choices, free will. I went on the trip that changed my life: Love of Travel! I was a kid from a small village in Ohio who had no concept of the big world around me.

I didn't know any of the other kids when we left Cleveland, but after that night I knew all the girls. There were thirty-eight of us talking all night on the dirty old Erie Railroad that is no more - we were bound for New York where the ship was awaiting us. My travel journal tells me "there were thirty-eight girls and thirteen boys, but I got one." My whole family, Jack and all my other boyfriends came to bid me farewell. My Dad stuck an extra five hundred dollars in my hands and a movie camera, which I didn't know how to use. But it was very useful in getting the boys to help.

The captain of our Scottish liner spent most of the seven-day voyage yelling at me, "Get that girl out of the crows nest." I had talked a sailor into taking me up.

We stayed up all night singing with the Scottish sailors, learning all their songs. I still know one I can sing by heart after seventy years.

Just a wee deoch-an-doris, just a wee drap that's a'
Just a wee deoch-an-doris before we gang a-wa'

There's a wee wifie waitin', in a wee but an ben
If you can say, "It's a braw bricht moonlicht nicht" ye a'richt ye ken

During the night we often visited the bakery in the bowels of the ship where the bakers gave us lots of treats. A few of us decided to go to A deck for tea dance time because their *hors d'oeuvres* were so much better than ours; we lived in steerage.

Someone ratted on us and the captain had us removed - back to steerage where we got no treats.

One day when we were pitching through fifty foot waves, I got the stellar idea of putting on our bathing suits, going on deck and getting washed down the deck by the heavy waves. A few brave friends joined me as we watched our perilous passage around the icebergs.

The captain again on his bullhorn yelled, "Get those kids off the deck." Our small Scottish ship was rolling and tossing. It was fun while it lasted.

I learned to eat haggis and fried bubble and squeak for breakfast.

One day I decided to shower and wash my hair. I put on my robe and slippers, gathered my toiletries and promptly got lost in the winding passageways. There finally was a bathroom. It was different. But many things were new to me in a Scottish ship after fried bubble and squeak. There were these strange sink things. So I took off my robe and prepared to wash my hair in one. In came a corpulent older man. All of the sudden I got the picture. These things had something to do with men. I fled. Much later I found out they were urinals and *bidets*.

One night we were asked to participate in a program. Some of the British folks did the "Lambeth Walk" and one of the boys and I did the "Big Apple." I think the captain forgave us.

We arrived in London late one night on two buses, the drivers had not heard of our hotel, the Newlaud. We drove around and around. I finally piped up, "Let's call Scotland Yard." When we found it we knew why no one knew it - or should know it.

Straw mattresses, dingy old hotel.

Our long-suffering chaperones, Mr. and Mrs. Duffy, somehow got us out of there.

It was then and again and again that we realized the woman who arranged the "Friendship Trip" was bilking us out of a lot of money.

I'd heard of famous Hyde Park having a small platform where people could speak about anything they wanted to. So, young, naïve, I gave an impassioned talk about God knows what.

Then the real adventure started. The plan was to spend three weeks traveling through England and Scotland by bus, two weeks living with a family, and seven days on the ship each way. My roommate and I were to go to the Wilsons' in Sunderland.

At the train station Lev and I trudged up several flights of stairs lugging our baggage in a dirty, dingy railroad station to wait for the girl we were assigned to. We waited and waited until midnight, tired and forlorn. Finally a girl appeared dressed in black: shoes, stockings, skirt, and cape. I whispered to Lev, "I think she's for us." Sure enough she walked slowly towards us. No one else around. She said her name was Irene. She looked at us and stated that she had two friends, one, a girl on vacation, another, a boy who hated Americans. Irene did something all day, I can't remember what. So we were on our own to explore. Cathedrals, cricket matches, etc. We played tennis. It was so cold I played with my coat on.

It was then that I discovered something about myself. While still in bed we heard Mrs. Wilson on the phone describing us to a friend. "We have two American girls, one talks all the time and the other doesn't talk at all." I deduced which one I was.

After a week or so the Wilsons' told us we had to leave. They had a relative who died. I think that was a manufactured relative. Poor Duffys. They had to quickly find a home for us.

This became the best part. We were sent to "Porter's School for Girls." They were dear, fun, taught us to play cricket, and talked with us about everything, except the looming war. Their first question was "tell us about the Indians." What did I know? Nothing.

The Porters had a Hungarian traveling salesmen boarding there, Mr. Jolly. He asked if we ever drank alcohol. "No." "Well, come up to my room around 10:00 pm and I will show you how." We showered, put on our pajamas and went. He had a traveling bar. He offered us a taste of everything.

The Lord protects the innocents.

The only thing my mother ever told me remotely about sex was, as I departed, "never talk to strange men." So I talked to every strange man I could to find out what would happen. Nothing.

Yes, the Lord protects the innocents.

My new sweetheart, my husband-to-be sent me letters every day. We had fallen in love the night before I left. Miraculously they found me. Miraculous: I couldn't find myself.

The Scottish bag pipers piped us out of Edinburgh at midnight as we steamed off to the U.S. Unforgettable.

It was 1938 and we were one of the last boats to cross the Atlantic before World War II. Still unaware of the horror looming.

I Love To Fall In Love!

LOVE

I Love To Fall In Love!

In kindergarten I fell in love with Pee Wee Eldridge. But all he did was push me off my tricycle.

In first grade I fell in love with Dick Siegrist. He had dark curly hair and black olive eyes. To show my feelings I pushed his face into the water fountain. He chipped a front tooth. He didn't tell on me, so not only was I stuck with guilt, but I fell in and out of love with Dick for years.

In the second grade I fell head over heels in love with Jimmy Scardon of the brown curly hair and big brown eyes. But he moved away and I never saw him again till a surprising event brought us together, many years later.

I fell briefly in love with Bob Harner with an embarrassing consummation. I told my friend Totsy to put my chocolate cookie in Bob's cocoa. He didn't like it and told our teacher Miss Smith, who was tall and beautiful but punitive. She made me sit in the front of the room by her desk the next day I had to face the class, with a sign around my neck printed in big red letters: "We have to watch Betty Lou." (I begged my Mother not to pack any lunch that day because I had a stomachache but she did it anyway). If I had been smart I would have dumped it out of my lunch box while I was walking to school. But I carried it along. My cross to bear. Totsy put the cookie in the cocoa but I was the one who got punished. (I learned that the idea person, not the doer, often gets punished.)

Years later, I was glad to hear Miss Smith got married and had twins. I thought that served her right.

In the second grade I was demolished by our teacher Miss Rex Roth who told us straight out that there was no Santa Claus.

In the third grade I had to sit between the Miller twins. The problem was their mother didn't believe that they should bathe during the winter because it would rob them of their strength. The odors got stronger and stronger all winter.

Our Mennonite schoolmates were our good friends. We taught them lots of games. However, when I was ten there was one game I never shared with Totsy or any other girls. Every day after school in the fifth grade, Dick Seigrist, George and Johnny Morrison and I would make a beeline for the giant fallen tree behind the schoolhouse. Somebody had procured a bottle and we were secluded by the canopy of branches with the best game in town: "Spin the Bottle." The only game I never lost. (I got kissed with every spin!). I had a monopoly on fifth grade men.

Years later, at a large party, Johnny Morrison announced that I was the first "woman" he had ever kissed. He was in the second grade. He said his brother George was supposed to watch him after school. George never failed to watch him when he kissed me.

I have no idea how this game came to be. Like so much of my childhood it is shrouded in mystery. Probabsly I invented it! But boy, oh boy, was it fun! I can't imagine why I left Totsy out of the game: she must have moved away and I had to console myself with the boys.

In the fifth grade Bob Harris came to town. He had marvelous deep blue eyes and a sweater to match. For me, it was love at first sight when our teacher asked him to stand up and introduce himself. On Saturdays, Bob (it didn't take long for him to be invited to my game) and Chuck Durbin took me ice-skating in the long-since demolished Elyseum in downtown Shaker Heights. I skated between them, gliding along with the music. Then we'd have lunch and go to a double feature movie. I sat between them, holding both their hands. We held hands down low so neither of them knew I was holding the other's hand. I think.

Then there was this gorgeous boy, Jack, we called him "Cope", better looking than anyone, a quarterback and captain of the football team. Cockier than hell. We fought all the time. In spite of that I fell in love with him.

One Sunday, I had to ride with him to Bob Bedell's cottage on Lake Milton, Ohio. Yes, I sort of fell in love with this Bob too. We called him Beetle. Helen, who worked for the Brown family, usually chaperoned us. We liked her because she always fell asleep. But that day she couldn't go. So none of the other kids could go. However, my parents were older and not in the same crowd as the parents of my friends so they didn't hear that Helen would be absent. They didn't question the outing. Beetle took my friend, Bonky, and so, dear reader, that's how I ended up with my husband. I remember whining to Mother, when I found I had to ride alone with Jack in his two-seater roadster, "Oh Mother, what will I talk about with him?" Well, he honked the horn on time to the radio and sang along like a dream. I didn't have to worry about talking!

He said he fell in love with me when he shoved a peanut butter sandwich in my face and my nose emerged. That may not sound terrifically romantic, but somehow it was to him. I sense that he decided I was a good sport because I laughed and laughed.

The trouble was I still loved Dick and Bob too, and when each one gave me his prize: a gold football won for being Portage County Champions I accepted all of them. Each of the guys thought I was wearing his. Each played his heart out for me when they caught sight of Betsy and Jeanie and me as we arrived from Hathaway Brown, our prep school in Shaker Heights. In the huddle, the word was passed, "the girls are here."

They were brave, our guys. They played in a cow pasture full of holes and nettles and they ran for their lives (literally sometimes).

It's been said that, "we live with our weaknesses and die with our strengths." My fatal day came when, on a dare, which I would never refuse, I wore all three gold footballs on my chain. I was sitting on the steps of Brownies' General Store and all three boys piled out of the car!

So, finally, I had to choose – kind of.

Jack was gorgeous and sexy as sin. What a dancer he was. He whirled me around the dance floor, crooning in my ear. My heart melted. It didn't matter what he sang- "Little Old Lady Passing By With A Gleam In Her Eye," "Stairway to the Stars," " Two Sleepy People By Dawn's Early Light But Too Much In Love To Say Goodnight."

He wooed me. I was fifteen. Sixty years later he took me to dance and crooned in my ear, he still wooed me, body and soul.

Jack had his heart set on going to military school, so in that fall of 1938 he went off to the Greenbrier Military School in Lewisburg, West Virginia. Thus began many years of long-distance courtship, actually six years. It is a wonder that our commitment survived the glitches and my predilection for falling in love. He went to Western Reserve University in Cleveland and I to Vassar College in Poughkeepsie, New York. We both dated, but he, the best catch around, talked to his dates about me, he said. I remember well standing in my Mother's rose arbor at our back door, choosing whom I would love most of all.

One night Beetle would say, "I love you, Gus" (my exquisitely feminine nickname). The next night it would be Dick saying in a husky voice of passion, "I love you, Gus." I loved him too.

Jack was dashing in his gray uniform. His long cape swung as we walked or danced, showing the bright red lining. The legendary lure of a military uniform surely worked on me.

The summer of 1939, Jack's parents, Mom and Pop Colebrook, at his passionate urging, invited me to go with them to Eireau, Ontario, to the cabin they rented yearly for two weeks in July. We fished all day and all evening and till after dark. I became an unbelievably good sport and so enthusiastic Jack didn't dream that fishing was not my idea of heaven.

That fall I went to Vassar, to spread my wings in a wide horizon. I loved it all. For the first two weeks, I listened to the heady description of the clubs: Political Science, Miscellany News, Hockey, Theatre, etc. I joined all of them. Then I spent the next two weeks trying to fit them all in my schedule. I dis-joined most of them.

Cope came to Poughkeepsie for prom weekends. An unforgettable picture of him riding one of the girls' bicycles with his usual aplomb, knees out, he looked like Ichabod Crane, wearing white tie and tails, his tails soaring, as I watched from a window in Main Hall, will be forever emblazoned in my memory.

The next summer, the summer before my sophomore year, 1940, the Colebrooks invited me to share their vacation again. This time my father put his foot down. "You two are getting too thick!" he declared. If he had only known. Pleading, yelling, crying didn't work. So I ran away from home – all the way to my sister's house, at least a half a mile away where they lived at the top of John Gould's Hill. I sobbed to my sister, "I hate Dad! I'm never going home – ever. He'll be sorry!"

The next day, Dad called. "We're leaving at 2:14 AM for Eaton's Ranch in Wyoming." His peace offering. I could not resist. Of course, I did go home.

When we arrived at the ranch the next afternoon, two boys from Cornell were standing at the entrance. One of them opened the car door for me – Fred Anderson. I fell in love when he said, "Would you like to go to the rodeo in Cheyenne with me?"

"Bye, bye Daddy," I yelled already on my way.

Poor Dad!

Fred persuaded his parents to spend an extra day at the ranch so we could go to the square dance. I felt like this was all I ever wanted. Fred walked me back to our cottage and when Dad caught us necking outside he said "Get in here at once, young lady!" Poor Dad, he had a wild filly on his hands. The next day, riding the Wyoming Mountains, Dad commented, "You know, Jack isn't so bad after all." (Hometown boy) Pretty soon I was writing letters to Fred, signed, "All my love." I considered becoming Catholic for him.

I developed another triumvirate: Fred at Cornell, Bill Belcher from Yale, and Jack who was at Western Reserve University giving blood to raise money to take the old New York Central Railroad up to Poughkeepsie for prom weekends. Meanwhile I was dating other guys. *Mea Culpa*

One Sunday night, a friend burst into my dorm room. "Betts," she announced excitedly, "I met a guy this weekend at Princeton who said he was your second grade sweetheart. His name was Jimmy Scardon." My heart leaped. I had never forgotten him.

He called that very night and wanted to come down and see me the next weekend. I cancelled my date with Bill saying I had to study for an art exam. He telegraphed back, "who's Art?"

Saturday morning I went to the grimy old Poughkeepsie New York Central train station, my heart fluttering, I scanned each tall, gorgeous guy as they got off the train. Finally I was aware of someone standing under my armpits. Jimmy! He hadn't grown since the second grade. He proposed to me and talked of a home with a white picket fence.

What a relief. I didn't have to fall in love!

Celebrating our engagement at the A D Phi House

The Engagement

In 1942, I was a junior at Vassar and Jack was a junior at Case Western Reserve. We had impulsively become engaged. I must have imprinted on my subconscious a family pattern that started with my Grandfather Gedecke. When Dad gave Mother an engagement ring, Grandpa made her put it in a drawer for two years while Father "proved himself." Mother, was a teacher. When my older sister, Kathryn, became engaged, my Father made her put her ring in a drawer while her *fiancé* proved himself. She taught piano lessons and played the organ at the community church in Aurora, where Herbert (her *fiancé*) was choir director and his father was the minister, and they then married.

I boarded the old New York Central train and went home to show my ring and announce my engagement to Dad and Mother. I was insouciant!

So we announced our engagement publicly and I talked my parents into giving a big party at the country club. I even talked my mother into giving me money for a case of gin to spike the punch (shades of grandpa). Dad declared it was going to be a non-alcoholic party (for fraternity men?). He never knew. Mother was a kindly soul, brave too. She had never had a drink in her life and referred to alcohol as the "devil's work." Dad didn't have any punch until the last bowl, which was almost pure gin, and never knew it. The next day we were visiting Uncle Rube and Aunt Lillian, Dad said, "We had a non-alcoholic party at the Aurora Country Club, a feather in our caps."

After we were engaged I called Bill from Yale and asked him to drive down. I had something important to tell him. We went to the Dutch Cabin and had a beer. He cried and cried. I cried too. Then he asked me to get him a date for the upcoming weekend. I wrote Fred at Cornell. He was stunned and wrote me a beautiful sad letter. His mother did too. She liked me so much and hoped for our future together. Fred had invited me to his home several times when he could get away. He was a serious academic. By then I wondered why I got engaged and missed out on a lot of fun. *Oy Vay*.

Our Elopement – 1943
Then Once Was Not Enough

It was Margaret Meade's fault or maybe it was Ruth Benedict's (those famous female role models of my time). I wanted to be just like them. In a panel discussion on "Love, Marriage, and Family" at our college, one of them said, "In wartime differences between partners those little irritating habits like squeezing the toothpaste tube differently don't matter." Wartime marriages were filled with passion and glamour. This sent my hormones racing! I took away the wrong message, instead of "be a professional in your own right." I dashed out of the auditorium and called Jack in Cleveland. "Let's get married next weekend in New York City!" I shouted, I had eight days off for a semester break and couldn't think of anything else to do. Fifty-five years later Jack asked me to get my own toothpaste. I wonder what that means according to Meade and Benedict. I wonder where my high-flown dreams went? I couldn't foresee that many years later what had been nascent dreams would come to fruition.

When I had called Jack in my impetuous enthusiasm, he was eager to get married. He couldn't stand the competition.

We wrote to each other every day for those six years. I wish I had saved the letters to know what on earth we wrote about every day.

We went into action: telephone calls and telegrams raced back and forth, often in Latin to disguise our mission. I had to find a church in New York City that would marry us on Saturday, February Sixth. Without parents. The Little Church Around the Corner wouldn't. The First Presbyterian Church on West 12th street would. But no organ music. That minister had his limits!

It was the usual stressful exam time but my friends and I went to work. One of them took me shopping for a wedding nightgown. My Doctor Dentons wouldn't do, they said. Another friend took me to a doctor to have a diaphragm fitted. His office was in his home in Poughkeepsie. I was twenty and embarrassed. I'd never had a pelvic exam before. I couldn't wait to get out of his office, so when I raced out, he called from the porch, waving my panties, "You forgot something Miss Poss." How I blushed and got quickly out of there.

We all struggled through our exams and went to New York for the big weekend. Jack arrived via the New York Central, the old Empire Express on Saturday morning, taking an overnight trip. We were to be married at 1:00 P.M. so we had very little time to dash around for our Wasserman tests and the marriage license. We kept asking for directions from people who didn't speak English as we raced around the city. At City Hall, we were told there was a seventy-two hour waiting period after the blood tests before the license could be issued. We flew from office to office in the courthouse trying to get the rule waived, to no avail. Finally, in desperation, just before Saturday noon closing, we went back to the license bureau with the same papers we started out with and this time we got our license without a hitch. They were probably anxious to close for the weekend. The whole scenario was romantic madness. I wonder now how my life would have been different if those fifteen minutes had been different.

I don't remember a thing about the wedding. I was in a dream world. Twelve of my friends from college were there, and Jack's friend Don Hamilton, came with him from Cleveland to be his best man. Don and his girlfriend got so carried away with the romance of it all that they got engaged. It was one of the happiest moments of my life. To be young and so much in love made me feel like the world was mine! I remember looking up at Jack, a foot taller than I and too gorgeous for words. "I love you so very much," I said. My girlfriends gave us a festive brunch at Enrico and Paglieri's in Greenwich Village. I still have the menu; the most expensive meal, steak and the works, was $1.95. We had champagne and everyone was ebullient. Jack and I were the essence of romance.

After brunch, the whole gang of us went to the Vanderbilt Hotel, where Jack had arranged for a suite. We spent the rest of the afternoon shooting craps on the rug in the living room and drinking scotch. What a heady time, so heady that one of our friends, who eventually became an author, dedicated her first book to the cab driver who drove her home. Looking back I can see that I did the most significant married thing in the 40's: I didn't play while all my girlfriends did. Not like me at all. Instead I watched my new husband play. Ah, the power of the cultural role we women inherited in marriage in 1943. And I considered myself an emancipated woman! A free spirit. Later, when we settled down with a baby in a rented house in Aurora, I gave away my ice skates. What a potent symbol! Fifteen years later I bought some new ones. It took that long for me to think of myself as an individual.

Our days in New York City were magical. We ate shrimp at every meal. I fixed shrimp cocktail in our suite, serving them in my new blue nightgown, eating them in bed. I felt like a paramour cum housewife. We went to museums and plays and walked in Central Park.

We took the old B&O railroad (Baltimore and Ohio) to Washington, D.C. to visit childhood friends; Bob Bedell had married Betsy, Jack's former girlfriend, while Bob was my former boyfriend. It was a most momentous trip for me. Jack took me to lunch in the dining car and ordered Ballantine's Ale and sliced chicken sandwiches with lettuce and mayonnaise. We laughed and flirted and talked. The fun was a revelation to me, traveling with Mother and Dad had been grim, task-oriented business. You didn't have fun until you "got there." Dad was always goal directed: the process was not important. I decided life with Jack would be an interesting experience because we would have fun along the way. (We still used to celebrate with chicken sandwiches.)

When we arrived back at the sooty Poughkeepsie Station on the New York Central, I had a call on the loud speaker. Betsy Bates was calling to say, "Don't come back on campus until you talk to me." Announcement of our wedding license had appeared in the Poughkeepsie paper, since I had signed that as my address. One of the maids saw it and alerted Betsy. A college rule I never knew about was that a student would be expelled if married secretly. I was petrified. My parents would never have forgiven me if I got expelled. Nor could I. I put my wedding ring in my lock box and the secret was kept by my friends.

Jack and I met whenever we could - Washington, Buffalo, Poughkeepsie, New York City, but I developed a severe case of guilt about being secretly married and not being straight with my parents. I kept ending up in the infirmary with terrible sinus infections, inhaling benzoin from a steaming pot. One day Dr. Bean came to see me: she of the English tweed suits and sturdy Oxfords. Her presence was daunting. She said, "You've been having these severe sinus infections. Do you have a boyfriend?" (Last thing I ever thought she would bring up). I stammered, "ye-es." Then she said straightforwardly, "There is a connection between the mucus lining of the nasal tissues and the lining in the sex organs. I was wondering if…" and she stopped right there while we both looked at something on the wall and I merged with the sheets. Sexuality was regarded quite differently in the forties. There was rarely any open dialogues or recognition of youthful sexuality – any other sexuality for that matter.

I wrote impassioned letters to my parents about wanting to get married. Mother said she didn't show them to Dad because he wasn't well. He never wanted me to get married. Enraged, I sent a letter, registered mail, to Dad's office. By God, I'd be heard, young and insouciant as I was.

"Dear Dad: I want to get married now while everything is sane and decent and honest!" What did I mean? I guess I meant I didn't want to have a secretive life anymore.

I was twenty and full of sauce and goal-oriented like my parents and Grandpa, who had run halfway around the world from his parents when he was fourteen. I prevailed. We got married in The Church in Aurora on June 12th at "half after four." I in a long white satin and tulle dress and train, Jack in a handsome white suit.

My friends complained, "Can't we get through another exam week without us helping you get married?" When people said we did it so well it looked like we'd had a dress rehearsal, we smiled gamely.

My father looked green in the photograph taken in the vestibule of the church. I was radiant. A neighbor lady had saved one of my decorative mud pies in her safe for all those years and gave it to Jack in the church. He lost it in twenty minutes, I don't think he was interested in my mud pies at that moment in time.

Jack was called up by the Marines while we were on our second honeymoon. So I did, in fact, become a wartime wife. I spent the summer with him at Penn State while he went through the V Twelve Officers' Training Program. Then I went back to Vassar. I never thought my parents would stop paying for my education, and I'm sure they were thrilled that I intended to complete my college to graduation.

It was a heady year. As I look back, I don't know how I got through it. Our college accelerated for the war effort. President McCracken said we would cover a smaller pie of course material, but we discovered it was the same pie with months less time to cram it in. I wrote my senior thesis on "Reconstructing Germany After the War," despite the reality that I knew nothing about the subject I chose. So my work involved research day and night; never considering that we, the allies wouldn't win.

I moved in with my crazy friend Erna. I decided I had to room with her in order "to know her better" so I could psychoanalyze her for another thesis. This entailed talking with her late into the nights and writing feverishly. Talk about taking on too much! My thesis director told me she was psychotic and needed prolonged psychotherapy. It turned out she was my first patient with anorexia nervosa. In my practice years later it became my specialty and ironically the subject of my doctoral dissertation.

Jack was sealed off in Parris Island South Carolina, the bowels of the earth, for three months of basic training. After this he would be shipped to Quantico, Virginia, a huge Marine base, for Officer's Training. Madly in love, we met as often as we could each get away: New York, Washington, etc.….

One weekend in Washington we decided to have a baby and we knew it was a *fait accompli*. We named "him" Michael. We went to the zoo the next day to show the baby the animals – such crazy kids were we.

I graduated eight days pregnant. The chairman of our Child Study Department, Mrs. Fisher, whom I adored, scheduled an interview with me after the graduation ceremony to talk about graduate school and career ideas. I remember that session vividly after all these years, another symbolic episode. I had sent my tan gabardine suit to the dry cleaners at the last minute and it wasn't ready yet. I was wearing my tan raincoat over my underwear, unprepared for the interview, or the possibility of graduate school and a career. Metaphorically so unprepared for a future on my own. Nobody had ever told me that I had choices - that I could "become." I told her I was pregnant. A female product of my time, I didn't dream I could have it all: be married, have a baby and a career. That summer I was offered the Directorship of Planned Parenthood of Ohio, with what was

Betts with cannon at Quantico Marine Base

then a great salary of $3,000. I refused, broken heartedly, explaining that I was "planning parenthood myself."

My new husband's life was spared through a fluke in the Marine Corps. They graduated too many second lieutenants and he was discharged the summer of '44 while we were in Quantico. The punitive Drill Instructor resented second lieutenants and drummed him out when he reported that someone had filched his canteen, saying he should take better care of his equipment.

So we started married housekeeping back in Aurora. I learned about life as we plunged straight into poverty. Jack made $120 a month, our rent was $60. Our parents never knew of our elopement. First we were too young to tell them, then we were too old. But when our children were older, we told them and they were titillated to think of our impetuous love. They said, "We wondered why you guys always went away in February."

We had survived the lumps and bumps of marriage and children growing up in a vastly changing world. With our mutual adaptation to evolving roles we were more intimately involved with each other than ever - like twins entwined in utero - but with our pursuits and personalities intact. We glided into our 50th anniversary and then our 60th.

I guess our elopement wasn't so impetuous after all.

A summer day while
still in paradise

A Housewife's' Ode To Her Husband
On His Twenty Third Birthday

Now that orange blossoms are left behind
And wifely duties are in my life
I swear by Clorox and Old Dutch
Though my hands aren't those you love to touch

Stacked towels have to come out white
And pants and shirts have to be just right

It's one half and one and a fourth
Until you think that west is north

In spite of fingers that always scorch
For you, Honey, I carry that old torch!

Mrs. Shakespeare Colebrook
(with apologies to the
famous bard)

*Betts, Jack and Pop Colebrook after receiving
his second lieutenant bars*

Don't I look frightful!

We Never Talked About It

I have written extensively about my home town of five hundred people: how it wrapped its kindly arms around us throughout our childhood and youth shaping us to be kindly people, and about our telephone operator, Bessie, who with her old fashioned switchboard listened to our conversations, and was a fountain of knowledge about everything that was going on. We loved her for all the information she gave us. How could I have known she would cause such calamity for us? I guess, trusting soul that I have always been, I couldn't believe our first brutal betrayal. This is a story about how Jack and I became pariahs in our benevolent town that I never told before to family or friends. Our party lines got news mixed up in telling and retelling. I learned how much people love to gossip especially with startling stories.

But the damage was done. Bessie spread the rumor that Jack had raped an officer's wife! An unforgivable offense and completely untrue! How could she have misrepresented the conversation he had with his father? Incomprehensible, for this gentle man I had married and with whom I was so much in love. He was discharged from the Marines and we were coming home. Such was the fervor of World War II that not to be in the service was a sin. He tried to enlist in the Navy and the Army and was turned down for medical reasons. This saved his life, of course, but we felt like he had lost it. Overnight, we had become pariahs in our town.

We never talked about it.

When Jack called his parents telling them what had happened and that we were coming home, broke of course, and with no where to stay, they took us in. His father took him to Washington to straighten things out (to no avail). My father said, "don't say anything to anyone." Rumors flew around, gathering falsehoods. Bad advice. He had an honorable discharge, but that didn't matter.

Jack and I never talked about it.

After we lived two weeks with my mother-in-law from hell I knew I had to leave to keep my sanity. We went to my parents until the baby was born. It wasn't long before Jack had to have emergency proctological surgery and sat for two days on a rubber doughnut in obvious pain. The metaphor was not lost on me.

He finally said, "There is not room for an old bull and a young bull in this house." He rented a little house for us in Aurora, close to both sets of parents.

When we left, my father stood on the porch shaking his fist with his forefinger pointed at me…shouting, "Young lady, you will rue the day you left this house." His ire settled around my heart like a concrete wall. The snowstorm was blinding. I was between the two men who meant the most to me. The noose tightened. I had to go with my husband.

We never talked to each other about how dismal our life was.

No washing machine, no refrigerator, washing diapers in the sink. I reflected on the six years of French, four years of Latin, and the messages of one of the finest colleges in the country. To carry the torch and become effective women, pass it on, but hold onto it firmly forever.

We were so poor. I was isolated and soon didn't even bother to dress anymore. I took care of my baby and felt helpless and ravaged and hungry.

We never talked about it.

Doors were closed to us. We were disdained, a dreadful way to start married life. When I produced our first baby boy, I put him in his carriage and wheeled him proudly to show him off to some mothers of friends I had grown up with, calling them "auntie." The doors slammed shut. The pain was excruciating. It was like a drop of bile infused into our relationship. Our hearts hurt.

We never talked about it!

Mother was dying of cancer; I was dying of numbness. I will never know what he felt. His suffering must have been incalculable.

Our first home

We never talked about it.

A concrete slab further encased my heart. What about him?

We never talked about it.

He died eight years ago near our sixtieth anniversary - so we'll never talk about it.

The Great Post Office Heist

How I Became A Heroine In My Own Hometown

In the early days of the 40's no one locked their doors. We didn't have any crime. Sometimes we didn't close our garage doors.

One morning when I was going to drive my children to school we went out to the garage and my station wagon was gone!

I called the police and they found it at the Post Office.

Some sophisticated burglars had studied the door lock at the Post Office and the alarm system and then needed a get away car. With our garage door wide open, they stole my station wagon. They hoisted the safe into my car in the dead of night and jumped in to escape. It was a perfect crime! Except my car (as usual) was out of gas. They fled into the woods where they were tracked by our police. So that's how I became a heroine in my hometown; saved all the money in the safe, securely nesting in the back of my car.

Moral of the story: always drive on an empty tank of gas.

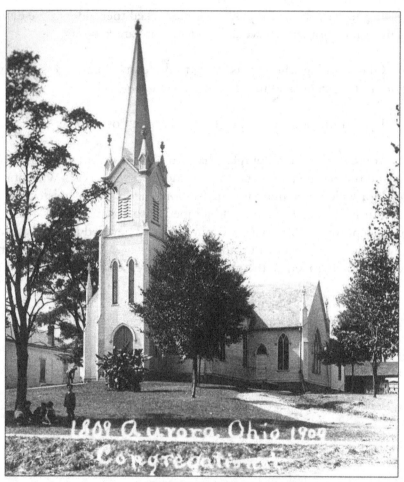

Church in Aurora

Surviving Suburbia

Ann and I in our early-married years decided to attempt to join the women in Suburbia. Bravely we went to the Missionary Society Meeting. There were only two seats left. There we were in the front row where we were observed by all the matrilineal ladies of Aurora where I would live the rest of my life.

First, I was in a maternity dress, just after I had a baby several months before.

Then, to make matters worse, I had brought my sewing box in an effort to join. When I opened it, two moths flew out!

I was found out. The sewing box is still sitting in a cupboard untouched after all those years.

PLUS CA CHANGE PLUS C'EST LA MEME CHOSE
AKA (The more things change, the more it's the same)

I vowed that when I had children I would never, ever scream at them as my mother had screamed. After all I had majored in "Child Study" at Vassar and knew all about everything regarding children. It was easy to keep my vow at first. That's why it was so shocking when the long-held-back scream came out of my throat.

All was peaceful - calm, perfect with my first baby. When my second was born fourteen months later, things got a bit hairy. Both babies cried hunger at the same moment. I thought, "What would Grandmother have done?" I resorted to feeding Michael in his highchair while nursing Suzie in my arms.

It wasn't until Suzie became a little person, crawling, reaching out for Michael's toys that he decided to massacre her on a regular basis.

One day, when Michael was exhibiting his terrible twos and Suzie was eighteen months old, he pushed her down a long flight of boulder-lined stone stairs from our terrace to the back yard while I stepped into the kitchen to get their treats. Like a kamikaze pilot she dove twenty feet. Unbelievably, she was unscathed. It was I who was a wreck and she grew up to adore him.

When child three and four appeared on the scene we were a "happy little family," but sometimes I was involved with children-saving tactics for their survival and mine. Happy little mayhem.

Now, finally, I understood why mother screamed. In extremis, my once buried genetic yell burst forth. My mother-cells combusted.

The "ah, ha" syndrome dawned. I understood more about why my kindly mother had morphed into a witch one day chasing me with her butcher knife. I dove into a bathtub where my sister was relaxing. "Sissy, save me," I screamed. The knife chase happened only once, but the experience was so powerful it haunted my childhood. Today, Sis says "Oh yeah, the knife caper."

I don't think I was a difficult child. I remember always trying my best to be good, to obey, to please. Yet, one day when I was in our small-town grocery store with my first two little darlings (who were acting-out in the worst way at the penny candy counter) an old-time friend of our family observed, "you deserve every minute of what you're getting now, Betty Lou."

Ah, ha. *Plus ca change plus c'est la meme chose.*

Not long ago in a family question-and-answer game Michael drew a card asking him what was the best and worst thing he had ever done.

He replied, "The worst thing I ever did was push Suzie down the stairs in her Taylor Tot. The best thing I have ever done was push Suzie down the stairs in her Taylor Tot." Ah, ha.

Deborah,Cope,Grand-Daughter Laurie,Suzie,Kristina,Me,Mike

We goof it up

Meditations On Clan Colebrook Going To School

At last, the youngest is sprung from the nest. Kris had laid her clothes out two days ago. The new shoes were waiting, lunch boxes packed, hair out of bobby pins and combed with care. Excitement and tenderness prevailed.

I watched the two little ones off (Deborah age nine and Kristina six) in alike pink dresses trimmed in lace, lunch boxes, school bags in tow. Kris proudly carried a hand-me down school bag of her older sister Suzie's of the Hopalong Cassidy vintage. It swung gaily, banging her shins. The new saddle shoes, looking sizes too big, as new saddle shoes always do the first day of school on growing youngsters, propelled them both down the street. They tried to walk, but a little skip and a hop kept breaking their pace.

Kris, highly impressed with the occasion, was poker-faced, trying manfully to suppress a smile as a neighbor waved gaily at her.

Debby is in fourth grade with Betty Hutcherson, Susan in tenth and Michael in eleventh. A momentous year in all our lives.

Michael, for the first time is on varsity football squad in Aurora. He's been training for several weeks - eating, breathing and living it. He's turned into a young lion -- giving the family a few growls occasionally. But he took time out of his emergent-man role to be concerned with the occasion of Krissy today.

Sue, having matured incredibly over the summer at camp, approaches the coming year with a newfound determination, much more self-discipline, and a real inner radiance. She's had a fling at dating, tried going steady briefly, has had more than an occasional brush with mascara, beer and cigarettes, and is happily back to playing touch football with younger fry in the back yard. We'll see what this portentous year holds for our dear little family.

Our Middle-Age Hearts Were Young And Gay

One night over *beaucoup* martinis Midge and I with husbands, Werner and Jack, decided that it would be a jolly good plan for Midge and me to visit Erna in Milan. Erna had been recuperating from brain surgery. Erna was Werner's sister and my college roommate. She was interesting and psychotic. So a plan was born!

Not so! First off Monday morning Midge called "I can't go. Werner and my father said I can't leave my four children and husband to go abroad." "I got the same Sermon on the Mount, Midge. There is only one thing for two intelligent women to do. Put on your black dress and pearls. I'll drive in and pick you up in an hour. We'll go to a travel agency and book our flight."

This was in the fifties when no wives from the suburbs would dream of doing such a thing. I would tell Jack "I got my passport today, honey." He kept on reading the newspaper. (yah, yah sure you did) "I got my shots today." He didn't look up.

A few weeks later on our flight day the husbands took us to lunch. Afterwards, we said "Now take us to the airport." They laughed. We boarded the plane and they looked at us open-mouthed, incredulous. Still didn't believe it. Went to England first to visit Midge's Aunt Sylvia and Uncle Eric. Uncle Eric was the second son of a nobleman in Spain. The first son stayed home. The second son was sent to a foreign court.

Uncle Eric Severino and Auntie met us at the airport in a thirty or forty year old Morris Traveller. Uncle Eric said "I hope it starts. I have to leave it in the right gear for it to start." With this auspicious beginning it finally started and we crept into traffic stopping only to buy two new metal hot water bottles which I learned to cherish. They lived in an old sprawling mansion surrounded by acres and acres of greensward. Uncle Eric showed me where our soldiers had built an encampment during World War II. We uncovered an outdoor bowling area with wooden balls. He said we could ride his horse "Nutty," but who was unpredictable.

The house had seventy cold rooms. No heat. I spent most of my time encamped in the huge fireplace. I asked Midge when entombed in my bed if I could crawl in with her. She said "on the first night?"

We visited other friends of hers. They took us to a pub for dinner and apologized for being in the "new section"; 16th century.

Off to Paris. We arrived around nine at night. Midge proceeded to unpack and put on her red flannel nightgown. "Midge, what are you doing? Paris awaits. I could never sleep thinking I was finally here and going straight to bed." She was afraid! Impervious Midge. I left and walked to a café opposite the opera where I could watch the beautiful people from my sidewalk table. I ordered an espresso and cognac and enjoyed my solitary self. Midge had our door locked and was asleep when I returned.

We arrived in Rome about nine at night. Anticipating the same reaction from Midge I hired a white horse and carriage that I spied across the street from our hotel. I yearned to see Rome. It was perfect swathed in amber light – the forum and cathedrals were haunting.

After a few glorious days we flew to Milan. Difficult and interesting days awaited us. We drove to Venice where Robert, Erna's husband, ever the scholar pointed out historical and artistic sites in detail while Midge and I escaped into shops.

We drove through the Alps at night on the windy, perilous roads at breakneck speed. It didn't help when Erna pointed out that Robert could only see out of one eye. We clutched each other and sank to the floor.

Cable car up to a mountain retreat where three stout aging matriarchs in black informed us that they had closed for the season. They took pity on us as we drooped with night falling and took us in. Lovely food with fresh strawberries and fresh whipped cream. Robert and I climbed an Alp and discovered a tiny remote church with fresh flowers on the alter. Where could they have come from? Who put them there?

When my flight arrived in Cleveland many adventures later there was Jack in a French beret with his hair sprayed grey. He was shaking when he kissed me.

When I went to the study club a few days later I discovered that I was the talk of the town. One of the reigning matriarchs asked me "what impressed you the most?" I thought a minute and answered "the whores on the square in Milan." In those early innocent days I had never seen women asking for sex.

Nobody else asked me any more questions.

The house Dad bought for us in 1949 at 101 New Hudson Road where we lived for twenty-nine years. Jack built a huge cherry porch on the back for a breakfast room and gathering room.
It was gorgeous. He built the floors, walls and ceiling with local cherry.

Mike today

Mike, Jess, Max and Rosie

Mike
It Was A Barnstorming Blizzardly Day.

It was nearly approaching the due date of our first baby and I started bleeding. I didn't know anything about "birthing babies." Mother's nurse said we must leave for the hospital immediately. No small feat. Aurora was encased in snow. No snow plows in those days. It was like driving through deep tunnels and sliding along three feet of icy snow.

Ours was the only car that got out of Aurora that momentous day, December 12, 1943.

I was put into a "Labor Room" like a padded cell – alone. I heard other women screaming in labor through the walls. I made a unilateral decision. "I don't want that, let that baby stay right in there safe and snug." I was twenty-one and had been reassured that having a baby was less painful than going to the dentist!

So I was put in a private room in the maternity ward. Dr. Glenn didn't want me to risk leaving in the treacherous weather. He stayed at the hospital too. Ensconced in my sky blue satin bed jacket, smoking the tiny-jeweled pipe Cope bought me because of cigarette rationing during the war; I was knitting soakers for the baby to come. Labor pains were intermittent for about thirty hours. So Dr. Glenn decided to induce the birth with "pit-packs" in my nose. I became an even more interesting specimen with these Q-tips sticking out of my nose.

Michael was born about three hours later while Cope was helping shovel a woman out of a snow bank where her car was stuck.

When he called his father with the news of a son, Pop asked what the baby looked like. Cope said "like a little Jewish tin can!" Who knew he would grow up to be the handsomest guy on the block?

I thought he was gorgeous. But I guess he wasn't, Carl's mother stopped in one day and remarked "well that's a baby, that is" Hmm.

He was a football star at Aurora High School and went to Hillsdale College. Around junior year he decided to be a beach boy in Fort

Lauderdale; soon he was drafted for the Vietnam War. When he finished basic training and was ready to ship out, he was instead shipped to Germany; which of course saved his life from the violent, ill-considered war and his future life. He was plain lucky.

While he was in Germany he was able to make numerous side trips in Europe for those two years. We flew over with Deborah and Kristina to see him during his two-week furlough. It was a grand adventure.

When he came home he married Rosie Rossi and had two children, Jessica and Maxwell. He and Rosie managed a teen/preteen store in Chagrin Falls named "Galie West." In time, sadly, it folded under the competition from the many discount stores that flourished nearby.

For years he has managed and maintained our one hundred and seventy-five acre family estate. Including a forty-four acre lake on Old Mill Road in Aurora. He loves every blade of grass and no one could do the job better.

His son, Max, does multitudinous tasks with his father summers when he is home from college, at Ohio University, where he is on the Dean's list majoring in Graphic Arts. He will succeed at whatever he does, because he's bright, responsible, disciplined and fun loving. Max will graduate in June *cum laude*. He said, "Well Jess put the bar high."

As I peer out a window I watch these two generations working together in harmony; my heart is filled with joy. Continuity of the bloodline is a fulfillment I wish Cope could enjoy.

"My eldest daughter Suzie"

Suzie holding Deborah wearing her nurses outfit when we brought Deborah home from the hospital

David and Susan

Suzie

Suzie has always been a madcap, the flame of the family. She is insouciant. Everybody loves her. She tends to each member of the family and I know when we are gone she will keep the family ties entwined. She succeeds at almost everything she attempts.

Suzie became an Otolaryngologist when she was in the second grade. One night when I was tucking her into bed with her dolls and her prayers she said, "Mommy, I put a bean in my ear today." She always had an adventurous imagination. As a small tot she loved to flush all the toilets. One day when my engagement ring went missing I asked her if she had flushed it. She said, "Yes, Mommy," looking up at me sincerely with her big brown eyes. Of course it was not so, but there were many instances like this and I learned early to be a bit skeptical of her stories.

The following night she said "I think that bean is growing." I believed that she was pulling my leg. The next night, she said, "Mommy, it really hurts." So, I got a flashlight and saw that it really was a bean in her ear. Off to our Otolaryngologist. He couldn't get it out. Off to the hospital where she was taken into surgery. Suzie explained that they were doing a project on beans at school and she decided to put one in her ear to feel what a hearing aid would be like.

When she was two she somehow contracted spinal meningitis, the bulbar kind, one hundred percent fatal until streptomycin and penicillin were invented. She was in the hospital for four weeks. We, at her side watching over her, begged her to take in just a teaspoon of fluid. As she struggled between life and death she was in the hospital for twenty-eight days. We were charged forty dollars. Them days are gone forever. Finally, she came home healthy, albeit with a deaf ear from the high fever and the streptomycin. The least of the losses we could have anticipated. So, she was trying out a hearing aid with the bean.

Suzie stated going to camp when she was about eight. She became a confirmed and ardent camper when she went to Firebird Camp in southern Ohio for three years. All of our daughters, grand-daughter, Laurie and great grand-daughter Eve followed. It became the "Family Camp."

When she was fourteen she went to Camp Bryn Avon in Wisconsin. One night she and her friends dismantled the equipment for every class. They hid all the arrows for archery, removed the bolts for the guns for marksmanship, took the bridles from the stables, the nets from the tennis courts, put all they had collected in canoes, and shoved them out on a lake.

The following year she went to a working ranch and loved it. She wrote "I've fallen in love – truly in love." I thought "Oh Lordy, Lordy – a cowboy." She said "his name is Ben and he is my horse for the summer." Whew!

Suzie succeeded in becoming pregnant at seventeen. Then she succeeded in marrying two Peter-Pan type men, but did not succeed in changing them.

Her motto, etched on stained glass became:

"Never try to teach a pig to sing,
It doesn't work and
Just annoys the Pig"

Divorced with three children, no vocational training and no visible income, she knew she didn't want to clean houses or be a cocktail waitress anymore. Nearly forty, she applied for a job at Harris Publications to work in Industrial Sales for yellow page advertising. She had two strikes against her: the Harrises were close friends of ours and feared hiring her, lest they might have to fire her if she didn't succeed. Secondly, she flunked a three-day battery of tests (incidentally normed on men). The results clearly showed, said Bob Harris, that she couldn't sell.

Suzie went back to his office the following day. She asked Bob, "What do you think makes a successful salesperson?" and "What can't be taught and can't be learned." He regarded her quizzically and she said, "I believe one ingredient that can't be measured is guts and I have guts."

He hired her.

Now she realizes that was her most successful sales call.

The first month she was the top sales person in the company! She, naively, didn't realize she was in a race.

In 1985, Ameritech acquired the Industrial Division and Suzie was the only person hired from the Harris Company.

When the Industrial Division became part of the Corporate Enterprise only two employees were hired from the former division to be corporate employees through a rigorous selection process. Suzie succeeded, becoming an employee in the corporate world. Suzie's free spirit encountered the inflexible, sometimes irrational discipline of a mega business. She succeeded resoundingly.

Deborah

She came out all pink and white, beautifully formed from a comparatively short labor, while Cope and my doctor were having breakfast. She came with me into a special room that was called in those days a new experiment "a lying in room." She was in her little lucite bassinette right next to my bed. We bonded there. We named her Deborah Elizabeth (I got second billing.) She was beautiful, round and rosy. I cradled her and walked her around the room. We couldn't go out of the room because I didn't want her exposed to other moms and babies for sanitation reasons. She never had to go out with the other babies. So every time she cried I was there.

When she was eighteen months old I was teaching nursery school; I took her with me. She learned to crayon and to socialize with other children who were much older than she was. She went to my nursery school until kindergarten. Then went to the public kindergarten that I had started many years before.

I have never ceased to be amazed - and sometimes terrified at children's propensity for saying the most improbable things at the most impossible times. One day I left four year old Deborah in the doctor's waiting room while I took the baby in to his office for a shot.

She had been following the usual pattern of the fourth year by becoming quite shy with strangers, even our friends. So I was naturally delighted when I heard her chattering away to the roomful of people. She was obviously having a fine time and so were her new found friends when I retrieved her after our visit.

I put her hat and coat on and grinned at her with unabashed pride while (I thought) all the good folks smiled at our lovely tableau - she - curly haired and pinked cheeked, soft brown eyes dancing, and I, the adoring mama.

We waved good-bye gaily and left. I asked, "Did you have a nice visit?"

She said happily, "oh, yes."

"What did you say to them?" I asked, not knowing when I was well off.

"I told them to blow their noses in their ham sandwich." Said my pride and joy.

I took Deborah and Kristina to a children's matinee when Deb was five and Kris was two. Deborah, of course saw the ubiquitous soft drink machine and pleaded for a dime. "You can't have a soda now honey, you have to wait until intermission." By the time intermission came, I asked her "where is the dime sweetheart?" She said, "It is up my nose. I couldn't find anywhere else to put it so I put it in my nose." I felt it, but I couldn't pull it out. It was surely stuck in there. So I called our faithful otologingologist. Of course the office was closed because it was Wednesday afternoon. Several other doctors were out too. I told Deborah "I don't have any more dimes left." Deb said, "well maybe if I just bwow my nose I can get this dime out for you." Oh my, how children solve the most complicated issues so simply.

Deborah can so easily recall playing in the lot behind the tent, making mud balls, drying them and throwing them at each other.

She remembers vividly setting up her little ironing board in the new porch room that her dad built. She would iron back and forth endlessly with her little red car wearing a red wool cap with a fringy ponytail and her flowered bathrobe.

Deb always had a little school in the basement just as I did when I was a child. She drew up lesson plans and had her attentive students sit in little seats. I heard her say to Kristina "wepeat after me Kwis – Wobin wed bwest," I just held my head in both hands.

She spent hours running around in her white polka dot tutu from Miss Betsy's school of ballet.

She was an obedient, cheerful budding *haus frow*. She stood by me when I was cooking and canning, watched and helped me at an early age as I had done with my mother.

In summers she and Kris walked all over town and played in the ravine behind our house and the golf course. She and a friend, Peggy Jewett, played in the sand box, on the swings and in the sewers of Aurora. I never knew about the sewers until they were adults when they told me all four spent their summers in the sewers!

Elementary school passed her by in a blur. In the ninth grade she started dating Don Woljevach and fell into teen love with him. Cope and I didn't think much of him, so were delighted and relieved when she went to college at Ohio University. We flipped out when we discovered that Don turned up there.

Deb only stayed for one semester; she found her courses boring. She and Don and most everyone their age became flower children, while we wrung our hands. When she was nineteen Cope appointed her manager of the teen and pre-teen clothing store that he bought in Chagrin Falls. She did an excellent job, but when she was twenty-one she announced that she "didn't want to be a capitalist anymore" and left for California with Don in his leaky van. The van died in Indianapolis, Indiana. They hung out there until it was fixed and then drove to Santa Barbara, California.

Deb worked for a family with four children who were in her charge. She called to tell us that she was getting married, but they didn't want us to come. I heard Cope begging her to let us come: "if only for five minutes, honey." She said no. It was the first time I saw my husband cry. In time, they got jobs in a huge estate in Montecito. They were given a perfect little adobe house. They had five chickens, one was named "Mother," etc. and knew each one by name. Their chickens laid double yolk eggs for them. When Deb got them a rooster they were so mad at her because the rooster was so horny that they stopped laying eggs entirely.

Deb started classes at Santa Barbara City College. She majored in nutrition. Her enquiring spirit was bored with just cleaning the big house. They grew apart in separate pursuits after four and one half years and divorced.

Deborah was working in a coffee café when Peter walked past, and with one glimpse of her, fell in love. He had planned to leave the next day

Peter and Deborah wedding photo by the lake

for his parents' home in Massachusetts, but stayed on. They lived together in the same big community house Kristina lived in. The variety of people was fascinating. Peter and Deborah camped during the weekends. Six months later they picked up sticks and drove for six months in the wilds and went white water rafting. I went crazy worrying about her with no means of communication. They took Peter's huge dog, part Husky and part German Shepard. Deborah got poison ivy; itching all over and camping with a big shedding dog in Deb's station wagon. I figured she would be able to survive anything with Peter and she has. Together they struggled through a year of Peter's aggressive cancer and treatment. She ran the business when he was virtually immobilized and drove him a distance to the Cancer Center. Today he is vigorous and cured!

Come In And Join Us
For Our Grand Opening, May 26 & 27.

We Bring To You The Finest Quality
Soft Wool Blankets, Imported
From England

THE BLANKET TRADERS
TREELINE TIPIS

Retail Location:
In The Country Peddler
Main Street, Box 496R
North Conway, NH 03860

603-539-4473
RT. 1 Box 192 AR
So. Effingham, NH 03882

Their first effort built in their dining room.
Later it has become a thriving business
known all over the world. Peter is reknowed
as the premier tent maker in the world.

"Questionable Dreams/ Unbelievable Success"

Deborah and Peter were married on a clear sunny fall day, September 23, 1982, by our lake. They looked like a Victorian couple as you can see. We had never met his family before, so I asked Deb how I should be with them. She said "Mom you are fine, just don't say "fuck." We had a huge white tent in the front yard with chamber music.

A few years later we visited them in New Hampshire in their rented log cabin. Peter was cutting a tent in the dining room. They hoped it would become a business: the most esoteric enterprise...

They were to become authentic period tents starting with the sixteen hundreds. They sold tipis and blankets. Today it has become a thriving business. They sell tents all over the world; and they have made seven movies for Hollywood.

Peter has a reputation of being the best tent maker in the world!

They have two grown children – men in their twenties and Chris's and Annie's little girl almost three, called Avelyn. She is a corker, so bright and intuitive. Eve, another great-grand daughter of T and Cait is so intelligent and creative. Deborah's total adoration of Avelyn is a joy to behold. When someone asked Avie who her best friend was, she said without hesitation "YaYa" (Deborah). Now they have a baby boy named Logan Peter.

Kristina the Potter

Kristina wearing Gram's
cherry hat we kept for her
in the closet

Momma and daughter

Life With Kristina

Our lives would never have been as rich without Kristina. I believe she invented herself – what a creation! Artist, potter, poet, now massage therapist, our youngest angel.

When she was a baby Cope asked me to make a list of things I needed. I wrote: "Q Tips, boric acid, baby oil and a boa martin scarf." He came home with everything! I danced on the kitchen table at midnight with nothing on except my boa martin!

One day, Kristina and her friend, Jennifer, ate all the blossoms off my tulips around the foundation planting of our house. Somehow, I always found it difficult to get angry with Kris. One New Year's Eve party, I ate half a dozen American Beauty roses from the centerpiece. I have often thought that Kris was my clone – greatly advanced. I see myself when I look into her eyes.

Krissy spent her early years in the window well of our house with her frogs and turtles. Kris imbued that window well with a sense of discovery, magic, and mystery as she dug up the little animals, finding turtle eggs, newly born frogs, and other surprises. There was a sense of wonder being in a secret enclosed space, digging into a subterranean world that entranced her buddies. Kris's window well became the most sought–after place in the neighborhood.

Then she started collecting gerbils and Guinea pigs. As they multiplied, Dad was co-opted into building new apartments, one after another. She tended them daily in our "permanent tent"-- thus called by neighbor Jill Wilson because our area in Aurora, the "Allotment," didn't allow any out-buildings. Jack had found a large piece of canvas by the roadside one day. He liberated it and made the tent in our woods. In time, he built walls and a ceiling inside the canvas, and installed electricity, so that the little animals had heat and light in the winter. Kristina's brother and sisters gave her new species of Guinea pigs and gerbils on special occasions, and everybody multiplied!

Kris named it "The House of Happy Talk" because when one of our cars came into the driveway, or when the animals could hear us talking, they would all squeak loudly. So her Dad made a sign above the door: "The House of Happy Talk".

Now that we have established residence in our Southern haven, we have the sign by our pool bathroom door: "House of Happy Talk II". And we squeak and chirp too!

Kris and I made weekly trips to the farmer's market to collect bushels of discarded lettuce and other vegetables to feed her burgeoning family. Gradually, the animals took over a large chunk of her life.

One day when she was thirteen and about to pube she came to me and told me she wanted to sell her little pets. I figured that she had decided to embark on adolescence. She put an ad in our local paper.

> For Sale: Long and short haired Guinea pigs and gerbils, lovingly bred and lovingly fed in "The House of Happy Talk". Call for an appointment.

Kris interviewed the prospective caretakers of her tribe. She sat formally in the living room, and served tea while she screened the potential adoptive parents like a social worker. Soon all the little animals had found good homes and new friends.

When Kris was nine and her sister Deborah was twelve, they went to Firebird Camp in Southern Ohio where their older sister, Susan, had spent many happy summers. Kris spent most of the first summer in the infirmary with a variety of illnesses. Maybe that was her way of creating a womb away from home. She had been a very sick baby with constant deep ear infections and high fevers. She could not sleep because of the severe pain. I often remarked that I carried her on my shoulders for her first three years the way some women wore their mink scarves. I rocked her in Gram's old rocking chair most nights for three years. I was bemused at how she fashioned a nurturing experience replicating her babyhood pain and healing when she experienced separation from us at camp.

Finally, a doctor who understood allergies moved to Aurora – both Kris and I tested positive on every skin test. It seems that I had transferred my allergies to her through my milk. We embarked on what turned out to be eight years of weekly allergy shots. During those years we stripped her bedroom of carpeting and curtains – any kind of dust catchers. Her diet was severely limited. No cow's milk or other dairy products were allowed; I went to a farm regularly to buy goat's milk. For years I packed her little lunch box for school with an oatmeal banana bread sandwich. At last she became healthy, happy and full of spunk.

Kris also had a degree of dyslexia that made reading very difficult. I took her to Dr. Rose, a pioneer in the field of dyslexia, which was a mostly undiagnosed and little understood learning disorder. He worked with us for years to help overcome Kris' distance over-convergence and close under-convergence eye coordination problems. In time, the eye-hand coordination lessons proved to help her immensely. She was always very bright, a searcher and a quick learner, but she languished in a typical academic setting.

So the next thing to do was to find a school where she could learn in her own way. "New Schools" flowered in the mid-sixties as traditional academia was challenged and found wanting. We enrolled her in the Kent State University Lab School for her first three years of high school. It was loosely run to say the least. When it folded, we toured New England to find the "perfect" school for her. She decided on Stockbridge School in Stockbridge, Massachusetts. A dear little town with a gentle way of life. The home of Norman Rockwell and time-honored traditions.

But the <u>school</u> was another story! We settled her in, impressed with the Headmaster and her teachers – so happy that we had found a safe learning milieu in which she could flourish. Our last child was launched out into the world.

Two weeks later she called us.

"I have to go to India."

I replied in a typical Mom fashion.

"But we just took you to Massachusetts!"

"I have joined the Divine Light Mission. Jumbo jets from all over the world are taking devotees to Maharaja Ji's ashram to celebrate his birthday. I <u>have</u> to go."

"You can't. You have just enrolled in your senior year at a fine alternative school. You need to buckle down and study."

"Mom and Dad, I <u>have</u> to go."

Knowing full well that the Headmaster would never allow this, we flew up to Stockbridge to settle Kris down so she wouldn't bolt. We arranged a meeting with the Headmaster, her Guidance Counselor, and teachers. The unbelievable happened. They said she <u>could</u> go for the entire <u>six</u> weeks, as long as she wrote a report about her experience. We were non-plussed – in a stupor. This school cost as much for a year as Harvard!!

The Guru Maharaja was a sixteen-year-old boy whose mother had anointed him after her husband, the old guru, died. I called everyone I could think of to get reliable information about this cult. The late sixties and seventies were the halcyon time for cults to flourish as young people, and older folks too, became disenchanted with traditional Western culture and religion, and sought spiritual guidance in the East. Scared and concerned for my daughter's well being, I called our ambassador to India, the Indian ambassador to the U.S., everyone I could think of. To a man, they said the same thing.

"There is a guru in every valley and mountain top in India. They are cashing in on the minds and monies of the naïve young people of the Western world."

However, Kristina went. I walked the floor nights, afraid for her health and mind. "Will we lose her?" was my refrain. We became even more anxious when she decided to delay her return by an extra two weeks without even calling to tell us! We had no way to communicate.

To escape our worries, Jack and I went to our place on St. Croix for some R&R. Unbelievably, and to our mounting agony, we discovered that a mother and son in the condominium above us had "escaped" from the Ashram and had horror stories to tell us. Stories of incessant hours of meditation each day starting at 4:00 am, laboring all day at menial jobs, pounding peanuts by hand in order to make their peanut butter, and undergoing hours of brainwashing sessions. There were no sanitation facilities. They bathed every day in the Ganges where feces, urine and dead bodies were absorbed by the putrid river. No one was allowed to leave. This mother and son found their search for enlightenment doomed, and slipped away into the night, past the guards.

We feared losing her to the cult – and feared for her very life. When she did return she told us we were only her "earthly parents." That was one of the few times I saw my husband cry.

Kristina arrived at Kennedy Airport without a dime, clad in flowing white clothes, carrying a bottle of sacred water from the Ganges as a special gift to us. Not even a cent to call us.

Predictably for Kris who falls out of trees on her feet, she ran into two friends whose grandmother had sent her chauffeur to meet them at the airport to bring them home. They took Kris with them to Gram's palatial home.

After India, Kristina went back to Stockbridge to continue her senior year studies. Her courses were "Pottery," "Thinking," "Mood Synthesizer," and "Slumber Lumber," (which as near as we could figure out meant sleeping with the boys in the woods) "The Question," "Yoga," and "World Religions." Where were the Math, Latin, Science, English and French? Years later I asked her what she liked best about Stockbridge and she said "swimming nude in the quarry, watching kids coming in and out of psychiatric hospitals and hitchhiking to Boston and New York." Jack and I looked limply at each other and swallowed our despair.

Kristina's graduation in 1971 expressed a bridge between tradition and rebellion. The ceremony was held in a lovely green bower of the Elizabethan Theatre. Kris somehow unearthed my mother's long white batiste dress decorated with lace and crochet needlework. She was beautiful – a statement from the Victorian Era in a much removed moment in time.

There they were – the graduating class, dressed by Goodwill and barefooted; one boy wore a tux and derby hat, but no shoes or shirt. The classic chamber music was lovely. In that bucolic setting, it all seemed incongruous, but so poignant. I wept.

In retrospect, we see that the career of her lifetime as an original potter and poet started with her courses in the milieu of Stockbridge. It was the embryonic pool for free thinking, combined with the journey inward that Eastern philosophy provided.

Kristina launched herself into the world. She was told to distribute posters on walls in the Bowery of New York City, the bowels of the earth, for the Divine Light Mission. One night she spent talking alone with a confessed murderer well past 2:00 A.M.! He told her she had a "shining aura around her." I think that must be what saved her. Kris has never lived "safely;" yet her spirit keeps her safe.

Her beautiful wardrobe had been tossed away. Only Goodwill clothes would do. One weekend we flew up from Ohio to visit and took her to Sunday dinner at a Scottish Castle. She arrived in an antique tux and top hat, looking like a diminutive Charlie Chaplin. Jack said, "What the hell will we do with her?" I just told him, "She's our daughter, let's go."

During the late 60's and 70's we did a lot of that "what the hell will we do with him/her." We had been taught that our parents' values were eternal verities, but our children in those chaotic years were throwing out most of them. "Everyone over thirty is dumb," was the general belief among the youth.

Cope and I tried to keep the love and lines of communication open. We all suffered through periods of separation while we each went through necessary individuation. We always came back together for understanding and nurturing, bonding together even more strongly than before. We realized that each offspring needed different catalytic wombs to grow through the changing time – and each moved at a different pace.

I was studying in Graduate School, working with the students, respecting their views. I saw so many young people angry and frustrated over issues of clothing, boys with long hair and the havoc their choices caused within their families. They were fumbling to make their statements about the rigidity and decadence of their parents and most of society in general. Many families were torn apart in uncompromising alienation and inability to communicate. We hoped that our family bond of love would carry us all through the changing times. We had already taught them what we could.

After Stockbridge, Kristina enrolled in a Rudolph Steiner School and studied pottery making with a very talented and famous instructor. The next fall, she went to live in an Ashram in Columbus. There she became a housemother and learned the drudgery of cooking constantly for a houseful of people. I don't think she has cooked since.

Kris developed her own liberal education – she worked as a chambermaid, on an assembly line at a lawn mower factory, etc. Somewhere along the way she needed a secretary wardrobe as I recall. And somewhere further along the way she decided to come home for the summer. Jubilant, I redecorated our son's old room with wallpaper of roses and vines, light blue bedspreads and curtains all trimmed with white ball fringe. I basked in the lovely aura of having our daughter back "in the nest."

After a short time she said, "I would like to have a 'Divine Light Mission Garage Sale' and sell all my earthly possessions – my furniture, my collections, everything. May I do that?"

The Divine Light Mission had already divested her of her hand-carved ivory sitar from India, her camera and rings her father had given her for her twelfth and eighteenth birthdays. Now this. We searched our souls for a few days. Her commitment was so meaningful to her. We decided that the beds and all were really hers. So we had a sign in front of our lovely Western Reserve home: "Divine Light Garage Sale." She operated in the garage for days until everything was gone. The money went to the Guru, and all that was left in her room was a lace-bedecked shrine with a picture of the Guru Maharaja Ji and her futon mattress. Jack drew the line at giving away her car and the trust fund she had inherited from her grandfather, so she wouldn't feel guilty. She thanks him now. It has facilitated her business and artistic ventures.

During this time many strange young people washed up at our doorstep. Yalie looked to be at least nine feet tall. I think he meant to live with us permanently. One day he made pancakes for our breakfast. I was delighted until I took a bite. He had seasoned them with sage and cumin. Standing in the kitchen flipping pancakes, wearing one of Deborah's old flowered bathrobes that came just above his knobby knees, showing off his long hairy legs, he was quite a sight. His *nom de plume* at our house became Cookoo.

Cookoo was predictably unpredictable. One day he used the new handmade bedspread from the guest room to envelop his tall frame as he meditated in a mud puddle. Pretty soon it became time for Cookoo to move on.

Then there was the time we heard people walking around on our back porch about 3:00 A.M. I found a boy and girl huddled against the wall. "Hi," I said, "Who are you? Friends of Krissy's?" "Yes," they chimed. "Well, come on in and go to bed," said I, tucking them in with glasses of warm milk.

I made breakfast for them in the morning and woke Kris.

"Surprise, honey, your friends are here."

Kris bounced down the stairs and then motioned me aside.

"Mom, I never saw them before in my life."

It began to seem that the whole world wanted to be friends with Kristina.

Her worldly possessions disposed of, Kris headed for California and left us with the shrine to the Guru and an empty room. She enrolled in New College in Sausalito with her two best friends. For several years she studied at various colleges and waitressed. Along the way she took six generation Chinese Brush Stroke painting from a master, learned to play the harp, violin, etc. The Socratic method of learning at the feet of a master worked well for her.

Once we visited her when she lived in Santa Barbara in the posh Riviera area. We couldn't imagine how she could afford it – then we knew. She had rented an old VW bus with no wheels parked in the back yard of a community house – a once elegant mansion of many rooms that had seen better days. Her rent was one hundred dollars a month, with kitchen, bathroom and washing privileges, and a corner of the music room for her harp. One of the many memorable times with Kris was sitting with her in her van, with nothing in it but a lace shrine and the futon on a rainy afternoon. Jack said, "Let's go out for a Bloody Mary."

The community house occupants were an odd assortment of all colors and types. A Native American attorney with long braided hair who lived in the house asked Jack how he felt about his daughter living there. To his eternal credit and my devotion, my husband replied, "My daughters have never ceased to challenge me and I have never ceased to rise to the occasion."

On our visits to Kristina, she selected the inn or hotel for us very carefully, inspecting the rooms and trying out the beds. One time we stayed in the tiny Sausalito Inn on the waterfront, in a postage stamp room with an antique bed that certainly looked as if Lincoln had slept there. The huge fern and its stand seemed to take up more room than we did. The room she selected had General Grant's bed in it.

We decided to go to the little bar below to wait for Kris to come from her late class. We watched for her from our table by the window. Pretty soon the bartender closed all the curtains and in trooped about eight transvestites, one in a long red satin dress slit to the crotch, others in velvets and silks in dramatic colors. They all had long cigarette holders, tons of make-up and mustaches. We forgot it was Halloween. I have never felt so under-dressed in my life, with my Midwestern forest green blazer and plaid skirt. It was a pretty racey scene for the seventies.

Soon Kris was living with Mark Watts in a tree house on Mt. Tamalpais. His father, Alan Watts, had been a psychiatrist and an Anglican priest famous for his studies joining Eastern and Western philosophy and religions.

Mark was exceptionally bright and the perfect person to help Kris sort out her belief system. She has used all her knowledge and experience to evolve into a fascinating, thoughtful, positive, joyful and healing partner.

Because of her connection with Grandfather David, an Elder in the Hopi tribe, she and Mark were invited to go with him to a conference on the Native Americans in Geneva. Elders from other tribes were there. It proved to be an impressing experience.

They spent six months hiking, and then driving, through Italy and Greece. Inevitably, the time came for Kristina to leave him when she discovered that he really was not a nurturing partner. After she broke her foot, it became hard to live in the tree house and he was not solicitous.

She came back home to Aurora to replenish her spirit and studied pottery for a semester at the Cleveland Institute of Art. Her creations were on a grand scale. She wrote poetry about each piece and worked it into the clay.

Then California called to her once more. From 1979 through 1981 she studied at the College of Santa Cruz, Santa Barbara Community College and San Jose State College. She supported herself by waitressing, but always Kris returned to her true passion – pottery. Each piece she made was symbolic of her evolution at the moment.

A dramatic turning point in her life came when she met Michael Kelley. It was "love at first sight" for both of them. Her world changed. They moved to Casa Grande, a desert town in Arizona, to be near his dying mother, Marion. With Michael's invention, a multi-wave osilator, and with their loving care, Marion recovered and lived for many years. It was an ugly little desert town. I often remarked that if you wanted to give the world an enema you should stick the tube in there.

Kristina and Michael rented space in a shopping mall and opened a lovely store selling all manner of electronic things – from satellite dishes to microwave ovens. Michael was an electronic genius. Kris learned accounting and kept the books, also learning about the technology of their numerous products. At one time she was celebrated as Business Woman of the Month by the Ladies Business Group. Amazing!

"The Satellite Center" was extraordinarily attractive. Together they created it – building walls, plastering, painting and mounting mirrored and lighted display shelves. They breathed love into it. They went to flea markets and garage sales and emerged with treasures.

Sadly, in 1992, after working every waking hour on their store for ten years, they had to close shop. The mall had become run-down. People gravitated to newer, sleeker malls and the huge discount stores. They closed the door on that chapter of their lives with no pension, unemployment benefits, etc. It was a very painful time for both of them and we hurt for them. They were bankrupt.

To compensate for the rest of their lease they concreted the outside walkway of the mall on their hands and knees, working from 4:am to 8:am, before the stores still remaining opened. They worked from November '93 until July '94 to pay off the remainder of the amount they owed on the lease – twenty-three thousand dollars. We couldn't believe that our diminutive one hundred pound Kris could sustain such grueling work and for so long. But no job daunted them. They are survivors.

Michael, while working for an air conditioning company, fell off a roof in '94 while installing a unit. He damaged both knees, both shoulders and his right hand. He has lived with incredible pain and has had two knee surgeries thus far.

Kristina had a stunning art gallery that, again, she and Michael created. She is devoting herself to her true craft and talent, pottery. All of her artwork is unique and an expression of her soul – angels, spirit vigils and always – her turtles. Her gallery was called "The Clay Speaks." Wisely, she had chosen other area artists' work to diversify her presentation.

In her winsome and determined way, she manages to get scholarships to every potter class at the colleges in the environs. She has studied also with the Indians there. She mostly produced stunning raku pottery. She writes delightful poetry and is a voracious reader now. The living room of their home is a crystal gallery. She remembers the name and origin of each piece.

THE CLAY SPEAKS

KC STUDIOS CASA GRANDE, ARIZONA

Kristina Colebrook

" When I touch the raw clay, my search is to speak through it. Whatever my life path is, at that moment, culminates through that contact with the clay. Each piece is a voice, each piece a journey unto itself. Each piece sings its own song. I am there to facilitate its speaking, to bring out its story. I enjoy working with the earths substance, its very nature. I welcome you to enjoy my work and hope you too, hear it speak ".
KC

Art Man Productions **Kristina Colebrook**
is honored to introduce:

Kristina has been working with clay and other media all of her life. She began at age six making clay turtles. "Clay is a giving and moving medium. We walk on it, it holds us up", says Kristina. Only recently, January '94, Kristina has offered her works to become available to the public. To Kristina, " The Clay Speaks ", and she responds to it. We welcome her works and hope to extend a part of her through the pieces she creates.

Kristina is a limited production artist. Each creation is one of a kind and she creates only when the clay speaks to her. With a very limited number of works in the offering, we suggest you carefully listen to each piece, and see if it is asking you to take it home. Don't pass up this opportunity to acquire something so rare and precious. We would not be surprised to see her works accelerate in value and see her name along side todays great artists.

Kristina has studied with such renowned artists as: M C Richards, David Middlebrook and Victor Spinski to name a few. Kristina has attended the Cleveland Institute of Art, the Miami Metropolitan Museum of the Arts, San Jose State College and the San Francisco Academy of Art.

Kristina is a 14 year resident of Casa Grande Arizona. She finds the desert an inspiration for her works. The peaceful open space of the desert brings forth the words and form to her clay.   ART MAN July '96

Desert Wind Singers

For more information about current show dates, questions, comments or contact with Ms. Kristina Colebrook, ask the showing gallery, or call Art Man Productions, a Division of Mobile One "Technical Services" by voice or fax at 520 - 836-6277 - You may also write to: KC Studios at P.O. Box 11321 - Casa Grande, AZ 85230-1321
The Clay Speaks © copyright 1994 all rights reserved.

KC STUDIOS
"THE CLAY SPEAKS "
Kristina Colebrook
P.O. Box 11321 - Casa Grande, AZ. 85230 - (602) 836-6277

Kris and Michael parted. After some time she met "Montana Bob" in a sweat lodge. They dated and fell in love in a permanent commitment. He had been a hermit living in a shack on top of a mountain in Montana since he was eighteen. So, now in his early forties, she de-hermited him and he goes to parties and dances and other events all the time. Such is the power of Love! He cooks for her! Hooray, she will not starve.

They moved from Casa Grande, bought a lovely sprawling adobe house on the foothills of the Tucson mountains. Kris has taken many courses in massage and is now a certified maso-therapist. She works in a spa in a fancy nude hotel in Tucson. They go to nude parties every weekend and have lots of interesting friends. Kris is ever a determined learner. She goes to workshops on all the varied disciplines of massage therapy and counseling.

As with all "hands-on" bodywork, people seep out their innermost problems to an empathic healer. She has evolved the ability to help with her native intuition and training. One could observe that Kris "loved to fall in love" too. My clone!

May they be strengthened by yesterday's rain, walk straight in tomorrow's wind and cherish each moment of the sun today and may the Great Spirit always walk with them.

Bob and Kristina

Mud Princess

Kristina with a hand made plate
with poetry in circles

Spiral Poem
About The Poetry - By Kristina Colebrook, my daughter

A spiral starts at the center
At the center ripples start.
Ripples move out from the center
our lives interweave
We think and the Mind receives
Time and time again, what you do matters
to me
your tone of living, touches my life
and the way I live mine
Yet, and oh yet I have my own unique freedom
My freedom to be my tone
Live, perceive, receive from nature
in her many forms and expressions
Perceiving, receiving, retrieving – Atoning –
These freedoms are my God given gifts
and my heart is thankful,
for these spaces in places....
Sometimes a place you've known for many years as just so
open= same place more space –
is this another dimension?
Creating a whole new roominess, an area –
unusual – the usual holds
- I just knew there was more
and I knew I wanted it.
I knew it was always right there before me.
Yet and oh yet, it took time
Time tells tales
Tells tales of times past, present, future.
Now it all meets.
Now it all exists.
The multitude of facets.
The Godhead sees mirror upon mirror
the many selves align – sighing, they all look from the center.
In a moment, they touch their heart of love and send it out –
send it out in all directions, in a breath, like a ripple from the center out.
Sometimes when it gets reflected, it spills back to the sender.

"A penny for a spool of thread, a penny for a needle and that's the way my money goes, pop goes the weasel"

A Father's Legacy

Cope with assorted grandchildren

A Father's Legacy

Cope had a sweet ritual with our children and grandchildren following in his father's footsteps. He lifted them to sit on his knees and sang; "a penny for a spool of thread, a penny for a needle and that's the way my money goes, POP goes the weasel." At the POP he bounced them on his knees and threw them up in the air.

Each child waited in anticipation for the "Pop" - their eyes popping out of their heads, clapping and hugging him, wanting him to do it over and over. I have some pictures of son Mike, his son Max, holding big Cope on their knees playing "Pop". I see them all carrying the ritual down through the extended family tree.

Cope thoughtfully says, "I think my greatest satisfaction in life is seeing my children arrive in good places in their lives as they evolve through the rocky times, the joyful times and to watch my grandchildren develop. It's a great joy to hear from my grandchildren that some of the values they develop are from me. That feels good and I am happy to see Betts evolve, on a new course in her later years. I share many of her interests. We often go to psychological conferences and I enjoy her memoir writing."

He thoroughly enjoys his retirement, his new artistic expression in sculpting: the thrill of watching the unknown of the rock evolve into a unique creation in his hands. He feels a sense of accomplishment with his golf. He has loved the game since he was nine years old, but faced an obstacle when the nerves in his right hand were affected during a quadruple heart by-pass surgery twelve years ago, leaving several of his fingers and part of his hand numb. To his credit he swallowed his pride about playing an inferior game after being a scratch golfer. It required a certain gracefulness and ego acceptance as he mastered a new grip. Later he contracted shingles. He was very sick: couldn't bear for anything to touch his chest, wanted so much to play golf when out of bed. I took some of his shirts to a dressmaker to cut the front down. I called him "The sex symbol of Longboat Key." When you are handed a lemon, make lemonade. He played with inexpressible pain and moaned about going out to "the torture chamber." But he played! I well remember how on one of our trips to visit Kris in California she insisted that we go to a "meeting" with her. We sat in a large circle and chanted "om" for three hours. Cope, the business man passed that test too.

Cope was pleased to hear his former secretary, whom we met in one of those serendipitous accidents recently describe how well liked he had been by everyone when he was president of a large storage company in Cleveland. She said he handled every person and every problem well. Never was a bad word said about him by his customers, his workers, or the union.

Most of all his legacy of love and kindness, his honesty and trustworthiness are carried on in the hearts of his children and grandchildren. Even his great-grand child, Eve, now nine who was one year old when he died, but adores him and yearns for him from the love her father, T, shows for him. She often says, "I want to visit Jack." Susan, her grandmother, takes her to the cemetery and they sit quietly by his burial plot.

His greatest pride was that people said he was trust worthy. His word has always been his contract. With age he knew more about who he is. He is a man of honor and a loving nurturer to all his family, who love him deeply.

Future goals?

"To make my wife happy and lower my golf handicap."

I'm glad I come in first.

I would give anything to hear him singing "Pop goes the Weasel" to his grandchildren today.

My Helpers Through The Years

First came a young Mennonite girl named Aldene.

Then came Maggie from a destitute family. I bought her clothes and had her teeth fixed. She stayed with us for a few years and we loved her.

Then came Martha Washington, a very large black lady. I hired her on the spot because she asked to go to the bathroom and when she came back she said, " Oh, that's better; I had to take my girdle off now that I think you are hiring me." I thought she would be good for kicks. When I asked her to wash the kitchen floor she said, "Oh I can't do that." So it was bye bye.

Then came Hazel and Elaine, two black ladies. When I picked them up I would end up with the one less drunk. Usually I had them come on separate days. One time in an emergency before Christmas I had both of them on the same day. Hazel, ugly as a mud fence, was finishing the gin. She erupted from ironing in the basement with blood in her eyes. "Mrs. Colebrook, Elaine is sleeping with my Charlie and you better watch out, she'll be sleeping with your husband."

The end of that regime came when neither one of them could stagger out in the morning. It was sad I really loved them.

Then came Julia, she had no teeth, but she could gum the toughest of foods. She arrived at 7:15 every morning on the Erie Railroad, walked to our house in blistering heat and icy snow. She worked for us until the train came to take her back to Garrettsville at six p.m. Her fee was eight dollars. She cleaned our large house, changed the beds and washed and ironed. Julia's once beautiful face was worn and haggard. She wore a babushka over her hair. If she was getting a cold she wore a large clove of garlic on a string around her neck, or sometimes a hot pepper. She smelled bad, but they seemed to work; she never got sick.

She could not read or write....but I didn't realize that for many years. She and her husband, still young and handsome looking, had seven boarders. She washed and ironed all their clothes, made their breakfasts, packed their lunch boxes and boarded the train at six a.m. When Julia discovered her husband was having an affair, she grabbed a clothes pole and ran around the outside of the house, smashing all the windows. Julia was not a woman to be reckoned with. At the end of the day we sat down together and she had two shots of whiskey for the road. Julia was an icon.

Once when Julia and her husband come to visit after she had retired I invited them to have a drink. The husband said "No thanks we have some at home."

My Helpers
Rebecca's Story:
She Did It All On Faith

A distraught Rebecca confesses the worst sin for an Amish woman: "I have committed adultery," she told her husband Andrew. "Can you forgive me?" "Okay," he said, not missing a bite of his dinner. She had expected a torrent of his usual verbal abuse followed by stony silence.

After twenty-two years of a loveless marriage, Rebecca had met a man who made her feel loved for the first time in her life. Her only indiscretion ended up tearing her apart.

She was thrice violated: by a lover who was a sex addict (whom she discovered had been having a nine year sexual affair with her best friend Martha, by a husband who didn't care, and by church officials who ordered her shunned after her confessions to the entire congregation. She sought guidance from God every step of the way realizing that the preachers' repressive rules were designed to control members from straying.

She had been taught that the "English Way or Yankee Way," as Amish call outsiders, was too worldly. No longer willing to live a life she didn't believe in, Rebecca felt trapped, yet she couldn't conceive any other way to live.

Many days she lay on the floor sobbing, tasting fear and desperation. Ann, her eldest daughter, then twenty, believed her mother was possessed by the devil. Andy Ray, nineteen, thought she was menopausal and made her promise to see a doctor. (as though he knew anything about female problems)

Her three youngest daughters were unable to formulate any opinion: they were severely handicapped and totally dependent on her. A genetic inheritance will eventually render them all blind. Laura, now twenty, functions at a nine-month level, while Tina has the capacity of a three-month old. She cannot feed herself or walk. They will always be in diapers and wheelchair bound. Rebecca's fourteen year-old daughter, tiny Becky can walk and talk but needs constant care.

She called me one Friday and was at the end of the rope. "Betts, I don't know what to do. I have to get away but no Amish woman goes away from her husband and I have no money and no place to go!" "Yes, you do honey. Jack and I will be over to get you in an hour." We spent an interesting week-end together walking and talking, taking her out to a Chinese dinner where she ordered two "peach pussies" while out of deference to her we drank periot. Her spirits lifted. Then we had a martini.

But when we took her home Sunday night there were two black buggies parked by the house. We could see the people with their big black hats in the living room. "Rebecca, I'm afraid you are in for a tough time now, but it wouldn't do any good for us to come in with you." I wrote in my journal that night "I see no way out for Rebecca. She is trapped – hating her Amish life, but can't see any alternative."

At 10:00 a.m. the next morning she called to tell me that she had taken the three children, withdrew money from the joint savings account, rented a house and gone to a lawyer to sue for divorce." Something that is religious and social suicide in the Amish culture.

I was, in a word, awestruck. The therapist she went to was a long-time colleague of mine. He said "I'm not surprised, after living with Betts all those years you were too smart to remain Amish and remain dependent.

Friends and even her older children are forbidden to have anything to do with her openly. Rebecca's actions threatened the fabric of the Amish community; the church authorities feared losing control over their parish, the men feared losing control of their wives, and the women feared assuming control of their lives.

Now, two years later, Andrew, lives trapped by the Amish rules that had propelled Rebecca's exit. He has two choices: remain celibate for the rest of his life or, should he have an affair, confess it and be excommunicated.

Rebecca has fared considerably better. She bought a house, moved walls, installed plumbing and started a craft and baking business. She enrolled her children in special schools for handicapped children, went to school board meetings, talked to principals to make sure that her children were not neglected.

Rebecca moved from a horse and buggy to a van, fax, beepers and the internet. She connects with physicians worldwide. After being born to a mother who made it very clear to her that she wasn't wanted, she needed love badly. But she decided that she didn't need Joseph in her life. Joseph had come into her life and was a soul-mate for a while, but then he changed into a hard, difficult man. She found the love that she needed within herself. So she asked him to leave.

Miraculously, people whose lives she touched have brought her everything she would need for her new life: clothes for her and the girls, furniture, appliances, a TV, video, radio, and microwave. A steady stream of people came bearing gifts for their first Christmas.

This unstoppable woman enrolled in night classes since in the Amish tradition she could not go to school beyond the eighth grade: too worldly. She did this heroic undertaking for herself and earned her GED.

We were incredibly lucky to find Rebecca and have her live in our house part of the week and do all the housework and child tending while she continued to live with us for four and a half years until she married. I went happily to graduate school.

While Rebecca was at our house I learned to respect her rituals. Tuesday mornings when she arrived, she would take off her big black hat and black shoes. Then we would sit at the breakfast table with two cups of coffee and some doughnuts and exchange news of our weekends.

The Amish young people were not allowed to date. But the time honored practice of "bundling" was allowed. The boy and girl lying in bed with a stack of pillows between them: while the parents sat in the living room.

After the four hour church service on Sunday mornings, men on one side at seats in a barn, females on the other, the young people were allowed to get together behind the barn and "play party" and drink.

The boys went to work at nearby factories and the girls were farmed out to do housework. All the money they made went directly to their parents.

I pondered; there is something wrong with our system. We pay and pay for our children and it gets more expensive every year because of college, clothes, technological stuff. Amish parents can retire and watch the money roll in from their children's work.

On Friday afternoons after Rebecca had cleaned the whole house and baked bread, we would sit down and chat while she drank two Harvey wallbangers (vodka and a smidge of orange juice). Then she was prepared again for culture in collision, i.e. bunson burner irons, scrubbing all floors, a kerosene oil stove, fixing the barn roof and so on.

Rebecca didn't have money to go to a dentist so I took her to ours. She needed a lot of dental care.

When her older sister, Mary was to be married her parents sent us a message making an appointment to come talk to us.

They hired someone to bring them the long way in a horse and buggy. Ceremoniously they sat with dignity and asked if they could borrow one thousand dollars for Mary's wedding. The payments would come to us from Rebecca's wages.

We had a special invitation to the wedding. Rebecca told us to come two hours after the appointed time since the ceremony would last at least four hours.

We were allowed to sit together as each preacher droned on. We watched the dust motes in the old barn, cows mooing below. At the first moo I heard, I whispered to Cope "did you do that?" He motioned below. I felt that I was in an old world culture: deeply moving.

This unstoppable woman with her newly styled and blonded hair said, "I thought I would have to give up all my hopes and dreams when, I realized my daughters would always need constant care, but God has given me these three children as gifts. He knew I could do what I must and He is counting on me. My hopes and dreams have taken on new meaning."

And she did it all on faith.

My Helpers
I Remember Deanie

One day when my household helpers evaporated and the frenetic activity of the pre-Christmas holiday was looming, I sent an ad for live-in help to our local newspaper. We needed lots of help: two toddlers, two teenagers, a big house and a ton of washing, ironing, and house cleaning! I got an unlikely response. She sounded so young. "How old are you?" I asked. She said, "Fifteen," in an Appalachian accent. "My name is Deanie Cross and I'm from Crosstown, Tennessee." I asked her for references. She gave her Aunt Millie's name. Auntie turned out to be sixteen.

In the interview at the house where she was staying, I asked, "What can you do?" in desperation. "Well, I kain't clean, I kain't wash, I kain't iron and I kain't cook." I said, "do you like kids?" She said, "Yes, I love kids." "You're hired!" Desperation sometimes lures us into interesting experiences. I figured I could teach her all the other chores, but I couldn't teach her to love children.

Knowing Deanie turned out to be an unforgettable experience. She brought a lightness of heart and unconditional devotion to our family through all the years as our children grew in and out of clothes and phases. We were the hub of the universe for the neighborhood kids and Deanie accepted all of them. Years later, she confessed that she had only answered my ad on a dare from Millie and never intended to go to work. She lived with us for four and a half years. Deanie learned how to do all the household tasks and helped raise our children with her good-hearted folk wisdom and humor.

Deanie learned all the skills of housekeeping, she said that I was her role model. I'm not sure who learned from whom, but we both profited. Deanie had an amazing potential for learning. There were a lot of glitches, but they provided good laughs and now nostalgia. She had never completed the eighth grade because her father wouldn't let her take gym if she had to wear bloomers for gym class. So, she ran away from home and ended up in Ohio. Mountain culture can be unexpectedly prim. Deanie had so little formal education, yet later, she inspired her own children to attain the honor roll through school and graduate from college.

One day she asked if she could leave early. Her cousins were going to shoot each other and she figured she could break them up. Jack drove her to the relatives. But when he came back quickly I said with all the heat of wrongful blame, "Why didn't you stay and stop all that?"

"Do you think I'm crazy," he said, "getting between the Hartfields and the Coys?"

Deanie did everything with verve. When she was washing clothes one day, she decided to throw all the clothes she was wearing in the washing machine. Then she leaned against the washer, liking the movement. All she had on was Michael's football helmet. I was blissfully unaware of the scene of her ample, curvaceous body, nude and sensually undulating with the cycles of the washing machine while her curly red hair bounced back and forth. Unaware, that is, until the meter-reader came roaring upstairs and out the door in full retreat.

Oh Deanie - how we loved her - every one of us! She developed a boyfriend named Peter. It wasn't too long before she confided, "Mrs. Colebrook, I think I'm pregnant." I took a good look and sure enough, she was at least four months along. Pregnancy without marriage was not acceptable in the fifties. But I swung gallantly into action. We would give her a lovely wedding and a reception at our home. My daughter and I went to Hough's Bakery where the finest wedding cakes were made and I ordered a beautiful three-tiered cake decorated with orange blossoms, and of course, the requisite patty shells for creamed chicken, and all the trimmings. I wanted everything to be wonderful for Deanie. She said, "But Mrs. Colebrook, Peter won't get married unless the ceremony is in a Catholic church and I'd have to turn Catholic."

"Oh, well then, Deanie, I'll take you to the priest in Aurora and he can give you instruction and you can easily convert to Catholicism." Deanie said, "Why would I want to do that? If I wanted to get divorced, I couldn't. I'd be stuck Catholic." I thought, she's smarter than I am and put the wedding cake in the freezer.

Weeks went by and Peter wouldn't budge. So I got her maternity clothes and let nature take its course. She got bigger and bigger as the months crept by. While Jack and I were on a fishing trip in Canada she called to say she and Peter had just been married by our pastor in our community church office with our children in attendance. "How come?" said I in wonderment.

"Well, Pete found out he isn't a Roman Catholic. He's just plain old Greek Catholic, and we could be married anywhere. I wouldn't have to convert." Terrific! Shortly after this she produced a baby boy, Michael, named after our son. She and Peter acquired a trailer in a nearby trailer park. All was resolved, except for the damn wedding cake molting stolidly in the freezer and the champagne cooling in the extra refrigerator.

I called my friends for support. "Please come to a baby shower for Deanie and bring presents, you see we have this cake…" They came through for me. I bought dozens of little pink rubber babies to tuck in between the orange blossoms. The cake was magnificent. One of my staunch friends viewing the interesting spectacle said solemnly, "Right on! Jonathan Swift said the answer to over-population was to eat babies." 2 Another said, "That's the most interesting baby shower cake I ever saw."

My Helpers

Lonnie Our Angel

Lonnie answered my ad for a housekeeper and became our angel for twenty-five years. She was our housekeeper, my dear friend and beloved by everyone in the family.

She became part of our family. There was nothing she could not do, especially showing love for us all.

Here is a Christmas letter she sent me in December of 2007.

Christmas 2007
My dearest heart,

For your Christmas request of a favorite short story, saying or poem; I forward to you my Christmas memories and "The Gift of Holiday Happiness." Be warned-it is not short.

I can't resist the opportunity to share my Christmas memories of you; before you lived in Florida for the winter months.

From the very beginning I marveled at everything you did! It was like watching a movie "LIVE" and somehow; in many ways, I was a small part of it all. You cannot even imagine how often these scenes play on my mind and in my heart.

I believe it started with catalogs. Hundreds of them! Catalogs that were shared with me. I loved looking through them. Many things offered in them I didn't know existed. What a discovery! (You are responsible for expanding my world in so many ways.) Some things I would purchase but mostly I'd get ideas of many things to make and create myself; from florals to paintings and many things from cloth. You and Mr. "C" would start shopping from them months before Christmas. Needless to say, I'd be on a first name basis with the U.P.S. delivery guys throughout the year. Once the packages would arrive, they would be opened and carried down to live in the infamous Christmas closet until it came time to wrap them. (I'd like to tell you that before I met you I had never received a delivery from U.P.S. to my home.)

I would watch you from a distance thinking, planning, pondering and anticipating with such thought and love, the holiday and your family's arrival weeks before they came.

Usually in October the wrapping would begin. You would set up the card table on the lake level with all of your wrapping supplies and wrap, wrap, wrap, to the tune of the football games. The wrapping table, that Mr. "C" built, lived for many years just on the other side of the lake level stairs. It served many purposes of gift-wrapping throughout the year for all occasions and for food and as a bar for the many times you entertained. My third year there you asked me to make a cover for it. The wrapping table now lives in the storage room and that cover is still on it today. As your health challenged you through the years you asked me to wrap for you. I've wrapped gifts on the lake level, in the kitchen, in the now living room and in Mr. "C"s study. You would have all the tags wrote out for the gifts and I'd be ready to go. It was such fun seeing what everyone would receive and I would envision the look on their faces as they opened them. My most beautiful gifts were received from you. My favorite is a gold necklace. My most treasured is the solar wind chime. My most useful is my sewing machine and Cuisinart. Every single thing I've received is heartfelt and received with such gratitude.

A few weeks before the holiday you'd start cooking and baking up a storm and then freezing your creations for the days the family would be home. (Oh the things I have learned from your cooking skills. Until you, I never had the opportunity to watch someone cook and want to teach me so much!) While you were busy cooking I would be cleaning the whole house and making sure there were fresh linens on the beds. Also polishing silver and brass, ironing tablecloths and napkins and making sure there were fresh candles to go everywhere.

Then it was time to bring in the ten foot ladder from the garage to get up into the loft above the kitchen. That first year there were twenty-three boxes to bring down that held all the Christmas decorations. In later years there were only ten to twelve boxes. I would unpack everything and set it out for you to see. I'd listen to you ooh and aah over the things you haven't seen for a year and tell the story of where it came from or how it came to be. You would strategically place those decorations all around the house. I do believe there was a decoration, a wreath or floral display in almost every room. So many beautiful things!! A few that will always stand out in my mind are those musical bells that would light up with the sound of the music. The wood-framed musical glass box that housed the most beautiful, tiniest tree I had ever seen; that you had received from your friend Carol. The "Colebrook" train that would stand proudly on the beam across the then dining room, (now the living room). This train inspired me to make our "Vorell" train that I display every year; although it is much smaller in size. Our third Christmas together you introduced me to the "*mache originals*" carolers; that I fell in love with. You remembered how I loved them and our fourth Christmas together you gifted me a caroling couple. Since then I have purchased several for all the holidays and believe I have approximately twenty-four pieces. I cannot help but think of you as I set them out with each holiday throughout the year. And then there was those stockings. There were sixteen of them my first year. All colors, sizes and shapes that were clipped to the wire across the biggest fireplace. I can still picture my favorite one, it was an antique looking, brown, heeled, Victorian shoe. So much for the standard plain red and white ones that I only knew! Lastly, those amazing centerpieces you created. You never ceased to impress me with your vision and creativity. What you could do with greenery and flowers is just fabulous! Usually over a weekend Mr. "C" would go out on the grounds and cut the perfect tree, set it up and put the lights on it. (I've never seen anyone put lights on a tree like he did; but it was always beautiful and I learned something). By the next time I would come you would have the tree all decorated. I was fascinated to see so many beautiful, unusual, different kinds of ornaments on one tree. You were kind enough to share that some were very old, some hand-made, some from all the countries you visited, etc…... The ones that really caught my eye were the crocheted snowflakes…. no two alike. It inspired me to crochet some and now every ornament on my tree is crocheted. (All kinds of things, not just snowflakes) When Mr. "C" was done with the tree he would go outside and change the color of the bulbs in the bucket lights along the driveway and put colored bulbs in the lights that shone up into the trees on the circle.

The most memorable tree for me was the fourteen foot tree that stood in the now living room in 1988. What an awesome sight with its height and width. It was placed in front of the floor to ceiling windows with all its splendor. When the lights were lit they would reflect off the windows and look like a million lights. One thing I never recall seeing was a tree skirt. After I would clean up the pine needles, being careful not to clog the central vacuum system, a sheet would be placed pretty under the tree to conceal the tree stand. Another thing I don't ever recall seeing is our Christmas cards ever being wrote out. I know you always did because I've always received one. Maybe you did them in the evenings after I left. The same year of the fourteen foot tree; Mr. "C" had created the nine foot by eleven foot wreath that he hung over the huge fireplace. The feat itself was not unusual as he had walked the grounds gathering all kinds of greenery, twigs, berries, etc… every year to create a beautiful wreath that he would hang over that fireplace. He'd place a bow either at the side or at the bottom. The bows themselves were larger than the normal size wreaths that I've seen. The size of this wreath was astonishing when I think about it being as large as one of the bedrooms in my house! It really was beautiful.

After the tree was up it was just a matter of days before one or all of the kids would arrive. I knew it was time for all of the very last minute preparation. With your instruction the table was set with all of your beautiful china, crystal, centerpiece and candles. Then it was time for the bedrooms. Turn the heat up. Put extra towels and a towel rack on the lake level. Sometimes you would place candy on their pillows and a special blooming plant or a small vase of fresh flowers would be placed in their rooms. Also a good book or an interesting magazine and occasionally a small bowl of fresh *potpourri* that you created yourself.

I remember first meeting each member of your family and through the years realizing just how unique and special they are. Such a gift to me to receive their warm hugs and smiling faces. The pleasure of witnessing their excitement to be at *"Bingen Am See"*. I remember their shared joy of getting Mr. "C"s pancakes and "my" joy of getting Deborah's *Kuchen* made from her grandmother's recipe. I remember the Rudolph nose Christmas. I'll never forget the China Christmas! (This was my first Christmas with you and you certainly broke me in right from the start) After the Chinese laundry trip; I barely had a few weeks before I had to iron all of those beautiful silk jackets and robes that we all received as gifts. The one Christmas memory that will always stand out is the Christmas "Lolly the trolley" trip around downtown Cleveland, also in the year 1988. Seeing the galleria and old enough to appreciate its architectural beauty. The square lit up. Those tall trees decorated with all those individual moving ornaments. The ride on the trolley itself and singing Christmas carols together. Wow…. the trip was so exciting!!

I know that all of these memories are also your memories and probably seem mundane. I treasure these memories. Each is so significant and I've learned so much. The memories you've created and the traditions you've carried on were life altering for me. Through my Christmas's with you I've been exposed to and included within a "Real" – "Live" – "Whole" – "Family" that feels like a length of a lifetime for me. You are responsible for so many firsts for me. I've witnessed things with your family that I've only dreamed about and thought only really happened in movies. Growing up I was never with one family long enough to experience any befores, during, and afters. You have worked hard through the years at teaching me to receive and to believe in my being worthy of a gift, let alone being thought of; without any repercussions of accepting it. That trolley trip memory has replaced my many weekly and monthly trips, alone on a bus, to see my social worker. My siblings and I were brought together at the social workers office, once a year, to see each other and that was for one or two hours on Christmas Eve. This is the reason we still celebrate Christmas on Christmas Eve.

On Christmas day I'm always busy taking down my tree and decorations. I have often envisioned your family together, gathering on Christmas day, opening their gifts, the laughter and shared joy and meal times together. My head would tell me, "it's nice to think of these things but you're not there." And then my heart would correct my head and say, "Oh yes I am! In so many ways-from the beginning to the end!"
That trolley trip I took with my extended family, Y-O-U-R-S, and my two precious daughters. I was with the "Family" that "I" adopted. I traveled with them! I ate with them! I sang songs with them! They included me and embraced me. I felt wanted and loved! They gave me the knowledge and power to create holiday happiness for the family I created and brought into this world!!

What a gift!
I thank you and yours!
Merry Christmas
I love you,
Lonnie

Lonnie at Longboat Key home

The house Jack designed and had built on our lake

Our cabin

Heaven On Earth

The driveway travels back
To a world unknown.
The house spans wide
Of rich earth tones.
Where the water always trickles.
The trees grow tall.
Where the animals roam freely
Both big and small.
A place that beckons your welcome,
Holds you tight in its embrace.
People dream of such beauty…..
Yes, there is such a place.
That will make you take
A deep breath
And slow your pace;
When you witness
All its nature
And endure all its grace.
A place where there is always a rainbow.
A place where the sun always shines.
I'm lucky to be a part of it,
Even though it's not mine.
It's the world of the most wonderful people
Mr. and Mrs. "C".
It's 'Heaven On Earth'
Here at 'Bingen Am See'!

By: Lonnie Vorell
November 4, 1985

My Helpers
Lovely Weezer
And The
Beautiful Sweet Potato

When Lonnie had to retire after twenty-five years. Sadness and loss prevailed, but another treasure came into my life, Kim Pease, "Mei Lang," I call her, "beautiful sweet potato," in Chinese. She brought with her Louise, "Weezer," who no matter how she felt, brightened my life. By this time Cope had died, leaving me with all the financial dealings he had kept for himself. To protect me, I guess, but left me utterly helpless. Kim became my business manager handling the multiplicity of complex details of running the estate: hiring, overseeing the work, running the household, when I wasn't able due to many surgeries and incapacitation. She came in the middle of the night for emergency trips to the hospital.

She types and retypes my manuscript working with her valiant husband, Scott, a brilliant photographer, putting it all on disks, doing technological things I don't understand. She buoys me up when I am bogged down, comes to visit on Sundays when I am alone.

Lang became my best friend.

To say "I love you" is not enough.

My Helpers
Heaven Sent

After we bought our home on Longboat Key. I needed help for some of our frolicking parties. I found Mary Lou Hamm or Heaven sent her.

She glided into being our housekeeper and through the past thirty years she has become my companion, dear friend and confidante. She is beautiful and always trustable. She cleans and attends to all my posies since I can't.

Now, at my advanced age, she has had to become my nurse, helping me shower and changing my bags which will be my lifetime companions after bladder surgery which remains unpronounceable and incomprehensible to me.

My Helpers
Maria Elena: One Of My Helpers
The Peter Pan Exodus
14,000 children sent by the
Catholic church in Cuba
to the U.S.

My Mother warn me that we might not see each other in a very long time, but I did not hear a word she was saying, as I was coming to the United States to see my brother that he was there already and I missed him so much.

It was 1961 in Havana, Cuba Fidel Castro had just overthrown Batista in 1959 and he was declaring himself as a socialist. My father was a friend of the manager of the Pan American Airways so it was very lucky for me to get a seat in one of the last flights from Havana to Miami Fla. Except it was the bathroom of the plane; I did not get care I was going to the U.S. to see my brother!

I finally arrived – only forty-five minutes but it seemed like an eternity. My brother was waiting along with my uncle which we were going to live with him; he was a bachelor! Children that came without their parents were called "Peter Pan". Biggest exodus in the world – fourteen thousand children.

It seemed like all of our cousins were sent to live with my uncle as he was the only relative living in the U.S. I understood much later, what a brave man he was – more like a Mother Teresa always helping everyone. We did not stay too long in Miami, Fl as my uncle was supporting all of us and there was not a lot of work, so we ended in beautiful Newark, N.J. I did not stay long in Newark as my brother being five years older decided for me that it was best for me to live elsewhere where there were women!

We, it was in Silver Spring, Md where these were friends of us from Cuba where we had a beach house. Went to Ursuline Academy where I finish High School and then went to Business School and became a bilingual secretary at the Marriott Corporation in Maryland which I met my future husband.

Who would have thought that a little girl that came in 1961 at eleven years old would have survived all of our trials and tribulations; Cubans are survivors and we live in the land of freedom and opportunity.

We have been married for thirty-eight years; good and bad times. Three wonderful children; now very responsible adults and five grandchildren.

My parents made it to the United States finally after eight years as they did not let my father come as he was a well-known pharmacist and was needed for the communist cause.

I explain to my children how lucky they are to have been born in the country and being able to have freedom and liberty!

Note: The Catholic Priests and Bishops arranged for this monumental exodus of children so they would not become communists under Castro's regime. (EPC)

Christmas
The Worst Christmas I Ever Had!

At a friend's house, with her help, I made a black taffeta skirt. My husband was so proud that he bought me a sewing machine.

He had it delivered to Bea Harris's house. She was so excited when it came. She wanted it and thought her husband, Bob, had ordered it for her. When Jack told her it was a surprise for me she cried and cried.

The huge Christmas tree was decorated. Along with the baubles were dozens of gold wrapped packages with red bows.

I salivated over the packages for days: a ring, a bracelet, perfume, a nightie - all the goodies a woman wants.

On Christmas Eve at 4 am, after we had gone to the candlelight service and a party afterwards and then hauled all of our children's presents under the tree, Jack started my treasure hunt through the house. It ended in a closet rarely used.

The prize was the damn sewing machine.

I cried and cried.

The once enticing gold boxes revealed pinking shears, extra bobbins, etc... things I never heard of and never wanted to. The worst two boxes contained eight sessions of making slipcovers and eight sessions of dressmaking. For dressmaking I had to disrobe and stand still while they covered me with hot wax, it became my mannequin. I felt like I was being burned at the stake. I left it there. Weeks later I asked stalwart friends to go downtown with me and get the damn thing. We boarded the streetcar with it in tow. People looked really interested in us. Today my unfinished dress, Mike's unfinished baby "soakers," and his army uniform recline in a drawer together.

The only thing I ever used the machine for was our children's Halloween costumes. It quit. The Singer sewing machine man examined it. "I've been fixing sewing machines for thirty years and I never saw one in this condition." I had broken the main shaft.

With an insouciant reply I said, "It must have been the pink elephants!" "What?" he said.

I had cut the elephant ears out of cardboard and sewed them to the pink material on the machine.

Sewing machines don't like to sew cardboard. My solution: I made it into a vanity table

The Worst Thing I Ever Did

Well, focusing on the worst thing I ever did is going to call up a host of "worsts." Perhaps a long chapter, now that I muse reflectively.

One of the "worsts" happened when Sis and I finally persuaded our father to take a vacation. He went to Florida and Cuba for three weeks with uncle Carl.

The two widowers had a good time. Dad was embarrassed only once, when Uncle Carl ordered a glass of milk at Sloppy Joe's in Havana, a famous saloon. Dad admonished, "Carl, you could at least order a ginger ale."

No sooner had their plane taken off the runway than Sis and I hatched a nefarious plot. Dad's house was getting dingy since mother died, and he either didn't know it, or didn't care. With unbridled zeal, we got rid of all the lovely old wicker furniture in the large sunroom and bought, in retrospect, dreadful, clunky contemporary blond pieces.

We employed Dad's housekeeper, Theresa's, brother-in-law, notably undependable, moody and a binge drinker, to paint the walls and get rid of the old wallpaper in the dining room and hang the new paper we picked out. Dad had always liked the old wallpaper, but we hated it.

We took his beloved easy chair, the only chair he ever sat in, to a Swedish woman in Cleveland. We told her it needed to be re-needle pointed and finished in three weeks.

What did we know?

We got Al Jurkowitz to take down the living room chandeliers and polish the bronze. Now, those two chandeliers were Dad's pride and joy. They had been imported from Europe and had shimmering crystal teardrops.

Al Fodor went on a bender at the height of the devastation. Theresa, on whom Dad was utterly dependent, couldn't stand the whole thing and threatened to quit. The project was in shambles: we were destroying his home and his helper network, instead of enhancing his life.

Al Jurkowitz got mad about the looming due date and our exhortations. He brought the chandeliers back and threw them on the living room floor in total disorder. We had forgotten about his reputation for being irascible. And how could we re-connect them? Another quandary.

Our audacity foundered. We got fairly desperate. Everything was a mess! The expenses became horrific. Dad's secretary, Marie, equally horrified, was paying the bills. She knew he, the consummate scrooge, would have a fit. Our faithful husbands looked on in consternation. They helped where they could, but their faces paled as the project got more out of hand. We were house wreckers. Theresa, dad's housekeeper, left. We didn't know whether she would come back. She did eventually.

I wrote a special delivery letter, telling Dad we were fixing up his house because we loved him so much. We wanted to care for him as Mother would have. Love poured out of my pen.

We got Al Fodor to sober up, mollified Theresa, fixed a gorgeous homecoming feast. And we waited.

When he arrived everything was beautiful and peaceful: a grate fire, new wallpaper up, draperies hung, easy chair resplendent. The plaster was still wet on the walls in several places.

Our father, to his everlasting credit, was a perfect sport. He was touched by my letter, thank God, and instructed Marie to pay all the bills. He didn't even want to see them. Remarkable for a man who had scraped a nickel on both sides to save it.

In his remaining years, Dad spent many hours sitting on his needlepoint chair in the redecorated sunroom.

The Infamous Church Dinners

It was an ill-conceived idea at the outset: for me to make the spaghetti sauce for the P.T.A. dinner, to serve three hundred or more trusting community members. I would save the school three hundred dollars which we had paid Mrs. Truce to make her famous sauce the year before. I had her recipe (more or less). What could go wrong?

EVERYTHING!

I was the brash young president of the Aurora Parent Teacher Association. Ideas erupted on a grand scale. I had a loyal cooking committee. No problem!

I bought the ground beef in five-pound packages and filed them in the church freezer a week before the dinner. Cases of tomato sauce, tomato paste, garlic, onions, Parmesan, herbs and tons of pasta, salad greens, and Italian breads were ready to jump in to do their part. I was organized!

Getting my friends together after church on Sunday the day before the big event was easy. Husbands rolled up their sleeves. Seven large electric roasters had been corralled. Now to brown the meat.

I had forgotten to defrost it! We banged each five-pound brick with hammers, cooking utensils, any weapon we could get our hands on. We played catch with them; they froze our hands. Finally we threw the bloody blocks on the floor.

Hours later, my still loyal (but teetering) friends had subdued the unrelenting meat blocks and revived our spirits with Bloody Mary's. The ground meat was sizzling in the roasters; we cut up an acre of onions, garlic, and celery. Now for the sauce.

The huge recipe called for between a quarter and a half cup of sugar per roaster. To save time I split the difference and added a third of a cup to each. I didn't think about adding it by degrees and doing the taste test.

When all the roasters were bubbling, we started sampling the sauce; the first roasterful was sweet! And the next, and the next. All sweet. I was horrified. My friends didn't look so loyal anymore, sweet spaghetti sauce. My cooking colleagues and husbands trudged wearily to their homes. I must say the husbands looked especially dubious.

That night I had wild nightmares of rats swimming in every roaster in the sweet sauce. I saw people take their first bites and stagger out of Fellowship Hall, vomiting on the floor.

In the morning, after seeing Jack off to work, and Michael and Suzie off to school, I scooped up three-month-old Deborah in her carrying chair that fit nicely on the seat of the car and then on the kitchen counter to keep me company. Possibly to save my sanity so I wouldn't jump off the cliff like the lemmings. We raced up to the church kitchen to taste my misbegotten brew. It was definitely, unequivocally SWEET!

It's not often in our lifetime that we are called upon to look at so many vats of mistakes at the same time. This situation was far worse than the time my cooking committee was reported to the Elders for drinking cocktails (shakers supplied by our sympathetic, loyal-to-the core mates). The nark! We knew who she was.

Even worse than the time we greeted the Kiwanians to serve their dinner, smilingly unaware that all of our tongues were bright green - a result of drinking the Crème de Menthe left over from the dessert recipe.

There was a time when we threw caution to the wind and our loyal, imaginative little band had collapsed all the tables in Fellowship Hall and made the Men's Club eat their Chinese dinners while sitting on the floor as we served in oriental robes. Aurora's own *geishas*! We painted Mandarin mustaches on the men as they arrived. It was a sight to behold: the young, the lean, the old, the obese, squatting on the floor as best they could, struggling with their chopsticks. That however enlivened their Monday night meeting (which usually were pretty dull, I can tell you). The stodgiest man told us, as he left, that he had never had so much fun in his life. Knowing his wife, I believed him.

Now this sweet sauce for three hundred trusting souls was definitely in another category. Calamity.

It was our biggest moneymaker of the year. But I wasn't going out with a whimper. Baby with me, I was off to the local store for some counter-ingredients. I started with lemons. Back to the kitchen, I squeezed one or two in each of the seven roasters. Stirred, tasted. Sweet!

Again to Hackbart's store. Canned, hot peppers.

Sweet!

Another trip to the store. Baby getting petulant. Mother desperate. Vinegar?

Sweet!

Nurse baby.

Baby sleeping, gurgling happily. Mother more desperate. Baby unaware that mother was about to commit suttee in sweet tomato sauce. Back we flew to the store for more desperate antidotes.

My friends and I spent the day setting tables, making the rest of the dinner, readying for the big event. I felt as if it was all preparation for walking the plank.

The sauce looked fine: thick, red, and shiny. I alternately prayed, faced Mecca, and swore under my breath, as I made constant tasting rounds. My friends strained to be supportive. Sweet! I was in a state of shock, too scared, too determined to panic.

Dinner was served at 6 p.m. At 5 pm, I did a final taste test feeling like the King's taster who knows there is a poisoner at the banquet. It was marvelous! All the guests remarked that it was one of a kind. Everyone wanted the recipe.

What do you know!

I was a wreck!

Galoshes, Galoshes

A friend begged me to take over her kindergarten class at a nearby city for six weeks while she tended her mother in post-surgery care. I was delighted. She said I could bring my two younger children. I thought, "what a great experience for them!"

I walked into the room to face fifty five year olds. Fifty little snowsuits and fifty little pairs of galoshes had to be removed. Many needed help with buttons, zippers and buckles. Finally class began. I remembered just enough piano pieces to accompany their singing.

Finger painting came next. Unbelievable chaos. Then time for a few more activities and on with the snowsuits and galoshes. They sat on the floor stuffed into their winterys. Then it was story time till the buses came. All of this had to be accomplished in three hours!!

Fifty-two pairs of galoshes later, we were on our way home. It was a long six weeks!

A Stranger Came To Town

A story from the 60's

His name was Elliott Waco, son of the chief of the Waco Tribe in Uganda. All of his brothers had been sent off to Oxford, but Elliott chose Hiram College, a small coed liberal arts college buried in the rolling hills of northeastern Ohio. I don't know why and there is no one to ask anymore.

He and my nephew, Lou Livengood, shared a room in the dorm. Soon Elliott took his place as part of our extended family.

Our Ohio winters presented a challenge for this child of Africa. Classmates could spot Elliott from afar in his long heavy black wool coat and earmuffs, his coat flapping around his legs as he raced around campus. He was very well liked by his classmates who evidenced no racial prejudice. In summer, Elliott's stark blackness contrasted vividly with his tennis whites when he played on our court.

He was appalled when he encountered the prejudice against African Americans in our society. He took to carrying symbols of his status with him when he went on shopping expeditions with me – a black leather briefcase (a parting gift from his father) and a black silk umbrella. Besides encumbering his shopping, I doubt they were understood or made any difference to those who would not treat him well. I began to resent my countrymen. Elliot wanted to survey the attitude of the culture in the U.S. more deeply, trying to understand the vein of racial-prejudices. He asked Lou to drive him to our state capital, Columbus. He asked Lou to come with him to a café and order a sandwich at the counter. A waiter broke Elliot's glass in front of him, smashing it on the counter. He was roughly treated and sent away.

Defeated and forlorn he came back with Lou: wiser and heartbroken, hopeless. The land of the free and the home of the brave was only an illusion.

Since destiny had given birth to Elliot in Uganda, it was impossible to take Uganda entirely out of Elliot. I realized how deeply his cultural beliefs under-girded his sophisticated education when he developed migraines. Sis took him to a neurologist at the Cleveland Clinic. The physician administered a battery of tests and pills, but the headaches continued. Finally, one day in dire pain he muttered to me, "If I could go to our village witch doctor, my headaches would be gone."

Living here was making inroads into his psyche. He was fascinated when I told him a story about a first-year teacher of social studies in our school. The teacher was trying to demonstrate the evolution of democracy in the United States. Taking down the flag that always hung at the front of the room, he threw Old Glory to the floor and stepped on it. He then told the class, "In the early stages of our republic, only the aristocracy could own a flag or touch one. Now, however, everyone has personal rights in our democracy, including civil disobedience." Elliot howled when I told him that the teacher had been fired before nightfall.

Elliot shared his story with me: one summer, when he returned to Uganda for vacation he discovered that his cousin, Henry, had become the King. At a ceremony in the village square, the people were obliged to approach the royal presence by crawling, their bodies flat on the dusty dirt in the town square.

Elliot said, "I couldn't do it. I had grown up with Henry. We played together, he was no better than me, so I merely bowed ceremoniously and walked toward him." That evening, the tribal elders met and Elliot was soundly rebuked.

When Uganda was about to be granted its independence from British rule on October 9th, 1962, it was in Elliot's home in Africa that the high-ranking chiefs of the four main tribes in the country gathered to work on a peace accord. They had been called there at the invitation of Elliot's father, who was a strong tribal chief. They were successful for several years.

On Ugandan Independence Day, my sister gave a party to celebrate. We all worked on a special centerpiece for the main table, a replica of the proud new flag of the new nation.

Sis bought a huge bag of peanuts and ground them in the waring blender. When Elliot walked in the kitchen he said, "Katy, what are you doing?" Sis said, "I'm making peanut gravy like your mother does back home." He laughed, slapping his knee. "That's because we couldn't get flour and peanuts grew wild all around us. She would send us kids out to harvest them to make the gravy because that is all we had to make gravy base."

Anyway, we enjoyed traditional African gravy that night. How hard we try without knowing why when we don't understand the culture.

Elliot loved parties. This was an especially momentous event. He was jubilant about his country's future, and the important role he would play in building its success. We celebrated with ebullient toasts and pledges to always stay in contact. He got quite drunk and very jolly.

"My family back home welcomes my new family halfway around the world to its capacious bosom." His ebony face gleamed at the white faces around the table reflecting his happiness.

The heady atmosphere and the flowing liquor, prompted Elliot to regale us with marvelous stories of his family and growing up in Uganda, treasures I should have remembered. I guess I was also, "ebullient."

Then some people began to ask him questions. One woman asked him, "What are your ideas on chastity?" He fumbled for the correct way in which to couch, for company, what he had told me previously in private…about the ten-year-old girls with their babies tied onto their backs, scouring the parched fields for meager life-saving manioc. And the ten and eleven-year-old girls sold into prostitution by their starving families…the younger the better for the customers' tastes.

Another guest asked, "How many brothers and sisters do you have?"

"Twenty-eight, don't you know?" replied Elliot in his proper British accent.

"My stars!" she exclaimed. "That's a large family!"

"Well," Elliot went on, "my father has four wives as behooves his position of tribal king."

After recovering from her initial shock the women went on fascinated by the subject. "How do the wives get along with each other?"

"Fine!" Elliot responded with a hearty laugh. "Everywhere except in the kitchen."

Despite my joy in his country's independence, I could only ponder ruefully at the celebratory occasion: a microcosm of our country's misunderstanding African culture.

This misunderstanding was to be the least of it. Little did we know of African and world politics: the tragedies to come. The peace was tenuous at best. As Britain and the other colonial powers relinquished their rule, Africa was carved into dozens of countries without regard for tribal loyalties and ancient animosities.

In retrospect, one can only wonder at the African peoples' monumental determination for self-rule, the overwhelming belief that they could establish and maintain orderly democratic government without experience or historic precedent. And, I must add, without the confidence of the West.

The Africans were considered ignorant and superstitious children by the colonial powers. At the United Nations, the Ambassador of the Netherlands confided to me, "What can you expect? They just got down from the trees!" I was furious, struggling with the pain of the impossibility of the hard times ahead.

It seems that the world powers did all the wrong things for all the wrong reasons. And what heritage had our politicians left in the minds of the novice leaders? How to be corrupt? The only hope was that there would be new leaders, men and women like Elliot.

When he graduated from Hiram, Elliot's parents sent my sister and her husband gorgeous ceremonial robes and headdresses that they would have worn. Sis and Herb were resplendent in the flowing royal garments of fine silk and damask in dazzling gold, purples, reds, and vivid blues.

When Elliot walked proudly across the stage to accept his diploma, we were not without tears. The audience stood up and applauded. There was nary a dry eye in the crowd. And, on his return to Uganda, we again were moved to tears when he wrote that because of his new educational credentials he had been appointed Minister of Health and Human Services. We were gratified that a qualified man, our dear friend, would be bringing his knowledge to his people, aiding them in their labors to lift themselves up by the bootstraps.

But it was not long before Idi Amin, a psychotic tyrant, waged a bloody coup and proclaimed himself President of Uganda. In his paranoia about ensuring absolute power, he ordered all the educated people brutalized and killed.

"No, No, No," we screamed, "not Elliot," as we watched the slaughter on T.V.

We cringed as we read newspaper accounts, and listened to the TV coverage. Men, women, and children were conscripted into the army, armed with guns (from America). These "soldiers" including young boys roamed the countryside looting, burning, torturing, raping, leaving common people, who lost everything hiding in terror, hungry and hopeless. There was no one left who was capable of administering a stable government.

For a moment in history a comet had blazed over Uganda, but it plummeted to earth disintegrating into ashes. Its orbit might have lighted a new path, but the stranger who had become our brother was no more: butchered in his office.

Betrayal
Another Chink In My Innocence

I write this story for my children, my hostages to the future, and for all of us who live and breathe in a country, potentially strong and idealistic enough to make a difference about accepting others who are different from us in color or creed.

This story is a part of me that I hold valuable and passionately hoping that it will live on in your own integrity.

I could not foresee how the web would be woven when a friend was asked to present a program for the combined women's guilds of our community church. Marion wanted them to organize a panel discussion; it was to be on the damage caused by prejudice. Her mutant conscience had been stirred by the book, <u>Gentlemens' Agreement</u>, about the WASP prejudice against Jewish people in a country club setting. Ironic because we lived in a small WASP community where the covert rule among realtors was not to sell to Jewish people.

This scenario took place in 1965. Donna and several of our liberal, intellectual friends (i.e. they read and thought) joined together. There were not many of us back then.

They researched and brainstormed; then presented a program determined to categorize and denounce prejudice in any form.

Nothing changed in our town, of course. Donna and I wanted resolutely to do at least one small thing to follow our path. She contacted a friend who was a white pastor in an all black church in the inner city of Cleveland. She asked him if we could volunteer our services in any meaningful way.

That was the summer after the Watts riots in South Central Los Angeles in 1965 where homes and businesses were razed resulting in four million dollars of damage and thirty-four deaths. It galvanized our country. Conditions of crowding in rundown homes and joblessness fomented the Blacks' anger at the lives they were leading. Gangs formed, crime rose. Out of this sense of hostile powerlessness a series of riots broke out around the country. Whites' fears were fomenting hatred.

Pastor Paul, a white minister in a black church: the Fidelity Baptist Church, suggested we bring food to the church on Mondays when the women had prayer meetings. I realize now that the streets were not safe. Some Aurora women would make grand casseroles but then said, "You know, I just can't go there and do that." So the bravest of us, Donna, my sister, my pregnant daughter Susan, myself, and several other women went. We ventured forth in our station wagons loaded with food and toys. I set up a pre-school for the toddlers and saw how much help they needed to be equipped for kindergarten. Interactional skills, verbal abilities and ability to express themselves and their feelings left much to be desired but it felt like a hopeful situation. The way the children needfully responded to any affection was proof that our efforts were needed.

The churchwomen were strong and smart and welcomed us when they saw that we were authentic in reaching out. They talked about how they were coached to "stoop and squat" and sing on sit-ins. Soon the men trickled in to stand around the walls. We invited them to eat and gradually to join in our discussions. The men were jobless and tangential. I realized that it was not enough to eat and pray and visit with our fold. Jobs were the answer. So another planning meeting with Donna; we designed the first Job Corps. It was not enough for me to eat and pray about the situation. "What kind of work do you do?" I asked the men. "Anything!" I made sign- up sheets for each job and each man signed every single sheet. It appeared that they really could do, "Anything."

I went back to the Women's Guild to persuade them to hire the good-hearted people I had signed up. Paul, the minister, sent the men out in vans from the church.

To say it was a failure would be putting a bright face on my fearless fiasco. The most liberal and beneficent suburbanites became upset, and some deranged, by the attitudes, sloppy workmanship and insolence of my troops. It was a cultural collision. We had to abandon our project. I had started the first Job Corps, but through the failure learned that it had to start with job training!

But we were not daunted! We connected with a group of like-minded people in Cleveland who were espousing Fair Housing. So we organized a meeting in our church's fellowship hall where the concern about prejudice had started.

At the Fair Housing meeting, hardly publicized, the fellowship hall was packed with people. Standing room only. It was that threatening to our local neighbors. Karl Bruch, a descendant of one the oldest aristocratic families in Cleveland, presented the Fair Housing platform. One of the venerated members of the church jumped up and screamed, "You don't see red birds and black birds nesting in the same tree! Birds have more sense." John's face was purple; he trembled with outrage. Then, he sat down, and became very white - aghast, I hoped, at his own emotionality. Probably not.

And so it happened, after a long heated meeting, that we had small group meetings until the church officers told us we could no longer meet in our church! My church, the church my family and I had gone to all of our lives and contributed heavily to. Dad had bought the organ in memory of Mother. Sis was the organist for over thirty years. I taught Sunday school, was a Deacon and a Trustee. The betrayal was one of the worst losses of innocence in my life.

The Methodists took us in. The pastor joined our group. How could I have assumed that there was no nascent prejudice. Growing up in my WASP country town with one large, token Italian family who had been there forever - there was always a Truce son cheered on the football team. I had been educated in a liberal atmosphere all of my formative years, and I assumed people in my town had the same principles that I had. But I had evolved in a larger tidal basin at Vassar and traveling in foreign lands and much to my father's apoplexy had become a passionate democrat. In fact, the town had to erect a democratic voting both for me in our consummate republican enclave.

When my mother-in-law was selling her house the realtor, a good friend of mine, said, "Gert, you don't want to sell to those people. They are Jewish." When mom explained to them that they wouldn't be happy in Aurora, they concurred and sent her a box of candy. I was furious, helpless, sad.

An Irish neighbor brought a petition to our house for me to sign against Fair Housing, outlawing Blacks, Jews, anybody different from us. He had ninety-nine signatures and needed mine for the hundredth; I looked him in the eye and with three daughters around me, tore it to shreds. Have you ever seen the color of a fat Irishman's outraged face? It's purple and blotched red. My daughters said they were proud of me, but afterward, I did think that I had acted pretty intemperately.

And so, as things came full circle, Dan, the husband of Marion, who had initiated the whole process, bought Donna's family's house when they moved, Dan was afraid they would sell to Blacks or Jews. They would have. Dan had a stoolie negotiate the purchase and Donna and her husband didn't realize what was happening. Dan later sold to "appropriate" people, who incidentally, let the house and yard rot! They were the founders of Earth Watch in the 70's.

Chaos followed for many years. Hispanics rioted in Los Angeles in 1970 and 1971. Riots accelerated worldwide during the 80's and 90's. Martin Luther King, the great Black leader, who inspired the people to demand civil rights by peaceful, but determined marches and sit-ins was assassinated in 1968. A deep sense of hopelessness grabbed the hearts of all who had dared to hope.

Dennis Hayes, speaking at my college reunion that fall said, "Never grow old. The only way you grow old is to give up your principles and think it's enough to pass on the torch. It isn't. We must hold firmly to the torch all our lives."

I have done that and I breathed fresh air during that Keynote address. The tone of the discussion that followed showed me why I had chosen Vassar College and why I value the education and experiences that taught me how to be more fully human; wiser in the ways of the world and passionate about politics.

I see my values living on in my granddaughter, Jessica. When discussing her second grade class in Winston Salem, I asked her how many African Americans she had in class. She replied, "Gee, I don't know? They are all so cute." The vines in my vineyard have grown fruit in my second generation!

Department Of Priceless Information
How To Stuff A Turkey

You go to an ecumenical service at your church, bring home your favorite next door couple and proceed to carouse till very late. Your table for thirty celebratory guests (most of whom you have never met) is resplendent with candles, flowers, favors, place settings awaiting my nephew Lou's wedding rehearsal dinner the following day. So you have worked your buns off to achieve perfection. Then you forget.

At about two o'clock in the morning your neighbor asks "What time are you serving dinner?" "Five o'clock." "How big is your turkey?" "Thirty-two pounds" you do a little math and realize it is time for Tom to go into the oven.

You apply yourselves to a vat of stuffing. You throw eggs over your shoulders, throw in onions, celery, sage and then you toss in scotch for more moisture, then more scotch. You stuff the bird from both ends and shake hands in the middle.

The guests all rave and want the recipe.

Your red face beams. My nephew, Lou's rehearsal dinner went on without a hitch.

Coming To Grips – 1968

Out of the cocoon

Thoughts of a fortyish woman on going to work at a full-time paying job for the first time. Behind me were years of child rearing and paying my dues to the community, including founding a nursery school, a kindergarten, establishing a community recreation program, adult education and so on. Feeling like a refugee from the volunteer corps, all I really wanted was to take a couple of courses at graduate school, unless I could get a top-level job at world-changing, from 10 a.m. to 2 p.m., with an hour-and-a-half for lunch.

I really wasn't sure what to do with my future, so I registered for a three-day vocational-personality test program at Case Western Reserve University, confidant that my path would be lighted.

The test results showed what I didn't want to own: that I was a fragmented, undisciplined woman, not well trained in any field, despite a B.A. in Child Development from Vassar. On the minus side, I probably was not fit to be a checkout person in a supermarket. On the plus side, however, Dr. Roulete said I had great desire to achieve.

He had arrived at this conclusion on the basis of my response to questions about whether I would rather write a best-selling novel, a best-selling play, or clean out my desk. To clean out my desk was never my answer. But that's the choice I checked. I thought the purpose of the question was to find evidence of inner discipline. The only clear conclusion I came to from the tests was that I needed glasses.

Patching my battered self together, I applied for a job at the Educational Research Council in Cleveland. Its aim was to write better teaching materials for schools. I failed their test too, miserably I thought. So I went home and cleaned out my desk.

Then I got the job.

When the director of the Educational Research Center called to say I had been accepted, I told her that I couldn't possibly start for two weeks.

After waiting forty-three years! I had to clean out the closets and the freezer I'd been meaning to clean for years.

Apparently Dr. Roulete's test results had made an impact on me. A desperate dash to self-discipline?

After a life of being the night-blooming cereus type, always the last to leave parties, reading late into the night, dragging myself out of bed mornings and bumping into walls, I became morning alert!

I took the commuter train at 7 a.m., getting home at 6 p.m. She was a grand steam engine called "twenty-eight" affectionately in Aurora, a bedroom community.

To insure a smooth home life after work, I decided - - organize the children. I made lists: when to feed the alligator, turtles, tropical fish, Venus- flytrap, the rabbit, the polliwogs, and of course, the kids must clean their rooms.

Instantly they grew up, developed hands, feet and brains. The eleven year old could start dinner; the fourteen year old supervised the cleaning woman. All could get their own breakfasts. My husband was non-plussed!

On my first day, I got up at 5:30. My clothes were neatly laid out from the previous night. For the last time, I fed my family; I made everyone a big, hearty breakfast. Then I kissed each goodbye, picked up my new (empty) briefcase and buoyantly mounted the steps to "my" train, smiling, talking to all the bland commuters. I was on an adventure. How could they be bored?

The first week I was so excited I couldn't sleep. The second week I was so sleepy I couldn't work. By the third week I got up at 6:45 a.m., dressed on the way to the seven o'clock train and slept all the way to Cleveland, grabbing coffee at the office.

I was assigned to write a social science textbook, to cover European Colonialism and its effect on India, Africa and the United States. I was told to cover Hinduism, African tribal customs, slavery, the infamous golden triangle of trading, slaves, tea, sugar, rum. Then Islam, China, the

Opium Wars. We had to include "Concepts" that were to teach the children "Big Ideas." All this for the sixth grade.

I hadn't studied geography since third grade; history (only ancient) in eighth grade; no social science. I was to write all this, including the disciplines of psychology, philosophy, geography, science, anthropology, religion, history and economics.

How did I deal with this? Well, I had developed a new habit: When things got tough, I cleaned my desk. Then I ordered supplies for my newly cleaned desk. Willingly, the supply person gave me paper clips, rubber bands, filing cards, legal pads. I couldn't think of enough things to ask for. Gradually I thought of more: a file box, a memo pad, a desk pad, a dictionary. A secretary brought coffee and doughnuts at ten o'clock every morning. I went out to a restaurant for lunch. I gained ten pounds.

Then the head of my department wanted my first chapter.

I ordered more file cards and sharpened my pencils. I gradually grew five inches shorter from lugging books back and forth from the library and the art museum. To plague my mind further, I worried about paying the employment agency fee. Even worse, I had bought an outfit at Franklin-Simon's that made me look like Marilyn Monroe. I will always remember it … a luscious concoction of white silken wool with an extravagant white fur collar that stood high enough for me to inhale it. I felt ravishing. A payment was due every month; I had visitation rights, but no custody. I paid five dollars a month for the rest of my life.

I studied and wrote and wrote. Got pictures from the art museum, like "David" to show the high development of sculpture in the Greco-Roman era.

The problems mounted, but the one that was insurmountable was the problem of the key to the Ladies Room. It seemed that I had visited one day and forgot to return the only key. I called a locksmith who made a mold and made four golden keys. I grandly presented one to each of the other women writers. None of them fit.

I quit the job when I realized that Jack, enjoying his retirement to the fullest, was playing tennis everyday with my buddies on our court.

A Sacred Tryst

We went to Europe taking Kris and Deborah to see Mike who had a furlough from the Army. We were at *Grindelwald* when our astronaut walked on the moon. Seeing it and hearing it in German was interesting. The next day we were in Zurich walking around and many people came up to us to shake our hands and congratulate us Americans on the remarkable exploit, as though we had anything to do with it.

There were two paths, we chose one path and there was Mike's best friend from college. They were both wearing the same sandals! Mike joined the guys happily for the rest of his furlough.

We drove on to *Bingen Am See*, my grandpa's birthplace; my sacred tryst with him. The roads were not built for cars so people walked about and visited with each other on the way. Vineyards climbed up the hillsides on both banks of the Rhine. It was a hot July day and we inhaled the sensual fragrances of the grapes hanging heavy on the vines with their voluptuous juice begging to be harvested. Now I understand Grandpa's vineyard in Ohio and the huge wooden wine kegs in the cellar, which we needed to taste every morning.

I wondered what his childhood had been like. Was this town oppressive or vibrant? As we walked around I felt the electrical current of liveliness. The buildings were made of stone, aged a mellow ochre. It felt like a good town, a safe town to grow up in. I wonder if it was. Did people love their children? Were they stern Germanic parents? Why did Grandpa really run away to America at fourteen? He told me it was because his father had severely beaten him and blooded him for spiking the Sunday school punch. That sounds like my grandpa alright! He taught me to play, such an important part of my childhood and adult life.

Forgotten memories of his stories pulled me along the streets. I tried to picture Grandpa as a boy running around playing games with his friends. I wondered what games they played in the 1800's. Old linden trees drooped with heavy white blossoms. A small green park beckoned. Maybe he played here.

Leaving The Cleveland Airport Bound For Our Odyssey

We stayed in a stone inn by the railroad tracks. Unfortunately we spoke no German; I only knew the German limericks Grandpa taught me as a child. But we found an ally - the innkeeper's small daughter studied English in school - she had a smattering of English vocabulary and was delighted to accompany us to the *burgomeister's* office where I hoped to find Grandpa's birthday in the register. I discovered there were three towns named *Bingen* - this was only one - the *burgomeister* was happy to look for the birth notice and luckily he found it in flowing German script, "Louis Poss, December 5, 1845." I couldn't wait to tell my sister. She kept saying that is was Possovitch or something long that the immigration officials couldn't deal with and shortened.

Jack asked our small guide to see if the portly *burgomeister* would let him take off his shoes and stand on the ancient desk to photograph Grandpa's official entry into the world. The book easily measured two feet by three feet and was thick and ponderous.

So I saw my roots and will never forget Jack standing six feet tall on that huge desk in his black socks, the *burgomeister* beaming, the little girl, Flora (also my mother's name) peering curiously at the ledger. I just stood very still with Deborah and Kristina and felt like I had come home.

Pretty People

Since I was a child in the thirties, just old enough to see beyond my own skin, I have seen and read of wanton acts of savageness in every corner of our world. But to be present at one, however small, soundless, stark, ineluctable, is to render it imprinted on my mind.

It happened at a Davis Cup Tennis Match at Clark Courts in Shaker Heights. The privileged people were in the stands, the people with money and power. Our first black mayor, Carl Stokes, was there with his then - wife.

A serendipitous feeling of the good life filled my consciousness. Yes, we had worked hard on civil rights. The stands were full of good people with gaily-colored clothes and white on black or black on white. We were seeing the best of the best tennis players from around the globe. No reigning sense of nationalism. Good sportsmanship was the coin of the realm in the best of tennis.

A chant and some movement from the street behind us diverted my attention; we were on the top row of the bleachers, a vantage point. A small group of people old, middle-aged, and children, repeated the chant, "Ho Chi Minh, Ho Chi Minh" protesting our war in Viet Nam. They walked in an orderly file. No one seemed to be watching but me.

A red truck with open sides used for picking up trash, "City of Cleveland," printed on the side, stopped and soundlessly, systematically grabbed all the people, (couldn't have been more than twenty, I can still see them) and threw them on top of each other into the truck bed. When anyone resisted a quick smack of the billy club rendered him or her limp and then loaded into the truck.

It was all over in the blink of an eye. One small protest against the longest, most unsupportable, unwinnable, brutal war our country had ever fought, (up to date) Vietnam.

The pretty people, the power people, hadn't taken their eyes off the tennis match, the waving at the friends, the chance to be seen at a select social event.

So now it came home to me: how easily, silently, freedom is muffled by whatever power is in control at the moment.

I don't know how our soldiers, brave, heroic, scared, ever get over the imprint of being death machines. Some lock it away in a secure compartment only to have it slip out at night in screaming nightmares. Some dull it with drugs brought back to the U.S. in the troop planes - that were loaded to capacity, at which our government conveniently averted its eyes. Some can't stop the acts of violence: killing people in other countries rewarded and sanctified by our government, they cannot dispel their violent behavior and are named criminals and are locked up by the same government.

This small event stays with me, to my horror, knowing that unknown injustice can flourish anywhere, even in the world's greatest democracy, "with freedom and justice for all."

Grandma Goes To Graduate School
At Kent State University

I timidly put one toe of my aging female self, into the sacrosanct, groves of academe by signing up for one course. Soon I was scheduling full time classes. It was in the late sixties: the time of protests mounting across the country against the prolonged and expanding war in Viet Nam. Students at Kent were enraged at having no voice in Washington, set fire to the ROTC building and sat in the halls of the administration building barricading the doors, so no one could get into their offices. The National Guard was called to restore order. Nobody took their presence seriously. One girl put a flower in the muzzle of one guard's rifle and danced around him. Suddenly, unbelievably the guards opened fire on students who were peacefully walking across campus changing classes. It was horrific, students fled in all directions, screaming, crying, blood flowing. Professors stupefied, didn't know what to do. Four students were killed many were critically injured, losing limbs. It was the first time our government killed our kids.

Students were sent to their homes. The great University was closed. We didn't know if it would ever open. Such was the rancor and confusion in our country. It wasn't till years later research showed that our President Nixon supposedly had given the order to open fire. Indignation, disbelief, horror. Now forty years later new evidence uncovered confusion about the incident. It is, however, true that the students protests that spread across the country contributed to the U.S. withdrawing from their war in Viet Nam.

Those were very strange times. Students who had led the riots were tried in court. Community opinion was extremely caustic about the students. The uprising had spread across the country to college campuses and into the streets: investigations, confusion, media coverage. The academic world was turned upside down, as were families.

During this time I was selected to be Director of the Student Activities Department.

Finally, out of the chaos Kent State opened tentatively in the fall. The campus was a spectacle. Professors wanting to appease students wore beads and sandals and sported long hair and beards. F.B.I. and C.I.A. men tried to disguise their presence sporting beads and sandals too. However, we could easily spot them. They were awkward and out of place on the campus.

Administration, here-to-fore lacking awareness of students' feelings and problems, created a Crisis Center. An intern, working on my doctorate, I was named Director. We had twenty-four hour hot lines to handle their problems and a drop-in center to deal with severe drug problems. We created a "problem pregnancy center" to deal with the young women who came in streams hoping for help to deal with their pregnancies. There were only three clinics in the country which provided safe sterile abortions. We created a liaison for the girls after carefully studying their cases.

This was one of the services; I believe that I helped perform. Many on scholarship, with no funds and a disappearing boyfriend were stranded. I paid for a lot of abortions gladly. A black girl on scholarship from the Inner City in her first trimester turned out to be carrying twins. If she had borne them, she would have returned to a life of poverty and welfare.

There were so many, but a few stand out in my memory. One young woman said her boyfriend didn't believe in abortion. So I told her to bring him in for her next appointment. He came with a book of poetry. "Okay, so you are going to be with her and support her financially and emotionally?" "No, I'm shipping out next week in the Army." I asked her to bring her mother in. Mother, who was Director of Birthright in a distant city, said "get rid of it. I'm not going to take care of it." When reality hit home a different choice was made.

Another young woman called about three A.M. when I was on the lines and told me she was pregnant. So, the usual question "what are your plans?" "I want to keep the baby and need pre-natal advice." I met with her weekly for the next seven months, and occasionally with her boyfriend. He could not help her financially and was a born loser. When the baby was born, I went to the hospital. The baby looked just like her mother. I was faint. My mother's heart was torn. But the young woman had all her plans in place. She wanted the baby to go to well-off Jewish parents who were cultivated and well-educated. So, it was done. Her parents were there. The father had a big position in government and agreed with her.

Classes were kind of funky. Before the opening we all carried on as best we could. Some of our loyal professors held classes in their basements, houses darkened, so we could finish our courses. As I drove past the great dark University and library tears streamed down my face. I thought "it doesn't take a Hitler to put out the lamps of learning." My major adviser was psychotic. When he was fired, he boarded himself in his office and wouldn't leave. He sued the most esteemed members of our faculty for devious sexual behavior. He called a meeting of our class on "Counseling the Culturally Deviant" at "Pop's Truck Stop" a shabby joint popular with truckers and prostitutes. He invited a lesbian and a gay man. An incongruous setting. Homosexuals were considered deviant. As their discussion got more and more graphic the truck driver's faces became more and more livid. To demonstrate the tenor of those times the lesbian lady said she had a one way ticket to go to Canada in case things got tough.

Finally, with another adviser, I completed my doctoral studies, and went into private practice. Slow going at first till I became well known and then flourished. My contact at the Philadelphia Child, Guidance Clinic Jamshed Morenos, my inspiration conducted week-end workshops for family therapists at my center: the little red building that Jack bought for me, I called "The Center For Better Living." I thought that name was pretty non-threatening for a small town.

In time, I studied hypnotherapy in Houston with Milton Erickson's trainers: went to Mayo Clinic to study their kind of family therapy, to Philadelphia Child Guidance to work with the three foremost structural family therapists in the world, Minuchin, Whitacker and Palozzoli, the Italian expert. I spent three years studying cognitive therapy at University Hospital. At the same I enrolled in a three year post-doctoral program at the Cleveland Gestalt Institute. It became my tidal basin. All this was while I was finishing my doctorate.

When I first approached physicians and ministers in the surrounding area they were unimpressed with my beautiful brochure and me. Later, they became my clients with their families. One minister told me he figured he was referring five percent of his congregation to me.

The Faithful Cabin Crew

Thursday Nights

An extraordinary seven-year experience evolved from an invitation to a mystery night. Jack and I were invited to Brad and Babs Holts' with Dan and Doris Frenz to meet with our new minister Bill Van Auken and his wife, Jane.

We had such an amiable time that we all said, "This is too good. We must gather again." Thus began a seven-year group meeting every other Thursday night in our cabin by the lake. No one ever failed to show up.

I began pursuing my doctoral degree at Kent State University and was accepted for a three-year post-doc program at the Gestalt Institute in Cleveland. Instead of just talking, I asked the group if I could proceed to use Gestalt Therapy with them. So, as I learned new Gestalt techniques each week, I "practiced" on them. We worked through dreams, psychodrama and whatever was going on in their lives. It was truly quite wonderful.

Years after we finally ended, I asked Dan after he had painted a piece called "Thursday Nights" what they had meant to him. He said simply "They saved my life."

Sadly, there are only two survivors of our brave band still living.

Unforgettable.

Cope's Experience In The School Of Architecture

Every medium in art that Cope studied through the years he excelled at: figure drawing, woodcarving, pottery, ceramics, sculpture, etc. Then he decided to enroll in an architecture course at his Alma Mater, Case Western Reserve University. He always should have been an architect. His life would have been so much more fulfilled. It was a love deep in his pores.

These were strange times, the early seventies. The world abounded with flower children. His professor, out of Berkeley arrived in beard, sandals and beads bearing a large bowl, a sack of flour, yeast and a pitcher of water. He proceeded to make bread dough while the class waited expectantly.

I knew him from the Cleveland Gestalt Institute three-year post – doc training program. In a word, he was nuts. He explained the importance of bread and how it caused people to build houses: a point he could have made in one sentence.

Cope soon dropped out in grievous disappointment. The professor because of a variety of rules, could not be fired. So the university terminated the whole architecture department.

So, Cope designed our new home on the lake, built an outhouse and a boathouse near our cabin on the lake.

The end of a dream. The creation of a new one.

NTL

One day while I was in graduate school I decided to go to a two-week summer national training lab therapy session. I told Cope that I would probably divorce him if he didn't come. I didn't always think things through in my halcyon days!

He went.

We took Kris along for a "growth experience." She was sixteen and the last one living at home. It was indeed a "growth experience" for her; swimming nude with the boys in the quarry at night, etc.

It was in Bethel Maine, some little hamlet tucked in the mountains of Maine that nobody had heard of. It proved to be intense work-therapy sessions all day and most evenings for two weeks. Cope and I were in separate groups of about eight people. I had rented a stone house in the woods by a big lake.

We had the week-end off. Kris was with friends, Cope and I spent all day Saturday on a couch watching the embers softly glowing in the stone fireplace. We told each other all the things we had blamed each other for; there was some kind of a special ethos that we never argued or fought.

We listened!

That night symbolically we went to the laundromat and washed all of our dirty clothes, stripping down the clothes we were wearing under our raincoats.

A cleansing rite *de passage*?

We had driven up to Maine on thru-ways and turnpikes. But on the way home we drove on little out-of-the-way roads – again symbolically....every time we passed a river or a lake we jumped out of the car with one accord and jumped in the water swimming gleefully.

I wondered how long this joyous free feeling would last. How does one hang on to that delicious freedom?

I opened my pratice when Cope bought this building for me in 1974

My Practice

When I was looking for a job after completing my doctoral studies, Cope said "you don't need a job. You can open your own practice!" "Are you crazy? Honey, people in our town know us too well and all my sometimes outrageous behavior."

Cope bought me a whole building I had it painted red (like the "little red school house) and I opened my practice. I called my building "The Center For Better Living," I thought that would not scare people off! I reflect now that I lived through the times of sexual discrimination when the prevailing point of view in the media, women's magazines, corporations, homes, etc. was definitively "The woman's place is in the home." If a woman ventured, out it was to be a secretary, nurse, etc… primarily serving men. That thought never occurred to me then.

My first three clients were a burnt out schizophrenic who couldn't pay, an anorectic/bulimic young woman who had gone the rounds in Cleveland of all the psychiatric treatments and was a determined anorectic, druggie and alcoholic, a young man on his way to college. I had beautifully printed brochures of my extensive training and workshops offered. I took them to all the ministers and physicians in the surrounding area who were not receptive. In time, the ministers and physicians and their families also became clients.

So my brave move paid off and I loved it. My clients were dear to me. In time, my client load grew so much I took in other distinguished colleagues.

While I was in practice I got serious about writing my dissertation the invention of the devil incarnate. I got a membership at the medical library at Case Western Reserve University asking them for all the material on anorexia nervous that they had in English. The librarian said "there won't be much." On the contrary bundles of research articles arrived daily. Someone provided a box for them. It looked just like a coffin: a strong metaphor. I drew cases from my client load of young anorectics and their families, read the ton of research. Many roadblocks too threatening to recall; there emerged my 350 page leather bound *Pièce de résistance*. I damn near died in the process.

I was often asked to give lectures on "Burn Out," did a lot of research on the subject and was popular.

I realized that I was burned-out myself. Physician heal thy self. I was forced to retire. My body was in ruins from the progress of the deadly, undiagnosed Chronic Fatigue Immune Dysfunction. I had worked so hard to break the chains of the suburban housewife and civic leader at no small sacrifice. I literally shed my skin and crawled out of a black hole that was slowly swallowing me. It had developed after a trip to China where I had contracted the Epstein-Barr Syndrome in 1983.

Now this! It broke my heart.

Mark Anthony

The young man in my therapy office was a major drug dealer, "on the lam" as he framed it from the law and the Mafia. We will call him "J".

The man in the waiting room, a policeman in charge of narcotics, was such a sweet, sweet man. He brought his daughter in to see me because she was hooked on drugs and was anorexic/ bulimic.

His only son's name was Mark Anthony, born to be his family's legacy. But born with an incurable disease, tube fed by his mother who used all of her available energy feeding him and changing his diapers. Obese, unaware of life, an unlived in body- no past, no present, no future. I expect the policeman would have killed J if he caught him or at least put the cuffs on him.

The young man was referred to me by a physician for "anxiety." J moved every day from one motel to another. The Mafia wanted him to pull off one last big deal for them for two hundred fifty thousand dollars. Enough to pay off the mortgage he had tendered for his parents' home and estate. He was terrified that he would be caught by the law. But if he didn't the Mafia would get him.

I suggested he turn to the law and plead for clemency. He felt that choice was as bad from his experience. Although I told him he could ask for a new identity and leave the country if he identified the big Mafia leaders.

J's probation officer called for an appointment. Therapeutic rule of confidentiality: I could tell him nothing.

The father called for an appointment. Was his son schizophrenic? At least I could tell him "no." He desperately wanted to know if J's promise of thousands of gold Krugerrands was real or the product of a disordered mind. In reality, a product of desperation. I could tell the father that I was very anxious and needed his family to show their love for him – if they could locate him. J's handsome face was carved of marble, no feelings shown. He had been incarcerated, slashed, and raped. I wondered who he would have been if he had chosen a different path.

Cocaine, he insisted was purely recreational, sold to judges, attorneys, and people in high-pressure jobs. I told him no drugs were just "recreational;" all were destructive to the mind and body.

Everyone stuck in impossible situations. As a therapist called upon to help people find surcease for pain and the problems of their complex lives, in this case my hands were tied. For a therapist this is the place of woe and soul searching pain.

He finally had to have appointments in the darkness and cover of night. My husband worried for my safety, alone in my building with both the Mafia and the law tracking him. He was right. But I survived.

Finally J disappeared; I will never know what happened.

The seventeen-year-old daughter gradually improved. The policeman, powerless and loveless in his home trudged on, his wife consumed with Mark Anthony. Mark Anthony in his vegetable patch, unaware of the pain he caused.

Beauregard

Everyone yearns to hear more about Beau's exploits. His escapades are quirky but entirely understandable when one is aware of his feelings. I would like to know more about his forebears. I know he is of royal lineage; Beauregard Von Franke is his full name.

He makes his own rules and is devoted to his family. This remarkable dog believes he is a person not just a boxer and I think he is too.

Occasionally he has to go to the Pet Hotel while Nancy and Dick are away for a few days. When he is liberated he spends precisely the equal number of days sulking in Dick's dark den. He only ventures out to eat and relieve himself. When he feels they are sufficiently punished, he emerges to join them.

Nancy piled the fresh laundry in a basket in her room one evening when they were going out. When they returned the yard was strewn with clothes. Beau had sorted through the piles but he only chose Nancy's to take outside. She was the one to be punished.

Sometimes when they went out, Beau scrambled all the cushions from couches and chairs around the floor. One time Dick decided to leave Beau in his convertible in the garage. Beau loves to sit in it – especially when he thinks he can become invisible and go with them.

Because he was so happy sitting up in the convertible, they left him there one evening when they went out. Dick had just gotten a new top for it. Beau was sitting there, expecting to tag along. When they returned they saw that Beau had eaten the entire canvas top. Not a scrap left: but no indigestion, no vomiting, no contrition or sulking around.

Once, when Beau was incarcerated in the garage, convertible safely driven away, they came home to an empty garage – no Beau. Standing there in amazement, they realized somebody was watching them. Beau, who had dug a three-foot-deep tunnel under the garage to escape, was proudly viewing the empty garage with them.

You see, Beau was presented to Dick and Nancy by one of their daughters, after Scott, a son, had died suddenly in his twenties from an aneurysm. Beau had to develop a personality that would divert the grieving parents and make them concentrate on him so he would become special to them.

And just think! How many of us develop the persona to fit the role needed by our families?

Raising Baby Deer

One of the precious experiences in our lives was when our sweet wild life manager presented us with a tiny baby deer, who was about an hour old. Her mother had been a victim of road kill and she lay on the side of the road to die.

I named her Begonia because she still had her infant white spots. We got baby bottles and infant deer baby starter milk. Our home had a barn and corral where she happily frisked and had shelter when needed. She was on a three hour schedule, then finally four. One of us came home from work to care for her regularly. We played with her and she ran about happily.

She was killed by a pack of wild dogs who had leapt over the fence to get her. How we mourned over her grave.

Undaunted, our wildlife friend brought us another baby deer some months later. He was only one half hour old. Ramon said he would be lucky to live. So we named him "Lucky Buck". He grew to become a fine deer.

When autumn came we knew it was time to let him go. Our home was surrounded by 180 acres where he could live his life in the wild. Reluctantly we let him go. But he followed us to our kitchen door. We got on our boat to go out into our lake. But Lucky swam after as. Afraid he would drown we turned back.

It was so hard to say goodbye. Lucky thought he was part of our human family never having seen another deer before. Finally, we got in our car and gunned it down the driveway. Reluctantly, Lucky gave up and we consoled ourselves.

On Christmas Day Lucky appeared proudly with his wife. Months later he came back with wife and child. He made regular visits for many years.

Ramon Hinchcliff called one day to tell us that he had been alerted by the local vet and asked to witness the stitching of an injured deer, a victim of a car accident. Ramon said the deer licked his hand. He told us no wild deer would do that. It had to be Lucky. He is all right.

The Robin Rescue Committee

These last few weeks we've been watching the nest mama robin built in the fern wreath on the front door. (which we haven't been able to use while she's in residence)

Babies kept falling out as they filled the nest and we kept putting them back. Kim finally tied the nest securely to the wreath and the front door knob.

Between us and mama robin faithfully feeding them they feathered out and flew happily to join the host of birds on our land. I wish it were so easy to cap the horrendous oil spill in our gulf.

Turd Coffee

Cope went to Tony's Camp to fish every summer with a bunch of Docs from the Cleveland Clinic. It was a ritual over Memorial Day. The Docs arrived with their bags: contents to cure all esoteric illnesses. But when one of them, the head of orthopedics, got a fish hook caught in one finger that couldn't be removed Cope was the only one with a pair of pliers, wire cutter and a band aid who could help him. He says to this day "See this finger; I have it because Jack Colebrook saved it!"

After they stopped going we went for years with Tom Gretter, a good doctor friend at C.C. F. and his wife, Joan. It was a ritual that we docked at a small island, built a fire and fried our fresh catch. Tom was the famous coffee make, which I dubbed "Turd Coffee." It was god awful but part of the ritual; so we drank it.

For many years after that we went with our children who were "hooked" on Tony's camp too.

Shore lunch where Tom makes his inevitable ghastly Turd coffe at Tony's Lodge in Canada where we went for many years. "It's tradition". Hail to good friends!

Family Gathering At Severn Lodge In Canada

Pooh said, "I have my friends.
I heard from one of them just
The other week."

We're on our way home with a vanload of dirty clothes, fishing gear, games, golf clubs and our grandson, Max after one week at Severn Lodge, a delightful lodge in Georgian Bay. The fifty-one of us. In age from one to eighty-four. All of Sis's and my progeny plus a gang of her extended family whom she gathers into her bounty.

Full of so many treasureful moments: gazing into babies' eyes and bonding souls, kayaking in the lake – (remembering how after sixty years), canoeing with my daughters, a seaplane ride, late-night confidences, games, daughters and I decorating each other with seaweed, a workshop led by my niece Elaine, sub-grouping, "knowing" family members who are distant geographically, wanting to stay connected. I've had soul-loving moments. I am full and quiet.

Severn Lodge was an ideal place to gather; the little ones could be safely independent, the twenty -plus-year-olds fiercely independent. They chartered a bus one night and took all the waitresses dancing. The staff so gracious about all of our exploits and misdemeanors. It was a haven for time-out from earthly concerns and duties.

My sister's off-spring have added one Native American husband, added and subtracted one Afro-American and one Arabian. We still haven't covered the Orient, but there's time. But we have a Mormon family and one schizophrenic.

I dreamed last night that I was Hillary and Bill's sex therapist – it was interesting that Bill came on to me – actually it was positively orgastic. Sis asked how I felt about him – and I said "today he's No. 1!"

My sister is so frail and almost blind, I fear this is the last gathering of the total clan. Now my doctor says that I, too, have macular degeneration, so it's kind of scary to see her limitations.

At The Lodge At Booth Bay Maine,
Our First Huge Family Gathering
Before Severn.

We gather at one of our cabins each night
to escape Mrs. "Strangelove"- our guardian.

She was a former head of a girls' camp and
we were mandated to respond to her whistle
and stand in line at the mess hall for our
meals.

We destroyed her the first night when Margie's
and Leslie's sink came off the wall-hot water
gushing everywhere!

But dreamers, my dreams this summer have been pretty flamboyant, so I'll be a lot of fun in our Friday group.

I wanted to stay in Canada – where some of us ventured into town I bought five lattes for fifteen dollars and got fifteen dollars and seventy-five cents back from a fifty-dollar bill. Like playing the stock market.

I'm bittersweet about going home. It's an incredible experience to discover or re-connect with people who share genes and see our similar and divergent paths.

Enjoyed all of your letters and calls and love each one of you.

Books to read – Wayne Muller, "How Then Shall We Live?" 3 Judith Orloft, "Second Sight."4

Letter To Family

To bring you up to date with me – since the Noetics Conference. I have been fascinated with E.T.'s – and what these visitations mean to our planet and, of course, why our government has chosen to zap all sightings and meetings out. After hearing Edgar Mitchell, scientist – astronaut, give his observations – I am embarked on new research!

In our wildlife refuge the deer, raccoons and all the assorted critters feel so safe here they have eliminated my gardens. Even the grape vineyard that Jack covered with strong steel meshing.

I'm going to tell them they may not be so safe! Just like Africa – civilization in collision with the animals that are a loving obsession with me but where the decisions will if necessary be made in favor of the people and their crops. The deer even ate the deer-proof planting/landscaping of last year!! I'm getting their message.

Our itinerant black swans had an early brood of cygnets that were eaten one by one by members of our food chain. We think it was the owl.

They produced five more babies and I was overjoyed. Now they are disappearing while the Dad ferociously attacks swimmers, the tractor, and our cars. I fantasized that he was the protective patriarch – I found today that the breeder says they don't want their offspring – so now we're running an abortion clinic.

Enduring Smokey
Damned If You Don't and Damned If You Do

When the decision became clear that Grandma, a.k.a. Great Tootsie, had to give up her apartment and go to a nursing home, we were in a pressure cooker. It was clear that Mrs. Wolfe's house, where Grandma's apartment was, had to be sold. Clear that in spite of her fantasy, she could not live with us.

When he was only fifteen, Jack told her he would always take care of her, but she could never live under his roof . . . a prescient awareness of things to come and of their relationship. Our marriage would not have lasted five minutes; Grandma had a highly developed way of destroying relationships.

Understandably, giving up her apartment and her independence was a cruel blow. Crueler still was the problem of Smokey; the cat had been her constant companion for years. Taken in as a ragged stray, Smokey, well fed and petted, grew into a fat cat, with a luxurious mantle of silky, black fur.

Smokey, however, couldn't go to the nursing home in those years. Months of agonizing followed: endless tears, hand wringing, pleading red eyes. Mom wouldn't give Smokey to anyone else.

Characteristically she reasoned, "If I can't have him, no one else can." Off to the death chamber she decided; he must go to the vet for a Kevorkian cocktail.

One of her friends made a little coffin for Smokey, but Mom called in distress. "The coffin is too small. Smokey will be forever cramped in the hereafter." So it fell to my husband to make a nice coffin that wouldn't cramp Smokey.

He took his measuring tape to Gram's to get Smokey's accurate dimensions, measuring the cat as he was stretched out full length while sleeping at Gram's feet. Jack measured him from top to bottom and side to side. I told him I was afraid to go to sleep before he did for a long time after that.

The casket turned out to be a thing of beauty; a lovely wood painted with three coats of white enamel, carefully sanded down between applications. It was fitted with gleaming brass hinges. Then the dutiful son went to the local fabric store.

"Mary Beth, do you have white satin?" he asked the owner. She showed him where to find the satin and asked, "Jack, what do you want it for?"

"I'm making a coffin."

Mary Beth did a double take. "Oh sure," she said, mouth agape, eyes narrowed.

Jack got out my long unused sewing machine. After Lonnie, our housekeeper, showed him how to thread it, he made a quilted lining. Liking the way it looked, he decided that a little coverlet would be nice, so he sewed one. Still having some satin left, he made a pillow for Smokey's head.

Off to the vet's clinic, we waited for the death verdict. Gram cried when Dr. Weible brought the moribund Smokey out to the car. She wanted Jack to take a photograph of the cat reclining peacefully in his coffin so she could remember him that way.

Breathing collective sighs of relief, we dropped Great Tootsie off and drove home. The phone was ringing. All was not so easily resolved. "Jack, the coffin is so lovely. I want you to make a plastic cover to preserve it."

This done, the highly emotional subject of the burial site had to be decided. Tootsie wanted Smokey buried in perpetuity on our property. Her son wheeled her around till she decided on just the right spot - - on a small hill facing northeast, warmed by the morning sun, and overlooking our lake and we thought our task was finished. The phone was ringing again. Great Totsie said "Smokey needs a proper headstone." So, dutiful but slightly exasperated son made a headstone. He dug the grave and inscribed "Smokey" on it.

We held a lovely memorial service. We formed a small funeral procession back up the hill, my husband pushing Tootsie, who was wearing a blue cardigan sweater I had bought for her. It just matched her wheelchair.

Finally, we thought, we could say the matter of Smokey was put to rest.

But no! Mom called. She had ordered crocus bulbs for us to plant on the grave so they would bloom for Smokey every spring.

And so, we can be sure that, for eternity, Smokey will be resting comfortably in his white satin bier, warmed by the morning sun, overlooking the lake, and with crocuses ever-blooming in the spring.

Great Tootsie ever the devoted fisherman in our flotebote on our lake. She fished till she was totally incapacitated. Cope built a ramp to accommodate her wheel chair

The Lump

We were making love

He said, "Honey, there's a lump."

Dead mother from cancer

Dead Aunt from cancer

Dead me from cancer

Cancer, cancer, cancer

Fuck it run from it

Nowhere to hide

Long Labor Day holiday weekend

Have to give the party

Cooking, cooking, cooking

People laughing, laughing, laughing

People playing at life

I dying?

See the internist

"Yes, you have a lump."

Not a cyst

A tumor

Hospital

The Lumpectomy

Biopsy

Nurse says

"If the doctor sits on your bed

You've got it."

We play cards

Waiting, waiting, waiting

Smoking, smoking, smoking

Ward off danger

The doctor sits on my bed

He quickly lops off my left breast

What did he care?

 He was a surgeon

Check nodes

Cancer contained

I forever mutilated

Transition

Fall has a magical effect on me – *tristesse*, I thought, but no, a sense of healing regeneration, a creative surge. Am I in tune with nature's photosynthesis? Each day at our home deep in the woods I see the colors of the trees get burnished; their images mirrored in our still lake, an impressionist rendering by nature's brush. The trees are drenched in a drift of colors: crowned blonde, brunette, titian, some umber, crimson and purple.

The poison ivy and Virginia creeper blazing, putting to shame with their scarlet tapestry the hosts they are ravaging. I can predict the colors of certain trees as they annually express their unique photosynthesis. My favorite, the ancient great oak, never fails me with its burnt sienna and I long for Italy, where sienna abounds. Some trees keep their summer green locks longer than all the others. The pines that Jack planted as little sticks have become giants; they stand out in their deep green, their limbs swaying in the autumn wind. They become ballet dancers. The beeches hold on to their umber plumage after others are stripped. Barren, their limbs silver or black beside their gaudy neighbors, they are part of the mosaic. Jack's metasequoias, emerald green against the blazing colors, declare themselves.

I wonder, if the leaves are like snowflakes; no two exactly alike. Randomly, I pick them up and find it true. Nature, in its infinite possibilities. Some, unlike us, are perfect. Like us, some are imperfect, but like us none is exactly like another. Thank heaven for diversity and individuality. We'd look like we were made by the same cookie cutter. Now how do the oaks all know we are going to have an unpredictably hard, long winter and need to grow more acorns to supply the little critters? Magic? Symbiosis? The deer are growing heavy coats and browsing in increasing numbers closer to our house.

The great oaks are pouring acorns onto our roof, the sounds crackling like rifle shots. I jump each time. They are ankle-deep outside. The critters are filling their cheeks and skittering to their nests. A ranger at Yellowstone once explained that some cones of the log poll pines bury themselves and immediately start reproducing. Others know they should

Transition

Exotic colors reflect on our lake!

bide their time for reforesting and wait until needed after a catastrophic fire. My prayer plant sits in a dark corner of the house, yet it knows when night is falling and folds its leaves in prayer. Magic? Nature's ineluctable process.

Now the brief radiance of blazing sunset reflects the scene of the lake changing from summer cobalt to shimmering silver at misty dawn, later to colorfully reflecting the riotous colors surrounding it, and brings me speechless to my knees.

The herons skim the water, the cormorants blithely fly in the middle, and the great hawks above like Supreme Court Judges. The Bald Eagle soars its solitary Kingship over all.

The crisp nutty fragrance of fall fills our senses. My posies are beginning to brown out. It's time for our annual migration to eternal summer. I know that I shall rejoice and plant all over again in our southern haven. So, I regenerate seasonally too.

The Land Of OZ

Yesterday, Jack and Michael brought in the new computer. We had gestated it for nine months and now were in labor. It was only a truncated fetus—not the whole computer thing or the printer.

I looked at the creature I had lobbied for and went to bed, slept for fifteen hours. You do that after labor. Only to find out that it was false labor; after all that dreadful pain! I didn't even awaken for four -hour feedings. The damn thing slept alone in the dark.

Now I'm told by friends who can do computer and also can turn on their Cuisinarts that I can't kill it, that it will do as it's told.

But they didn't know that I was right-brained and the creature was a left-brainer.

Yet, I believed them as I had believed all that I read about "you and your baby." That should have been enough to teach me a lesson. No wonder I'm daunted by the "dot com."

Then came "sending messages." Somehow they all came back. It was like baby two, three, and four. These accretions are left-brain additive goings-on. They are squared, multiplied, and cumulative. Even our faithful cocker spaniel, wee-trained, peed on the rugs each time I brought a baby home. He did it with the computer!

Once I had honors in math and Latin on my college boards, but all that's gone, too. After four children you forget. You forget math, Latin, French, science, current events, carrying the torch, and keeping track of your checking account. My beloved was bemused, if not totally frustrated, over a check stub that said "Cookie." The dog had eaten my check.

You also collect dogs, cats, rabbits, goats, gerbils, hamsters, iguanas, tropical fish, and you board white mice for a child's friend. To say nothing of large ducks swimming in your sink, the aftermath of the blessed Easter - and parental stupidity.

Survival is what you pass on or fail. Some days it's nip and tuck.

I learned in my major field in college, "Child Development," not to intimidate my children. Then I found out that I was the one who was intimidated; yes, compromised.

It's a tricky business to participate in the dynamics of mother-father-baby-more babies, who grow into children, then adolescents, escaping parental shackles.

You get into a League of Voters' Right of Self-expression. And when they become adults, the situation calls for a Red Alert.

Actually the whole thing is impossible. We become subversive. But one of us, hopefully a parent, becomes chairman of the C.I.A.

Notwithstanding your best intentions and desire to make them your best friends, someone will turn you in.

It takes a long time from the breast to the pill to launch a semi-reasonable adult child and to find out what the hell was going on all those years; like telling us that they grew up playing in the sewers of Aurora.

In reality, I don't think we ever know; or should know.

First, these unformed little creatures we would give our lives for are totally dependent on us ignorant folks until we prove ourselves culpable. Then they resist, sneak, and challenge all our inherited eternal verities. Finally, after they have survived Genesis and their own infants, if we're damned lucky, they become our best friends.

Now you can turn to the Beatitudes.

And then the grandchildren will teach us computer-aerobics so that we can E-mail to them.

Poor sodden initiates, are we in the Land of Oz.

We move to the Book of Job as a whole new total computer arrives in huge boxes three days in a row. The installer discovered that some of its vital internal organs are missing.

It is massive and grows and finally sprawls all over Jack's study. We may have to geld the critter.

I wonder if gazing adoringly at its big screen and stroking its mouse will bond us in the same way, as it was when we gazed adoringly at our infants and stroked their sweet baby-smelling cheeks.

The Road Most Traveled

Twice a year - spring and fall - we birds of passage are on the move between our homes in Ohio and Florida. Musing, I reflect about the tiny hummingbirds migrating from North America to Mexico or South America with their little hearts beating over five hundred times a minute. Little wings wheeling, carrying nothing on their backs, while we, or I, which turns into "we," carry our homes on our backs like turtles with ungainly carapaces.

For our invasions to the other camp we equip ourselves like troops in the Spanish Armada. Our first expedition to establish a southern beachhead was as our grandchildren say "awesome." Jack managed to pack in our van and in the clamshell on the roof: an antique Dutch sink, two end tables, a coffee table, bedding, two sets of china, several paintings, boxes of pottery, baskets, a coffee maker, a cappuccino maker, a Cuisinart, a spice rack and heaven knows what else or why. Now I know everything in kingdom come can be found in Sarasota, but Jack established himself as a packer in perpetuity.

So I pack mountains of clothes, books, writing and painting materials, boxes of my mother's letters of sixty years ago. Never left behind, rarely read.

Time disappears in bustling happiness in both homes. Then comes the ten-day agony of selecting, packing, loading. Bonsai, orchids, jade plants want fresh air and water every night and are grateful when deposited in the shower at motels or friend's homes en route.

Ten days to pack. Ten days to unpack, sort and find tasteful resting places for our stuff. This agony to be repeated twice a year. That amounts to forty days out of three hundred and sixty-five.

Friends en route take pictures through the windows of our van in disbelief. When we arrive at each home, I want to put a bomb under the van. We should have it Feng Shuied! Daunted, we dragged ourselves to bed without unpacking when we finished our pilgrimage to Longboat Key, in October. Cowards! Ostriches!

We awake the next morning to eleven huge boxes on our doorstep, courtesy of UPS. I had packed them up north and conveniently developed amnesia about them.

Clothes unworn, books unread, recipes unused, photographs unmounted in waiting albums (there will always be time in the other place).

We swear we won't do it again. Come the next primeval urge to migrate and the great beginning. "Don't leave us, you'll be sorry."

The research article that surfaces from one of my piles says, "There is hope for people suffering from obsessive-compulsive disorder (OCD).... high levels of anxiety will occur during treatment.... while there is no cure for OCD, medications and behavioral therapy can help control the symptoms."

We'll see if this psychotherapist is treatable. I want to be a hummingbird and fly freely, not a turtle dragging a carapace.

Mary Lou

Grief (Journal Entry)

Two days ago Mary Lou died. Jack got the call while I was resting. He took both of my hands in his: his face crumpled, his voice broke, tears slipped down his cheeks. We were in our home on Longboat Key, Florida. He said "Honey, I already have our tickets for Cleveland, we leave tomorrow. This! In spite of his relentless pain and deterioration with shingles. What a guy!

I was reading a letter from Mary Lou, saying, "now you can worry." It had just arrived telling me that she was having a rough day in the hospital with her bone marrow transplant. I screamed for about an hour, I guess I was keening. It was spontaneous, maybe because she was Irish? "She shouldn't have died," was all I could say. "Stop. She was one of my dearest friends. I can't live without her." "She didn't deserve her cancer. She loved her life." She and Tom had the most loving compatible marriage I know of. Multiple myeloma usually occurs in African American men in their fifties. She was sixty-six. Tom and Mary Lou would have had their tenth anniversary in ten days.

When she told me of her diagnosis and prognosis (grim), she said, "I can't die, Tom can't live without me. We wake up in the mornings and hold each other and cry together."

I am sick with grief. I realize that it is the first time I have truly learned to grieve. Mary Lou was the best friend a person could possibly have, best tennis partner, mother. I shall never forget her yelling when she hit a tennis ball into the woods. Out of her early Catholic upbringing, she screamed, "Jesus, Mary, Joseph – but that's not enough Goddamit to hell." All of us who loved her will always miss her. She had an interesting blend of little girlishness and ancient wisdom - maybe her grandmother's who raised her?

An unspoken family rule - no grieving. My father held court telling funny stories to friends who came to call while Mother lay in her casket in the adjacent "sun room." It was macabre.

The minister was under the spell of the rule. He never said a thing about her - her life of giving to others, of founding organizations, her faithful service to the church. Dad gave a wonderful new organ, the finest, to our church in her memory. Then he went home and cut down the cherry tree behind the house. The only time I ever saw him do anything in the garden. I never knew why. Had she loved it and he wanted it cut down and she wouldn't allow it? Had he always resented her preoccupation with gardening? It was her greatest delight and creative expression. Was this deliberately aggressive act a metaphor for their power struggle? Or was it a physical outlet for grief?

Grandpa died first in the string of deaths in the family, then Mother, and then Aunt Julia, Grandmother and finally my father. I never cried. Dad's death was heart breaking because of our bitter alienation in the last months of his life.

Our friend Dick Wilson died after a long struggle with cancer. That was the beginning of meeting the wall that disallowed my grief. Now I am sick with the pain of losing Mary Lou - my buddy. I hear her ready laugh, her jolly voice plays in my head. I am raw with vulnerability. There is no protection. Shirley said, "I cannot afford to lose another friend." This will go on and on at our age.

Now, Shirley died.

We are helping Ann and George host a picnic for Mary Lou's family tonight. I dread seeing their suffering. The service is tomorrow.

And now my most intimate, trustable friend, Carlla. We shared everything and anything with each other. I treasured our time together. A letter from her arrived saying it was her last – incoherent.

I stayed up all night drinking wine and watching T.V. with my caregiver. I knew I would never sleep. Some people are irreplaceable.

Stirrings

What is this stirring in my breast
That like the grass of greener years
Sways in advancing waves
When I am half asleep
And washes weary times away
While gently promising
Sweet summer days to keep?

How can it be this sorry stone
Begins to pulse and feel again
The heat, the breathing in and out of life,
Sweet laughter in the smallest thing
And best of all the hope that joy itself
May lie beyond the hill where swallows wing?

Beware, my simple soul!
You yearn for more than God has planned,
Seek golden shafts of sun in every rain.
And yet it's good to know, though Autumn's chill
Will surely nip your blossoms in their finest blush,
There's warmth among the roots again.

Spring 1988
Anonymous

December 20, 1989

Dear Friends,

I've never written a "group letter" before because I hated to think of myself as one of a group of receptors. However now 1) I've run out of time for cards for the people I really want to write notes to. 2) I've injured my back so badly that it hurts to write and 3) I've enjoyed the group letters that some of you write so thoroughly and feel more in contact with old friends I don't see often.

Thus launched, I will hit the desolate high-heights of '89. You'll soon see why I don't like to repeat them. I was finally diagnosed as having "The Chronic Fatigue Immune Deficiency Syndrome" early last march after being so ill I had to depart quickly from the sybaritic island of St. Bart's. It's a deep viral infection involving most systems of the body (once called Epstein-Barr). It appears that I have been struggling with it for many years - so it was both a terrible blow and a tremendous relief to find out what was going on in my body that made me feel that it was out of my control. Mark Iverson, President of the National CFID Association remarks, "it erases lives."

Anyway, it seems that I manufactured the perfect disease for myself as we often do, to make me re-examine my life - because there is no cure, just remission possibly with REST, nutrition, vitamins, herbs, and a few medications and INNER GROWTH (which means, that I have to stop going into phone booths and putting on my cape and think that I am inextinguishable, like superman.)

After many months in bed, except for testing every cell in my body, MRI, barium up and down, sigmoidoscopy, colonoscopy, giving gallons of blood (which nobody paid me for), EKG's, echocardiograms of the heart, thallium stress tests three CAT scan's, surgical insertion of a pacemaker which was removed the next day, and other things blessedly forgotten - oh that's it - crippling memory loss and deep depression, I finally feel "better." So, we went to the Southwest in November where-upon I did this back job riding pink jeeps up and down mountains and buttes and climbing into Anasazi caves and swinging ladders (I actually started lifting tall buildings while we were creating a Japanese garden in the fall). Now I'm going through injections and wearing a transcutaneous electrical nerve stimulation contraption constantly. Day and Night.

Someone else has to do the limbo and wear the bikini at Stanley's.

Hopefully, I am avoiding spinal surgery.

The good news is that I'll be out of bed for Christmas and it looks like I can go to Tortola for the two months we'd planned (all my physicians have volunteered to accompany me). We're taking the extended family for a post-Christmas holiday.

You see, after some dismal months, I realized that I needed to retire from private practice, and somebody else would have to save the world while I saved myself. This was one of the hardest things I ever did. I was extremely attached to my clients and concerned about them. I missed the deep sense of fulfillment I felt when helping people turn their lives around. I didn't know who I would become then.

My tall bunky has promised that we will travel and have fun and he wants me to write etc. And etc. I don't know how I feel about retirement yet - I haven't had the energy - but I haven't had enough energy to be bored either.

We loved Arizona and New Mexico and Jack chomped at the bit to buy a winter home in Sedona where the sun shines three hundred and fifty days a year and the red mountains gleam. Of course, we're living in a fairyland right here in Aurora albeit frigid this morning in our woodland retreat.

Meanwhile, Jack has cooked one thousand meals - no slouch - he even removed Heinen's dressing from a turkey the other night; made Grandma's old fashioned stuffing and roasted it in a new convection microwave oven without directions - no easy trick - it was delicious. He has become an intrepid cook, but sometimes falls into bear traps. In his premier attempt he bought chicken wings and put time in the oven at 2:30 pm. I didn't get home till 8:30 pm. He tried!

He has walked the one hundred fifty round trip steps from our kitchen to our bedroom twenty thousand times and washed enough dishes to reach the moon. He has fed me in bed, spent days, weeks in hospital waiting rooms, has dressed and undressed me (this is not a replay of Romeo and Juliet- I figure they would have eventually divorced anyway).

Jack has in fact, tended to my every need! We have given up one hundred ninety-five parties, evenings at the theatre, ballet, symphony, trips with friends, tennis, lunches, and all our good companionships. In other words, this extreme extrovert became a hermit. But, in the process, we have become imprinted on each other. It will be forty-seven years in February.

I am so lucky to have him as a true nurturer, to have a number of competent compassionate physicians, to have finally claimed Medicare, to have wonderful friends and a direct pipeline to and from my good bookstore, and most especially to have adult children who care and aren't bored with us. All of our children are happy and well at the moment. We are passionately devoted to them and while the going is good, I'm going to get this to the post office.

Deborah and Peter live in North Conway, New Hampshire, where they have their own company "Tentsmiths." They have Christopher almost five and Nathan almost two, both terrific kids.

Michael and Rosie live down our country road with Jessica eight, a real beauty and sweet as can be, and Maxwell Andrew, one and a half, the only male Colebrook progeny. He will explore this world. Mike says he needs a leash but they're ashamed to buy one. He loses himself in crowds, examines everything in sight, and took a bite out of a sand dollar the other day.

Susan lives in Mentor, Ohio. She is a very successful senior account representative for Ameritech. Of her children "T" terrific is still at home, in college and a ski instructor. Michael enlisted in the Army and instead of the promised Intelligence Service in Germany got plunked in the middle of Kansas. He is changing as many Army rules as possible. The bad news is that now he has been sent to Kawait for Operation Desert Storm. Her daughter Laurie is in college, doing beautifully, and will probably change the world by being a psychologist.

Kristina, our youngest, the artist and poet, has her own electronics business with her partner Michael Kelly in Casa Grande, Arizona.

So we wish you a blessed Christmas and 1990 and peace in our time. We think of you often with love and caring.

Betts and Jack

LES SALLES DE BAIN DU MONDE

Around The World In W.C.'s
A Scatological Venture

It didn't take Jack and me long to discover that our three daughters might grow up to be sewer inspectors.

Wherever we took them: by plane, boat, car, or train - to restaurants or resorts, as soon as they had settled in their seats, they rose with one accord to visit - the Ladies' Room! A second visit soon followed. And yet another. Like a flock of sea gulls after their prey, they flew off to make another round of inspection.

Landing in Cairo Airport unbearably encumbered with purses, tote bags, water bottles and booty, we steered directly to the Ladies' Room.

There we were met by a male attendant dressed in a flowing *galabayya*. He handed each of us a long-stemmed red rose. From various stalls came shrieks, "Mom, what should we do with the roses?"

"Put them in your teeth, I guess. Think of Carmen." The floor awash with reminders of previous visitors, we clutch all our various carry-ons to our collective bosoms.

"How shall we wipe?"

"How about the rose? Watch for the thorns."

We discovered that most bathrooms in Egypt and Tunisia are not equipped with toilet paper. Afterwards, we stuffed tissues in our purses for necessary stops.

In the Roman ruin of the city complex of Dougga in Tunisia- we explored the large lavatorium with twelve marble toilets (or holes) forming a semicircle. Apparently this, to us a private function, was a social affair several thousand years ago.

When you gotta go...you gotta go

Suzie ventures first into the public toilet, a new crudely erected small building.

"Is there any toilet paper, Suzie?"

"Yes, but there isn't any toilet."

We clumsily adapt to holes in the ground, like Ichabod Crane on his famous ride, our bundles flopping around us.

While we stay in a remote hacienda in Yucatan, we run out of the precious commodity in all of our rooms. Trying charades with the maid that I blush to consider, finally Suzie, the only member who has studied Spanish, gets the message across. The maid runs toward us triumphantly waving the sought after rolls. We stay on and keep risking Montezuma's Revenge until our plane deposits us in Ohio. (Strangely, the Mexicans get *tourista* in the U.S. We'll probably be mingling our bacteria as we melt increasingly into our pot.)

In Paris at the Eiffel Tower I try, *"ou est le pissoir?"* I'm directed to the shoulder high enclosure framing an array of males faces smiling or frowning in concentration.

I find a British lady and explain my dilemma. She says, "Oh my dear, ask for the W.C."

I am greeted by an amiable matron dressed in pink who hands me three pieces of pink toilet tissue. To my acute embarrassment, a gentleman dressed from head to toe in dove gray with a derby hat, three piece suit, and spats, opens the door next to his stall and doffs his hat. I am to perform there.

Enfin, the final disaster at the close of our Chinese adventure.

In the Forbidden City of Beijing, I asked our guide for directions to the women's restroom. She looked at me quizzically. We had exchanged thoughts about our diverse cultures and had a good relationship.

She questioned, "Have you ever been in a Chinese restroom?"

"Oh, no problem," said I, and forged into a huge tunnel of mud and five thousand years of excrement piled up by faithful servants of The Middle Kingdom. I fled and may never need to relieve myself for another thousand years.

The next daunting experience was on a twenty-four hour train ride: a hole in the floor, no tissue, no Kleenex and a raging sinus cold.

Last spring I ventured to Italy with my darling adult sewer inspectors. W.C. visits went fairly well. Occasionally one would emerge with a pale face. We learned how to stoop, squat, pinch our noses and aim as precisely as we could.

Nothing simple in W.C.s around the world. But that will never dampen our ardor to explore.

*Cope and I by a Foo Dog
in Guangzhou*

Stir Fry

How I Came To Sleep With
Five Chinese Soldiers

We went to China in 1983. Ann was our Chinese-American guide. She had grown up in China, daughter of a famous general.

When China was decimated by the Japanese, her whole household with many servants hid in huge winding caves called *yaoyong* in the towering Karsts. Her father, as befits a man of his aristocracy, had a harem of concubines. Ann's mother, a woman of charm and vision, took care of them buying sweets and presents to make them happy. When her husband came home from one of his military exploits, she charmed him with stories just like Scheherazade and with sexual delights so he never got around to the concubines. She had to keep them content. If they went to their families as virgins they would be punished and banished.

After the opium wars all opium was illegal in China. Ann's father (the General in charge) had to stop his parents from opium use, common in aristocrats. They soon committed suicide.

We were fogged in *Xian* where we had visited the tomb of six thousand Terracotta warriors, an awe-inspiring sight. Emperor Chin who united China in 200 A.D. had this immense tomb created underground, horses and carriages decorated with precious stones. All the slaves were in chains yet they created unforgettable men and horses. He decreed that the tomb would be sealed up with his body resplendently adorned. The price of ego and the value of human life! The workers were sealed in forever.

Ann told us we most probably would be fog-bound for days in *Xian* so we had a choice of trying to get on a midnight train bound for Beijing that already was filled to capacity. We chose the train.

Most of us carried many bundles of loot purchased along the way. We climbed rickety flights of stairs in the dark, boarded the train and stood in the aisles thinking how crazy this was.

Peasants eating chicken, live chickens fluttering in cages. Ann, a true general's daughter, dislodged people to make room for us. We couldn't understand how she could do this. She said they were so used to living under communists' rule that they obeyed authority without question.

Later she tapped me on the shoulder and led me to a stateroom where Chinese soldiers were sleeping. She had cleared one bed but the rest were sleeping in three decked bunks with straw mattresses and rice pillows. That's how I came to sleep with five Chinese soldiers.

One of them awoke and offered me some of his tea from a beautiful pouch. Old women were walking the aisles with huge kettles of boiling water and poured us some. This man spoke some English so we had a modicum of communication, very welcome. I had a small can of orange juice and some dried fruit that we shared. Jack was somewhere sitting all night on a small stool. Jack had brought a case of beer along, an uncomfortable burden. It seemed like a good idea in Xian.

In the morning, after a night on the straw bunks and rice pillows, I found some of our sturdy crew playing cards in a compartment with lace curtains and antimacassars. Strange dichotomy.

My bunkmates were still sleeping unaware of the fun they missed.

Our next foray was on a Chinese airline the stewardesses wore little white embroidered aprons. They served no drinks but woke us every ten minutes to give us candies. There were lace curtains on the windows. Such an anachronism. China presented us with studies in contrast, "free markets," selling emaciated dogs and cats destined for cooking, and birds, snakes and many indescribable, very smelly vats full of stuff that smelled just awful.

We toured the Forbidden City: nine hundred and ninety nine buildings surrounded by tall brick walls. (No more buildings or rooms because only God had one thousand.)

As we passed the newer headquarters of communist power it looked exactly the same. *I mused, plus ça change, plus la même chose.*

First Day In Kenya
And Almost The Last One For Cope

We were guests at a Masai festival. The warriors were in a line aiming at targets with their sharp sisal sticks. One turned toward Cope who was videotaping the event. With deadly aim his weapon hit Cope on his head. His glasses and the camera saved his life. It was almost our first and last day in Kenya. Although the Masai were paid for their appearance, their pride was affronted.

They were proud Masai warriors at heart.

Another Day In Kenya

"The ellies are coming. The ellies are coming."

We had started the day at Amboselli Game Park in Kenya, ready, waiting for our small plane. It was two or three hours late, then the pilot, a Brit, had to have his cup of tea, so we waited some more. He was in no hurry. So we decided we weren't either. We made an emergency landing at a small field. We weren't told why. The "fire engine" was ready, painted a blatant pink, put together with strange parts. It looked like a pot-bellied platypus. We could do nothing but laugh. A group of villagers gathered under the shade of an embracing yellow fever thorn tree. They approached the plane tentatively, pressing hands and faces on the windows, babbling. Our leader said they didn't know what it was. It had no udders, so it couldn't be a cow.

A man rolled out his tiny plane, said he built it with stray parts and used his wife's sewing machine as an engine. Taking off jauntily, waving to us, *Mirabile Dictu* it soared.

Next step was loading Jack and me into the Land Rover, sloshing though mud and water. Our driver stopped, "Here you are." It was nowhere. "Where are we?" "Across the river to the other side; stay on the path." Climbing down a rope ladder, grabbing a rope to pull ourselves across the river, climbing another rope ladder, we ran straight into two stout typical British matrons with their ample bosoms waving. "The ellies are coming," they shrieked.

Not understanding what to do, we keep on the path, "what on earth are ellies?" Sure enough there were two large elephants waving their ears, swinging their trunks, signs of attackfulness protecting a baby who looked like a little animal cracker plodding between their legs, trying to keep up. Elephant mothers and aunties have instinctive and fierce devotion to their babies.

We backed into the brush thankfully, giving them the right of way.

Soon our tented camp stood staunchly ahead. Jack said, "I don't know about you but I need a bloody mary." I agreed. A smaller elephant rubbed his trunk against our tent pole a few feet away from us. Jack ground away on his video camera. Shortly the bartender came over, "this elephant is not entirely tame you know, he just likes to hang around the camp, better back up, Sir."

Governor's Camp was on the Masai Mara River. Hippos splashed a few feet away from our tent, baboons screeched, monkeys jumped from tree to tree.

There was a bathroom attached behind our tent, so when we wanted to shower, we had to let someone know and a native would appear, pouring buckets of water on us from the roof.

Being curious, I asked to see the kitchen. Three mud humps with tunnels in them. I told Jack I had no idea what we'd eat. We couldn't believe what emerged from those mud humps. An elegant dinner and *Grand Marnier soufflé* for dessert.

Nestling into bed after a sing-a-long bonfire we heard some big thing pushing against the screened opening alongside our bed. I said, "Honey, go out and see what that is," like asking him to see if the neighbor's cat was at the door. "Are you crazy?" he said, burrowing under the covers.

Next morning I discovered from the spores that it had been a huge Cape Buffalo, the largest, and most dangerous and unpredictable African animal. I made an inspection of the dung outside all of the neighboring tents. We had the best!

So Marge and I wrote a play about the previous night's adventures to produce for our friends to the tune of "What Kind of Fool Am I?" We sang, "What Kind of Dung Is This?" I was cast as the dung. That's life on the fast track. Some come-up-pence for a reader, writer and quasi actress. I discovered that it's easy being dung. No lines to learn, not much acting required.

Thus ends a typical day in Africa.

Queen Of The Jungle

Conversing with the baboons at Samburu in Kenya

The next morning I was to go up on a hot air balloon over the Savanna, the jungle and the mountains. So excited, I had reserved one six months ahead. The Frenchman in their jaunty berets and boots were tending the fire, blowing up the gorgeous multi-colored balloon. I was hoisted up into the basket and off we soared. I immediately was filled with surprising panic. Don't know why. I had never had any fear of heights before. I grabbed onto the edge of the basket and gritted my teeth. We took off and flew above the earth and the migrating animals.

Finally, our Frenchman said, "We may not have enough gas to get over the mountains ahead. We could try or we could land."

I shouted eagerly, "Oh yes! We should land here." The follow up cars with Jack (the coward) came right away with champagne in chilled flutes, chicken salad, and gorgeous dishes accompanying it. I cannot drink champagne but I think I drank a bottle of it.

This endeth another African adventure.

We loved Africa so much we went three times.

Island Bliss
Reminiscence of a family gathering on our favorite Island of Tortola –
forever beckoning us to come back.
By Jessica Colebrook 12/6/99

I cannot believe it is already over. Even though we have already
lived here for ten days, it feels like just yesterday I stepped off the small
plane into the fresh tropical air. The warm breeze hit me in the face like
the smell of fresh baked goods when walking into a bakery. The breeze, so
warm and refreshing, smelled like a summer day.

Now I was banished back to the cold, cloudy, dark, dismal recesses
of an Ohio winter. A season of deep snow, which made it impossible to
obtain the daily "Plain Dealer" from the paper box at the end of the
driveway without the accompaniment of a heavy jacket, boots, gloves, a
hat, and a big red metal shovel. And even if the paper was retrieved, the
snow from the snowplow that went by every morning usually drenched it
in snow. Then as soon as the paper hit the warmth of the indoor, the
snow all melted and the ink on the frozen paper bled, making it difficult to
see the words.

I had just become used to seeing the sun everyday, shining brightly
down on me every step I took. In the mornings, I would watch the sun
rise in the east over the volcanoes and rich lush tropical rain forest from
the balcony outside of our condominium. The balcony overlooked the bay
where we would soon relax after we finished a small breakfast.

After the daily fifteen-minute tropical storm that left no trace of
precipitation, we would pack up our beach toys, towels, and snacks and
head off to the beach. We would walk down the volcano that our
condominium sat on, passing billy goats on the way. Once we reached the
bottom, we would cut over to walk along the beach. At one point along
the shore rocks stretched out from the beach into the water, so we had to
walk out into the ocean up to our stomachs in order to continue our
journey.

Once we reached the spot on the beach we always sat on, we would
smother our bodies in the coconut smelling sun block. Our spot was
directly by a slanted palm tree with a tire swing. I would always attempt to
climb the palm tree, but never made it extremely high. I ended up jumping

off and landing in the soft comfort of the sand instead. My uncle would push my cousins and me on the tire swing; the warm wind hitting our faces as we swung back and forth. The unforgettable days of sitting on the beach without a care in the world were now over.

Times of basking in the sun from the hot, soft, sandy beach and becoming so hot I had to have a Popsicle or an ice cream cone just to keep from breaking a sweat were over. It was too hot to lie in the sun, the reason why I kept to the salty waters of the ever-so-blue ocean.

My time of snorkeling around in the clear ocean had ended. Swimming through the water watching the tropical salt-water fish and finding pieces of coral and seashells was no more. I now had to resort back to burrowing through snow mounds, occasionally finding a lost summer toy, or a rotting walnut from the black walnut tree. I was going from building sandcastles on the beach to building snow forts in my back yard. My yellow pail, which I had used for over a week to fill with sand and make sandcastles, was now going to be filled with snow to construct snow forts.

I was leaving the sunsets of inexplicable beauty. The sunsets of purples, pinks, oranges all splattered in a dazzling array of colors. Watching the sun as it slowly sank into the ocean. I was leaving this to go back to the gray skies where the sun never shone and the wind chapped the skin and froze the esophagus with every breath taken.

As the sun began to set, we would head back up to our temporary home. We would prepare a meal and everyone would shower as much of the sand as possible out of his or her hair and off their bodies. After our meal we would head back down to Stanley's, a restaurant on the beach where we would dance to the music of the steel drum band. Stanley's was an open building with minimal walls so the cement floor was covered in sand dragged off the beach from feet and shoes. After dancing for a while, my cousin and I would sneak out and take walks along the beach under the moonlight. We would walk just close enough to the water so when the waves came in, the water would rush over our feet. If we found a stick we would draw pictures or write our names in the sand and watch the waves gradually come closer and closer to our drawing until the water eventually erased it.

The time had come to now return to a December in Ohio, where the sun never shone. No beautiful and colorful sunsets to watch, no ocean to swim in, no steel drum band to dance to, no beach to walk along. The extraordinary vacation had ended. Our clothes, retaining a part of the beach, were packed tightly back into the suitcases along with other memorabilia we had picked up along the way. The tank tops and shorts worn all vacation would not see use until the summer months. Little gifts picked up along the way were also packed safely amongst the sandy clothes for the long trip home.

As we landed at the Cleveland Hopkins Airport, the snow was falling and covered the earth in a white blanket. I sat in my seat on the plane and gazed out the window. It gave me the chills just looking at the snow. I looked down at the short-sleeved shirt and pants I was wearing and realized my days of warmth were long gone. The summer months still someways away would eventually come and bring with it the heat but, unfortunately, without an ocean.

Rosie and Max on Tortola

Romance on Virgin Gorda

Jack and I coming home to Cleveland
from a Carribean trip

It's Bye Bye America
Italy floats its siren song to me

I finished reading *A Year In Tuscany*; called Susie, "we have to go to Tuscany." "We do? Okay." Then Deborah, "we have to go to Tuscany." "We do? Okay." Then Kristina, a happy affirmative. I booked a 17th century stone villa in Gaiole and a flat in the old Trastevere section of Rome for the second week. Took a crash course in Italian whereupon I proceeded to speak French in Italy. Got passport. Bye bye to non-objecting husband who had to suffer through house renovations in my absence. Off we went.

Daughters meeting me from Arizona, New Hampshire and Ohio. No hitch, except I had lost my ticket by the time we were ready to board at Kennedy. Tears. Hands were wringing. Miracles work; off we flew!

It was a marvel of an experience. Old churches, wineries, poplars, rolling hills, cappuccino, wine and inevitable lingerie shopping for Kris who was meeting her sweetheart on her return.

Eternal Rome. I cried at my second view of the Forum. Our apartment in Rome was a funny little four-story apartment. One room on each floor and a roof garden. Our first adventure was traveling around Rome in a white horse and carriage. Elaborate lunch on Taverone Square with its three Bernini fountains. All the waiters hovered over us announcing that they were gay.

Laurel and baby in a Cadillac buggy joining us from the Netherlands, much to our joy. Mother's Day in St. Peter's Square with the eternal Pope. Zillions of people parading, singing out "Mama Mia."

Homebound with tears and memories.

Two Years Later

I read another book; Italy called with yet another invitation and off we went again. This time to a dark antique filled villa in Stra. The bathtub was so deep I had to call daughters to haul me up.

And Venice in all her glory. I wanted to spend at least twelve years there.

Home again to new buildings, fast food places, cranes and outlet stores; the land of tee shirts and hamburgs. No Vivaldi or romantic *gondoliers* enticing us.

My farewell to beloved Italy where I fear at eighty-seven with flying problems I can no longer respond to her siren call.

*Cope and I at Grindenmould on top of a mountain
with Jungfrau looming*

You Can Go Back
But It Won't Be The Same

"I'm looking for the Grand Hotel here in Grindelwald. It sits high on a mountain and looks across at five mountain peaks. Could you please direct me to it?"

"This is the Grand Hotel Victoria Regina," said the desk clerk.

"Ah, but no, it can't be," I said. "The Grand Hotel was set back from the road with a lofty entrance and an elegant lobby."

The two receptionists, a man and a woman, exchanged glances. Not to be daunted, I pressed on.

"You see, we were here in 1969 when the first men, Americans, walked on the moon. We watched this phenomenal event in the television viewing room; it was being described in German by a commentator."

"Yes, yes," said the receptionist, too young to remember the breathtaking moment. "Be our guests. Look around."

Puzzled, displaced, we wandered into the dining room. Having described the elegance we had witnessed to the couple we were traveling with, we were anxious to show off the treasure we had unexpectedly found: the embossed china and silver, the sparkling white linens, the view from the floor-to-ceiling glass windows of the Jungfrau, Furst, and the other three majestic Alpine mountains. We remembered the dazzling colors of their cloaks, changing with the sun's path.

Today the windows were dirty, the mountains dull gray. The disinterested waiters looked like unmade beds in their rumpled tuxedos.

"Of course, this is the Victoria Regina," they grunted. "It's the only hotel in Grindelwald."

We found this hard to believe. In 1969, we had stumbled into this four-star hotel after a tiring eleven-hour drive, corkscrewing up the Alps with our son Michael on leave from the Army Tank Corps in Frieberg, and our daughters, Deborah and Kristina. Tired hungry wanderers, we were received by the grandest hotel we had ever seen. Treating us like visiting royalty, the chef had served us a beautiful repast in our rooms long after the dining room had closed: big juicy red strawberries with real whipped cream, a delicate venison steak with fresh mushrooms, and waiters in attendance to our every need.

What happened to the magic? Where was the symphony of boys and girls, apple-cheeked in their alpine outfits, families hiking up the mountains with their picnic baskets, the echo of the alpine horn wafting through the mountains and valleys?

In the years between, had my vision grown beyond measure with each telling of the tale of our magic mountain hotel? Here it was, small, a bit tawdry, crowded with down-at-the-heels furniture, with but few guests.

Somewhere inside me, in a place where I store precious memories, my box of treasures to peruse and finger as devout Catholics touch the beads of their rosaries, I felt the sting.

The loss of a lovely illusion: that kind of thing that makes one question other experiences. Is my storehouse of sweet memories an illusory thing? Do I need to explain each one?

I think I will keep each positive memory in my treasure box sacred, until I'm forced to face it differently.

A pyramid at Giza and the Sphinx on guard

Their Mom Is A Power Person

When my three daughters went to Machu Picchu on a Caroline Myss workshop, she told them their mother was a power person because I had planned trips to the power places in the world for the family. Chichen Itza in Mexico, the Great Pyramids of Giza and St. Croix where there are many vortexes, sacred places.

Cope and I embarked on a five-week adventure to Morocco, the Seychelles Islands and another Safari in Kenya. Memorable moments in Morocco were stopping at a small private tea service. We were surprised and delighted to be welcomed to join. The Tableau: the chief or headman presided as we sat cross-legged around an oriental rug under the shade of a magnificent ancient tree. One of his servants poured warm water over our hands from an ancient copper pot before the tea was served. Each act was performed in silence and solemnity – like a sacred rite. We bowed and folded our hands before our hearts in deep respect. The moment, the scene, is still deep and clear in my mind.

It was not until the first night in a venerable Harem that we realized we would be the only English-speaking people in a group of Parisiennes. Only one man spoke a little English. The Harem (Club Med) defied floor plans, winding corridors and stairways, no keys. The elite gay manager told us *"Ici, c'est ne pas vous, c'est tu."* They used only the familiar or intimate address to people. The salon was filled with opium alcoves and a gigantic bar; we stood or sat around on gold cushions during cocktail time.

Waiting the next morning for our leave -taking from our harem in Marrakesh overlooking the sprawling souks, I opened a suitcase and, to my horror, discovered that the chalky Kaopectate bottle (prescribed to deal with the ubiquitous international *"tourista"*) and my hair spray had opened and sprayed all the white stuff indelibly over my clothes while flying over the Indian Ocean from the Seychelles.

Catastrophe.

We had the Morocco junket and a Safari in Kenya ahead of us. What to do? We had a strange bedroom – two opium dens (aka..beds) on either side of a small rock lined pool. So, I plunged in with all my clothes – sweaters, blouses, slacks, underwear and tried to wash the stuff off - glued on firmly. I emerged with a wet gooey load of clothes for my trip.

We went to a huge henna kasbah, rising like a castle in the mud and sand, visited a newborn baby and mama and had a sumptuous feast. One big copper pot sat in the middle of the table into which we reached for handfuls of the lamb stew with couscous and bravely tried to get it into our mouths, no plates or napkins.

The last days we crossed the Atlas Mountains to a lush oasis in the middle of the Sahara desert. The French, we thought, drew straws to see who would eat with us, but we couldn't decide if we were the long straw or the short straw. As it turned out, it was always a hilarious time. Cope communicated with charades; I with my forty-year old fractured French, probably saying all kinds of funny, screwed-up things and probably in the wrong tense.

Moments To Remember
The Land Of Pharaohs, Gods And Goddesses

Ten strong we boarded a plane to Egypt. It had been my magnificent obsession ever since I took ancient history in the eighth grade. Egypt had waited a long time for me – bursting in glory five thousand years ago, then slumbering in the sands awaiting archeological digs.

My first sight of the Great Pyramids of Giza. I melted. Galloping Arabian horses with abandon in the sand around the pyramids at dawn. I felt like Lawrence of Arabia with my family together on the adventure. The most memorable event of my life. Afterwards I went to the stable to pay. Another adventure awaited us. Lo and behold it was full of treasures; Alabaster chess sets, Egyptian gowns in endless array. Treasures found their way to our rooms. My long suffering husband said "I thought you went riding!" "That was just the foreplay."

Standing in the pale cerulean blue light of dawn at the registration deck of our hotel on Tahiti, I watched a far island rise from the sea through the mist in all its opalescent glory as blazing dawn illuminated it.

Bali Hai – the forbidden island, beckoning me, stirring a longing to get there, just as it had in Lieutenant Cabot in "South Pacific." I felt weak in the pit of my stomach. Tears sprang to my eyes. I held to the desk to keep from fainting.

Having a bloody mary at Amboselli Game Park in Kenya, with a Masai warrior who looked like he was nine feet tall, skin covered with henna cloth over his shoulder and loin. With his spear and shield a formidable person striding across the plain. I invited him into the bar tent for a bloody mary. It was beyond amusing since the Masai diet is the blood and milk from their beloved cattle. We sat amiably not needing or able to converse. He bowed and walked back to the Savannah.

The Great Pyramid of Luxor in the Yucatan gleaming in the shafts of sun: climbing up the steps to the top, we saw murals of Viking vessels in the ancient pyramid. They were there several thousand years ago!

On a Victorian curtained train riding across the infamous, once fearful, Bamboo Curtain in its decaying fierceness now fallen into shreds. Once separated China, the "Middle Kingdom," from the rest of the world.

My first sight of the glorious Parthenon in the rear view window of our bus.

Elderly women who had come down from the mountains in Bora Bora with flowered wreaths on their heads and many layers of leis sang the most beautiful songs. The workers were all wearing hibiscus on their ears. The whole resort resonated with anticipation of the arrival of the new French owner and his blond mistress to arrive in a long boat.

Odds And Ends, Mostly Odd

In Tahiti I suggested we hire a car from a bilingual driver and tour the island. We hadn't been to China yet, so I innocently asked our Chinese driver if it was true that the Chinese ate dogs.

"Oh yes…now that dog not good to eat. That dog good to eat." Pretty soon I was learning and said "that dog good to eat, that dog not good to eat."

On the island of St. Kitt's a young boy named Clinton approached us on the black sandy beach. He was selling bird houses he had made from cocoanut shells. I guilelessly bought two. After this he came every day. He told us that he was an orphan who slept on the doorstep of a house. He went to school every day and got all A's. I became fond of him and very sympathetic.

We visited the school. The teacher told us that Clinton rarely came to school and when he did he flogged him. I said "no wonder he doesn't come to school!" Then he told us that Clinton owned several cartels on the island and was extremely influential and very wealthy. I gathered that he sold more than birdhouses.

On Bora Bora the children were naked and playing in the mud. The mother wore only grass skirts. Their houses were made of mud and wattle. But there was always a long loaf of French bread in their mail boxes. A tiny store with little to sell revealed one box of Stouffer's macaroni and cheese in the tiny refrigerator.

Our first 50th anniversary celebrated on Tortola

Our second 50th in Aurora. Sometime we'll get it right

50th Anniversary

To celebrate our first 50th anniversary (or as friends dub it - our 99th because we celebrate both our weddings each year), we flew down to our beloved island, Tortola, in the British Virgin Islands to be with dear friends, Carol and Doug Roberts.

Carol had prepared a sumptuous feast and all our friends were there.

They asked me to talk about our elopement and marriage. I said the fiftieth was the best year of all.

Carol jumped up and shouted, "You peaked too soon!"

Jack and I have come to harvest our plowing and reaping. We struggle to learn how to love and not control or be controlled. We struggle with the roles and boundaries we brought with us like carapaces from our families of origin. We have worked at learning how to express our dichotomous gender roles valuably. We have learned how to be safe, keep each other's vulnerability respected and so we are able to risk.

For me, the most remarkable feeling is that he has steadfastly been there when I needed him. We have learned how to care for the other as much as the self.

We arrived on Tortola February 4th, as I was finally released by the cardiologist the night before with exhaustive heart tests after gripping chest pains. We were tired, but excited and grateful to be escaping yet one more bow to our aging vulnerability.

Douglas patiently met us as we dropped down at the tiny airport on Beef Island, and we tumbled into the arms of Carol and friends at Stanley's Beach.

We drove up to Doug and Carol's house clinging to the mountainside looking forever out to the Caribbean Sea - Jost Van Dyke, St. John and St. Thomas in the distance.

As always, I was stunned by the blue sea and the verdant green mountains, the roads, rutted and pot-holed that double perilously back on each other looping around the peaks of the mountains. We brace ourselves all the way.

I had forgotten! I keep saying, "I don't believe this road!" Now there are trucks loaded with building supplies competing with Land Rovers and Jeeps on this tiny, sometimes dirt road already occupied with goats and their kids of every blend of color and velvety, burnished cows.

Though it has been two years since we've been on Tortola, it feels like a home place. All of our family have joined us here for two vacations, except Michael Colebrook and Michael Kelley, who had to tend their businesses.

So now, this turns out to be a celebratory year. The family will gather at our place in Aurora in June for the "Official" Golden Anniversary. Deborah, Peter and sons, Christopher and Nathan, from New Hampshire, Kristina and Michael from Arizona, Suzie and David and her children Laurie, Michael and T from Mentor, and Michael and Rosie and their children Jessica and Maxwell from next door. A year to remember a reason to celebrate us all. They all love each other and are presently happy and the love goes back and forth in all directions. I think that is the severest testimony to our marriage.

Stanley

Memo To All Staff Members:

(On the second celebration of our Fiftieth Anniversary – June twelfth)

Dearest loves,

How can we thank you? Let us count the ways.

Thanks to Rosie and Suzie for going through dusty, moldy old boxes of pictures in the storage room and scrapbooks and the wedding book in "The Closet," the records of the decades. And for looking through two thousands photographs and sending off thirty-eight pounds of memorabilia to Kristina and Michael, clear across the country for him to create a video, narrated and set to our music. Thanks for – the production of the master film of our Lives – the treasure of a lifetime for us – by that dynamic duo – Michael Kelly and Kristina – such expertise! The Chief of Staff and Chairman of the CIA deserve another gold medal for super sleuthing and performance beyond the call of duty. (Did we ever give you the first one?) Thank you, Rosie dear and Sweetie.

Thanks to Michael Murray, the excellent bartender and entertainer. Cheers!

Thanks to T – the faithful parker and unparker – you are a sweetheart!

Thanks to all the ladies for the lovely food you produced – beautiful and so tasteful – the salmon, the shrimp, the tortilla nummies, and the creative little pastries!

Thanks for decorations – from the geese at the front porch, to the deck and all through the house – a lifetime of pictures gathered and bedecked with begonias. Thanks for the flowery "Just Married 1943" sign, the picture of the bride and groom, and the two red roses – our eternal sign of love. And for decorating the rabbits, ducks, chicken and frog carvings around the woodland of our home. They tried to look decorous and ended up looking silly for us.

Thanks to the ladies for producing and managing all the gorgeous food and the whole party while we just relaxed and had a marvelous time with our friends.

Thanks to Rosie, the experienced hay rack planter for helping me with the planting of the English hayracks. They're gorgeous.

Thanks to Kristina for helping in the construction of and planting the beloved pyramid – and for the hours she helped me pick up sticks all over the property after the storm.

Thanks to Deborah for leaving her husband and children to be with us for this loving occasion. And thanks to Peter for taking over!

Thanks in spades to Suzie who had all kinds of wonderful foods planned and prepared after driving to a stressful sales meeting in Columbus round trip on Friday. (Hooray for Chief of Staff, the Pearl Mesta of our family!)

Thanks to Laurie for coming from Pittsburgh to celebrate with us and bringing us a videotape of our year of the wedding and for the especially meaningful card.

Thanks to Michael Kelley for fixing the satellite (who broke it?) and the warning signal at the gate that the hired ding-a-ling couldn't fix. And kudos for rigging my little tape player up to the sound system so it sounds grand. Also thanks to Mike for putting salt in the softener and making one thousand cups of *Cappachino* and for many other acts of kindness.

To Deborah and Kristina, the Secretaries of State and Commerce – many thanks and eternal appreciation for your unfailing good humor and good sportsmanship and the making of at least one hundred tiny little biscuits for the rotten ham. That was a last minute debacle. We had to dump it.

Thanks to David for his steadfastness, fire building, bringing of the food and general charitable attitude in putting up with Colebrook women and their fertile ideas and on-going celebrations. (Gird up your loins for August, David!)

Thanks to Michael C. for being around and helping out and to Jessica for helping in every way and being gracious in the doing of it. Thanks to Max for taking part in the festivities.

Thanks to Hillary and Bill for their cordial anniversary card.

And thanks to all of you for loving us and caring about us and making our golden anniversary a memorable and romantic event. Our friends were delighted with all of you and raved about the party.
Dearest love,
Mother/Betts & Father/Jack
Look Me In The Eye

The videotape will bring us a lifetime of memories and joy as we watch it through the years.

xoxo

Addendum: To all Staff

I must hasten to inform you that this meeting was so successful that we are looking forward to another ad hoc meeting in August at the Liniken Lodge in Maine with the entire Cabinet comprised of the Senate and the House of Representatives.

Accommodations are secured for everyone. There will be a heated pool in addition to the ocean beach and linens and towels are provided.

This meeting promises to be more relaxed than the June meeting since Cabinet members are not required to cook or do housework. This should allow ample time for activities of greatest importance on our agenda: ie..

Shopping
Sightseeing
Talking about people not present
Sunbathing
Singing old camp songs
Thorough discussions about hair, skin, movies
Games of derring do
Doping-off
Reviving the ancient art of bean bag
Christmas
Healing arts and angels
Discussion of family secrets
List can be completed by the ad hoc staff members.

Max the drummer

Max

Adventures With Max

Max, my grandson, was six going on seven in the summer of ninety-five and he has never forgotten anything that happened to him since he was born.

Two years ago I had taken Max on an adventure to a petting farm out in the country. "Oh, the fun we will have, Darling." Then I proceeded to get us lost. Max was not to be cajoled when I told him I had forgotten the map, but I figured it out. He looked at me querily and started rocking back and forth as hard as his seat belt would permit saying in his Max decibel, "I'm not having fun now! I'm not having fun now!" he speaks in one decibel- LOUD. When he is in the supermarket with his mom or dad, we not only know he is there when we walk in, but which aisle he is in. You can see his little throat straining as he belts out his thoughts.

This adventure was turning sour. I had to grab at straws. "How would you like to go to McDonald's?" The magic potion, how did it come to represent all good things? Immediately salvation was at hand and we talked and sang the rest of the way. Thank heaven a McDonald's can always be found.

One evening the next summer I took him to a youth theatre production. He lives and breathes whatever happens on the stage. When he went to "West Side Story," with me a year ago, he sang all the songs in bed far into the night. We had so much fun that night that I asked him if he would like to go on another adventure with me. He said, "Yes, Grandma, when?"

I said, "Soon, Darling." He called me the next evening to see if we could go the following day. "Oh Max, I'm sorry I have to pack for our trip to Montana."

We had to cancel our trip because my husband was so terribly ill with Post-Herpetic Neuralgia that he could not do anything.

Max heard we weren't going so he called me up and said, "Now that you don't have to pack and go away, let's go on our adventure tomorrow."

I said, "Oh, Max, I decided to file all my papers from my boxes and I have piles all over my study that I have to take care of."

He paused and said, "Okay, but don't file the map."

Soon we had a perfect day to go. I can't bear to disappoint Max because he'll remember it the rest of his life. Off we went - Max decided on the Cleveland Health Museum and the Natural History Museum. I was born with no sense of direction, but I knew that I could find the museums in the dark after many visits with our kids, and I took the huge Ohio atlas to keep him reassured. He held it and paged through it with delight. Away we soared - or so I thought, singing merrily along the freeway. Then Max said, "Grandma, why is that light flashing on and off on the dashboard?"

Almost daunted with a sinking heart I said, "Oh, Darling it's the gas gauge telling us we are almost empty, but we'll get off the freeway straight away and find a gas station." Oh, *mea culpa*. His parents, my son and daughter-in-law, would never run out of gas! With grateful relief I found a gas station. But it was all "self serve," Woe! I haven't used a "self serve," since Jack taught me how years ago and I broke a fingernail on the clamp, so I never tried it again. I thought, "Okay, I'll handle this efficiently and Max won't know what a technological drop-out I am."

I couldn't open the cap. Max gave me a look of disappointment nearing incredulity, but he helped me and got the cap off with a flourish. I put in the hose and started pumping feeling pretty adept. After a while Max said, "I don't think any gas in going in Grandma." With what almost amounted to a prayer, I said positively, "Oh surely it must be". I feel some pulsing through the hose."

Max said, as he took the hose from me, "That's enough, lets' go inside and ask the man." Still with a little verve left I asked the attendant how much I owed.

He said, "eight cents," then gave us a long look and came out to help. I hadn't released the lever on the pump. We filled her up and paid. Sweet humility, relieving success.

"No more problems, we're off on our adventure," I said as we got back on the freeway. Whew, I thought, nothing can stop me now. All's well - "Do you want to hear a story, Max?"

After a minute or two, Max said, looking at me with more than disappointment, sad disbelief, "Grandma we're going to wrong direction, we're going back home."

"Deliver me," I thought and made an illegal U-turn at the next median. I could tell Max didn't approve. Finally, we made it to the Health Museum. Max raced through the museum talking at his piercing decibel with a tiring grandma in tow. But first he dragged me into the gift shop where we had a grand time. I discovered that Max had clearly inherited my shopping genes. Did we ever shop! Then on to the next museum. Finally, I said, "Max, I can't go another step. I need to sit down and get some water and something to eat." Unfortunately the museums are located in a seamy part of Cleveland. McDonald's was not the answer. So I took him to the restaurant at the Cleveland Clinic where I figured the food would be sanitary. I told him this was like a little United Nations as we watched the sheiks pass in their robes and turbans followed by their entourage of wives and children and attendants. So we dined in the hospital setting. I longed for a bed! I could imagine him telling his parents, "Grandma took me to a hospital to eat." We talked about what we saw at the museums. Max's eyes widened as he heard how much I knew about history and archeology and the human body. Perplexing. Was this the same Grandma who couldn't find her way out of the driveway?

A few weeks later Jack invited Max to take a ride with him in his big red truck. Max paused and said, "Okay, but do you have enough gas?"

This wonderful child. I'm afraid that Max for all his love of me will always look through a little cloud of skepticism about an adventure with Grandma!

P.S. He has forgiven me and next month will graduate cum laude from Ohio University with a degree in Graphic Arts. He will succeed in whatever he does!

Max: College Man

The Clan

Nate

We Count Our Blessings

1995 Family Reunion

To Deborah for bringing grace and
protection to our land and providing
a new thoughtful family ritual.
The blessings of the Labyrinth
and the Deva goddess of our land and water
the energy of love surrounded us
like an aura
and lingers
thanks for the many thoughtful bounties.
To David and Suzie for bringing
the Pig to The Party
and all the other foods
David in his grass skirt
and coconut boobs at his
Birthday Luau
we won't mention the
twenty-five piece "Geauga County
Leftover Band"
Since I first heard them they had gotten
so old
they couldn't stand up to play.
so we had to give them
our chairs
and we stood up while they
played discordant music to us.
(one of Betts' worst case scenarios)
The pig and trimmings were a lovely
dining presentation
---and the special music for each
occasion – Thanks David!
And the elegant French toast brunch-
---- Heaven ----
To Michael K. for the family film
--- enduring 239 mosquito bites
joining all the activities on

his poor bandy knees.
To Kristina's loving, cheerful presence
at sink or play
the three white mother turtles
lovely blue racu bowl.
To Michael and Rosie for
saving my life twice with pizzas
and Rosie helping through the
last night with cabin cleaning.
To Laurie for her exquisite artistry
stained glass gifts
many, many thanks
appreciation of the time and energy
and thoughtfulness
in caring for all of us.
To T – our cabin resident – our summer buddy
working on the land, shoring up the lake
with rocks - - I hear him pounding now.
To Michael M. who braved
sleeping on the floor
to be here with the family.
Thanks to Deborah and Peter
for the chairs so perfect on our new dock
my heart warmed at the fullness
of their new love.
Knowing children were safe
in their water ability
swimming, floating, boating
the cool respite of water on our sun-drenched bodies
so many blessings in our family!
For us, the folks at "Bingen Am See,"
it was the most welcome respite from the siege
that ravaged my dear buddy all summer
It was a scary, lonely time
Wondering if, indeed, he would ever recover.
So many thanks for your coming and
filling us and the land with your good
Energy!
We can't omit paying tribute
to the midnight cowboys

where men became boys
and bonded over heroic
feats of water terrorism
until dawn's early light.
Salute!

Ever-loving
Caring
Mother/Betts/Elizabeth

Epilogue To 1995 Family Reunion
Letter to a friend

Dear Carol,

Our home looks like a fraternity house- family encampment for two weeks now- I never know how many. It varies. Damp piles, backpacks, foodies. It's the best so far Kris tells me, lots of loving and happy stuff going on.

I had a little late night meeting with the ladies and said I can't do it all, you take over, and they have.

Last night they staged a "Thank you" party for us - candles, flairs, all singing when we were invited to come in, red roses, and balloons.

I'm beyond exhaustion.

"Life is grasping the hard fact that time runs only in one direction, that we already had died a thousand deaths and will die a thousand more, and that there is no remedy for it but love, though we are sure we have never seen love except in the rearview mirrors, in the sad and tawdry puddle at the bottom of the glass"

"Her life is a skiff whose bilge is never dry, and she is too busy bailing to ever set sail." *Anonymous*

Love You,
Betts

Reunion
By Kristina Colebrook

The faces and sounds of bloodlines
in common
While separate boats we row
in the current
of the river of life
Now we are brought together
to share, compare notes
and just meet
Sharing of our time
is our biggest gift
to life
This is where lessons
can be learned
Patterns of day-to-day living
can stretch and
be friends to change –
Changes are a given
in life
Family and reunions
are gifts

The Abyss

January 28, 1996

I feel as thought I've been dropped on an alien island. People are speaking in gibberish – my husband, friends, my family, T.V., films, theatre. I strain to understand the words. It is exhausting, defeating. I want to retreat to a cottage by the sea or an A-frame on top of a mountain where I can yodel and wait for my echo – that may never come back to me.

I had an extensive, experimental ear surgery three weeks ago. The fourth operation on that decrepit ear. All the parts surgically removed and replaced thirty years ago were taken out and new prostheses installed with laser removal of recent calcium deposits.

A social animal, I now retreat from the usual large gatherings. Mostly to bed where I read and try to be patient in the healing process which was to take weeks.

It seems an oxymoron to say that I am working with clients and various therapy groups. I move next to the person who is pouring out his/her soul and pray that I will interpret what they are saying correctly.

My doctor says it will take six more weeks to know whether I can hear. Six weeks! It looms like a lifetime sentence. I prepare myself with lip-reading lessons.

Several years ago I told my otolaryngologist I would rather be blind than deaf. Then I discovered that I have strange growths on the backs of my corneas called corneal guttata that will keep growing. Cataracts in both eyes have been removed and I have new lens implants. But I wonder if I will ultimately be blind. Beware of careless wishes! There are no immediate answers. Will I, the extreme extrovert whose life is people and visual delights, live in a silent dark world? Have I outlived my body with so much more living to be done?

I pursue my journey inward, hoping for food for my wayward soul. Is this, indeed, another betrayal? Again by my own body? Can I trust my remaining senses to help me complete my life's journey this time?

I turn again to the things that nourish me. My family's love, my work, gardening, reading and music to inspire my soul's journey. Jack is thoughtful in multiple ways: seats in the first row of the theatre, keeping a record of quiet corner tables in restaurants and reserving by number, deciphering what has been said that I miss. But when he doesn't understand that my problem is discrimination of sounds, not volume and raises his voice loudly, I cringe. I am pulled into my child's memory of my father who treated my increasingly deaf mother, suffering from the same congenital otological disease, as though she were dumb. My inner child is scared and angry, feeling for her all those years, embarrassed.

Mother was so beautiful with her prematurely white crown of hair, so bright, so ready for every new experience: study groups, theatre, opera, parties. How dearly it must have cost her to be silent about her deafness. I never realized until this moment how much she must have suffered in silence. Her deafness was never discussed. Like hiding the idiot child in the attic. I see the deep core of my embarrassment. Why is it so difficult for me to explain my problem to people? I smile when that seems appropriate to the speaker's facial expression or frown if he/she looks sad. Heaven knows whether she is saying, "My husband is dead" or "I took my dog to the vet." Last week I commiserated with a client who kept saying, "I am lovable" with emphasis. I thought she was saying, "I am vulnerable." Woe!

Last week the bomb I dreaded dropped in my lap. My surgeon said, "the surgery didn't work."

"I knew it."

"In fact you have lost all the hearing in that ear because we took all the prostheses out and the replacements aren't working."

"I know it."

"And your other ear has about the same deficit."

"I know."

I go home and crawl into bed and pull the cover over my head. I need to make a snug little womb for myself for a while to keep sane. Then I will pick up the pieces of my life again.

How to preserve the goodness of life, the hopefulness of a new day?

At the end of the day I am exhausted from straining to hear and read lips. Lip reading proficiency comes to me slowly. It is a daunting, frustrating experience. The other ear isn't so hot, even with a hearing aid. I lost the one that, damaged though it was, discriminated consonants.

Clear enunciation is rare. People variously turn their heads away while talking, cover their mouth with a hand, talk out of the side of their mouths, forget I can't hear and whisper confidences, speak loudly as though talking to a stone, spit their words out, chew at them or throw them away. Oh, the bewilderment of the vagaries of speech.

My two hearing aids give me access to my world, although loud noises pierce through them and I flee some situations. I wish that people understood that loud sounds drive me away. I am lost in cocktail parties where the ceilings are high and the crescendo increases with each drink. I can give them up for the duration.

My eldest daughter, Susan, encourages me with her story of success over loss of hearing with high fevers and resulting nerve damage when she survived bulbar spinal meningitis at age two – formally a fatal type. The savior medication was streptomycin, which in the large doses she needed can cause the damage. That was the least loss to suffer. She came out of a long coma with her life, after four weeks in the hospital. We were grateful beyond belief to take our little baby home. She had learned to talk during those four weeks: mostly in medical language like "lets check her temperature," "thank goodness she is sitting up," "lets check her reflexes," etc.

Susan says she learns so much about people using her other senses. Watching body language, facial expressions, mannerisms, intuitive information about personalities and behavior.

Susan's livelihood depends on reading people. She is a big-time successful sales person. Words often obscure communication, she reminds me.

Theatre has always been a passion of mine and I still love to go, although mostly I discriminate a small percentage of the words. They are spoken in Sanskrit. Tears silently course down my cheeks until I reflect that I can understand the body language of the actors better than hearing people.

Being in transition is a constant for women. I have reinvented my life many times. I suspect this will not be the last rendition. My reinvention only requires the same resources I used in past transitions: adaptability, education, for the next step and optimism. "*Educere*," the Latin root word of "education," means to lead forth the innate wholeness in a person. So in the deepest sense, that which truly educates us also heals us.

The process of working through this crisis of faith by writing it out has helped me heal...

Fear Of Aging Dissolves

How The Fear Of Aging Turned Into A Pearl In My Naval

Suddenly all of our children decided to come to us in Longboat for my seventy-fifth birthday and my sister's eighty-fifth in Naples. Assured by friends that plane reservations should have been made months in advance of the holidays, magically it all happened. They came from Arizona, New Hampshire, and Ohio. Everything worked. They came! Eleven of us fit into our home in joyous chaos.

When my three daughters and son invited me to lunch on my birthday, I realized that had never happened before. We went to the Alley Cat Café and lunched in a sun-dappled arbor. Each gave me a long - stemmed red rose, the symbol of the love in our family - Jack's romantic creative tradition. I will always remember balloons filling the house, the beautiful dinner Jack arranged in a private room at the Colony. Phone calls. Presents from their hearts. An outpouring of love. My soul is in warm water. How can I not treasure a birthday like that?

I Discover Myself

Gertrude On My Dock

I Discover Myself

Sitting on the warm grass looking out at Sarasota bay in the last light of a numinous day, I watch sailboats in a regatta, tiny toys near the far bank. Pelicans swoop and dunk for their plunder. Gertrude, our resident pelican, austerely surveys her domain, stalking slowly on the deck. No porpoises today, our three have strayed away. We miss their cavorting.

This feels like a time to take stock and reflect. My thoughts pulse through my hands to my pencil.

Jack's and my bodies got old this year.
Wrinkles and ripply skin in once-taut limbs.
We forget.
We have little pot bellies.
We get irritated at interruptions.

We sign up for an "Improving Your Memory" research project. We are rejected. We haven't had the requisite stroke.

Like our skin, our personalities have lost some of their flexibility, their *jeunesse*.

Regrets:
Looking back I mostly regret wishing things were different, wishing he were different, wishing they were different.

Why wasn't I different? Given the times – how different could he, they, I have been?

My face needs lifting, my boob too, I suppose (singular because I sacrificed one to cancer). I should be grateful for the twenty-two years of my survival since then. How can I overcome the feeling of being mutilated? My sexual feelings have never been quite the same. What became of my passionate youth?

Wishes:
I wish I had listened more intently.
I wish I had asked more questions.

I wish I had treated each day as a treasure instead of being so task-oriented, so often sad, yearning, hurting. A sense of loss.

Wanting:

Waiting:

My polarity – adrenaline, living intensely, collapse. But I want to grab each day and hold on for dear life.

I have survived the disease of no-name, a thousand names, as the Chronic Fatigue or Myalgic Encephalomylitus is called. Stupid names for the complex of myriad disabling symptoms. An elusive, thus far incurable, debilitating illness with no known sure treatment. A kind of disease that renders the soul empty and in need of reinvention. As Marc Iverson, president of Chronic Fatigue Immune Dysfunction Association of America says, "It erases lives."

In 1986, when I was struck down with unaccountable symptoms, I was scanned and "Magnetically Imaged" to the bone. I enrolled in graduate school in my late forties. Then I limped along to keep my hard-won psychological practice going. A late bloomer, my career was desperately precious to me. That life had been filled with vigor and activity.

I gave myself a three-month medical absence and collapsed. Finally, I declared myself healed and scheduled two appointments. Just two! When they were over, I slipped to the floor sobbing. I was drained – knew it was all over for me.

I had to cave in and retire myself at sixty-three. I was too tired to be depressed or to get out of bed. Life passed by in a blur. Jack must have fed me. He nurtured me with loving understanding. Sadly, many marriages are sacrificed to Chronic Fatigue Immune Dysfunction Syndrome. Because it is disabling and undiagnosed, it seems illusory and "all in our heads."

When I could be up and out of bottomless pain, I finally found a medical study that described my *mélange* of seemingly disconnected symptoms. Dozens of physicians at a large prestigious clinic had scratched their heads and prescribed all manner of medication for me. Little wonder it is called "the disease of a thousand names" – so many puzzling symptoms are its handmaidens.

I had been a psychologist with seemingly psychosomatic symptoms. Humbling, humiliating. Finally my internist and the head of Immunology at the Clinic confirmed my diagnosis. I felt validated. Any diagnosis would have been a relief, even as Waztlowick's story goes, "*Moribundus*." The man in a terminal sate was told they could cure him if they had a "diagnosis." A specialist from Vienna was sent for. After examination he proclaimed "*Moribundus*" (A.K.A. dying.) The man jumped out of bed saying "I knew I would recover if I just had a diagnosis."

Most physicians and great medical centers disdain us, treat us "PWC's" (people with CFIDS) as pariahs. They don't have a marker for the disease or a cure. Doctors don't deal well with ambiguity or helplessness. No wonder we don't trust our own symptoms. It is, after all, basically a women's disease. I had to go through the process of owning it, making friends with it, dropping the victim or guilt stance.

Now I see that it was the perfect disease for me: Chronic, Incurable, Baffling. Something had to stop me dead in my tracks. I lived with an intensity that defied the hours of the day. I treated my body like a machine – didn't want to gas up. Jack brought me a rose one evening (after many heart to hearts) the card said, "I am hopelessly in love with you, but I need more than the crumbs."

I had to retire and re-invent my life. My heart hurt at giving my hard won career up. Now I try to trust the body that I thought was my betrayer. Instead, it is my wise barometer. I have a happy busy life doing all the things I love to do. But I am realistic; keep a supply of good books for the drop-dead time. Jack makes chicken soup, and I disappear. Everything in life is a trade-off. I no longer feel invincible or so angry at my limitations. I had to resolve the cauldron of anger and regret at giving up my professional identity. I was once again in an embryonic state – my protective covering of skin intensely permeable.

The chairman of immunology at the clinic diagnosed me and offered what turned out to be a miraculous "cure". Infusions of gamma globulin every four weeks. I became human.

I can give to those who are disabled ways of healing and hope – an elusive commodity when in the pits. My husband at seventy-eight had survived a heart by-pass while on vacation, many ambulance runs, a life flight, etc. I still quivered with fear when he had ominous symptoms. But both of us bounce back – like teeter-totters. Fortunately we have become very good at caretaking each other.

Practice:

We are re-learning how to be good to each other when healthy. Giving and receiving nurturance is the workbench of healthy intimate relationships.

We have survived fifty-six years together, not without daunting struggle. We <u>know</u> each other. I often think of us as Siamese twins in utero. Once in a while each needs to stretch and kick, claim more room. Individuate. We have ridden the waves and troughs and are committed. A soulfully contented feeling. We no longer wish the other were different, more, better. I can even think of us growing older together – with all the losses involved.

Now at seventy-five for a few more days, I begin to grasp how <u>I</u> can be different. "Too late," you say. "Not so. I will not live as though my life were infinite…" I will treasure each day.

As I sit on the bank by the bay in the last patch of sunlight, the warmth of Mother Earth washes through by body.

This is a blessed moment. Please, God, or Goddess, whatever you are, let it continue. Contentment has been the yearning.

I found this in my archives. Since then Jack died and it puts my soul in warm water to recover how I felt, after the sad travail of his last years and my anger at him for beginning to die. .

My Grand-Daughter Laurie

For My Grandfather, Jack L. Colebrook On His 80th Birthday

As morning dawns sky soars,
reflecting my heart.
Memories like lightening flash.

Through the mist
Wide-open spaces become well-tended paths,
and you my guide.

You showed me how strong love can be,
constancy your greatest gift.

Your presence always with me,
lessons become etched in my soul

love family, be kind to animals, plant trees
create with your hands,
always give 100%, never bet more than a quarter,
stop and take time to enjoy the moment
and, even pickle washers have worth.

You bestowed upon me a forever,
childhood gifts perfectly seated in my heart…
a sand box, a tire swing, a toy box of my own…
and you with a warm lap on which to rest.

As night falls my heart glows,
embers of time spent with you dance in my heart…
and I know I am loved.

I speak to God softly, with purity of heart,
thanking the Universe for the
You I so love.
Love,
Laurie

Dearest Family And Family Of Friends,

(December on Longboat Key)

Thank you all for the joy we received from you at Christmas. Our holiday down here was filled with love and celebrations. Kristina and Michael were here on an extended visit- such delightful fun- but still so many things left to do.

We are so excited that she impressed some excellent galleries her with her beautiful pottery and she and Michael are working on setting up a gallery for her art in Casa Grande. My friends were enchanted with Kristina and bought some of her vigils. Michael has promoted her so well! Good team.

We decorated our little Norfolk Pine and hung our stockings Christmas Eve - reading a very funny Christmas book aloud to each other. Santa found us. Our stockings were filled!

We went to the stunning "Splendors of China," near Orlando-wonderful time. Michael put a red velvet bow on the front of my little Toyota and I think I'll keep it till it falls off-now I can find it in parking lots.

Jack gave me a three-foot in diameter Gardenia bush- and I am enchanted with the scent of the house. Better than potpourri or perfume! (P.S. It stopped blooming and is out by the pool in intensive care - leaves and buds are gorgeous - but no blossoms. Oh dear.)

I have been in perpetual motion since we arrived in mid-October-with the new addition to our home unpacking boxes, boxes, boxes, shopping, shopping, and galleries - oh how much fun life can be.

I had embarked on a series of three holiday lunches for my various circles of friends - that proved to be a lot.

Then we had a "state of the art," New Years party. Jack made a bean bag set and we played in the living room - they are all aficionados now, one way to keep people until mid-night down here! No easy trick! It was a costume party and everyone was outrageous.

Two six foot gorgeous male friends entered the living room with nothing on but their pampers and big, oversized diaper pins, enormous baby bottles (full of gin), and a silver streamer across their chests saying, "Happy New Year," and top hats. Some Entrance!

Our kitchen server lady, who had never been here before, entered right after them. She took one look at them and ran away! I ran after her, "Mary Lou, this is not going to be a lewd and nude party, please come back." She said, "Oh, I was just telling my husband I was in the right place." What a sport!

I'm having one of the most fulfilling times of my later life.

I'm even discovering some latent creativity, taking classes in fabric printing with flowers and leaves. I love it. Then three years making pottery with a master. I made a set of dinner plates and salad plates.

I joined the, "United Nations' Feminist Group to Help Women in Developing Countries," saw Alice Walker's stunning movie, " Warrior Marks," about ritual sexual mutilation of women in Africa and around the world. So cruel. Again- another way to punish women for our sexuality. Surprisingly there are ten thousand cases here in our country each year. Alarmingly this custom is passed on by mothers and aunties, in African and some Arabian cultures.

Then I joined the "Suncoast Women's Caucus," and the "National Women's Caucus," and of course, "Equity by 2000." Next world meeting is in Beijing.

I am volunteering at the Women's Resource Center. My group on "Healing the Inner Child," is fascinating- I am also seeing most everyone in the group privately. Such love pours forth in the painful healing process. The receptionist at the Women's Resource Center said, "What do you do to those people?" I said, "What do you mean?" She said, "They all come in here dragging and leave with their arms around each other laughing and hugging." I am fulfilled knowing I can still help people. It turns out that each of the twenty-three women had been sexually molested as children. That presented me with a huge therapy challenge especially for those woman who had buried the incest before this. The staff prevailed upon me to have a weekly group therapy for them.

I told Jack all I wanted for my birthday was to go to the Royal Lipizzaner Show and Ringling Circus before it left on tour. The Lipizzan Show was unbelievably beautiful – staggering - those gorgeous white horses dance, change pace with each step and walk on their hind legs.

I got tickets for the circus, but was too sick to go: it was in St. Petersburg, I was crushed!

My Friday Group, which started out as a class on, "Women in Transition," turned into a lunch gathering of seven of us. Sharing our lives and souls. It then became a dream workshop and now we were going to write an erotic dream book. We met every Friday without fail for seven years, until an unfortunate schism developed.

I send off this "collection of the month packet," to you with all my love eternally. I am longing to see each of you and share our winters and hug and laugh and catch up with each other's lives.

Who does the next family letter? Please don't stop.

Kisses,

Mother/ Betts/ Mama

Millennium Musings

There were several things that made this particular family gathering different from all the other family fests. We invited everyone to our Florida home in Longboat Key to celebrate the historical millennium. They all came. They left their homes, their jobs, their pets and jumped on airplanes! Now we own the airlines. They came from Ohio, New Hampshire, and Arizona. Seventeen altogether. Jack rented the house next door.

It was like fielding and feeding and joining a marching band. Noisy, chaotic, exhausting and wonderful. David once said after he married Suzie, "Deborah's right, this family is a fucking zoo." He also said, "You are a piece of work. But you're worth it. I've never felt so much love in my life."

The motif was a celebration of the "Force One Baby." T and Cait decided to have a baby with each other. They are planning marriage after the baby is born in April. This is part of the changing times. It seemed like the thing to do was to have Millennium Baby tee shirts made for everyone: "Millennium Baby 2000," "Millennium Baby's Mother 2000," " Millennium Baby's Father 2000," Grandmother, Uncles, Aunts, etc seventeen of us.

And that brings up the third phenomenon. We are instant Great Grandparents! Cait has a seven year old, Jacqui. Jack, now The Great, has always wanted someone in the family who was propagating to name a child after him. No one did. So T went out and got one. We like her a lot.

The fourth phenomenon was that Christopher wanted his hair colored blue for his fifteenth birthday. It was electric and everywhere he went he said he felt like a celebrity. So we all smiled, gamely proud progenitors of a celebrity. Now he's back in rock-ribbed New Hampshire and we hope President Bush saw him and has something different to talk about.

The fifth happening was fearsome. I discovered what I knew as a truism long ago, but forgot and it emerged as a grim reality. I am a generation older than my children! It was torture. They could stay up all night and party and be ready for fun the next day, while I found myself with my soul mate creeping ta-ta to bed in spite of the siren calls of the shrieks of laughter and splashes in the pool. I hung onto my mattress as soft voices sharing lives wafted into our windows. I knew I was growing old. However, I got a birthday card that said, "You aren't getting old." Ha, saved. I thought. I turned the page and it said, "You were already old."

The sad part was our son Michael whooped it up with us for two days, then went into self-imposed quarantine for the rest of vacation with a vicious flu. When T announced, "Mr. Michael Colebrook will receive select visitors," three sisters flew up the stairs. Kristina said, "Mother, there we were, only the four of us together. It was somehow holy."

Now that the confetti and tinsel were raked up we were left with a glut of funny foods: frosted flakes, dazzlingly colorful Popsicles, casseroles and stuff I had so lovingly prepared were found hidden behind gallons of milk, wine and cases of beer. They presented a fascinating study of molds. Clouds of billowy white fluff rose from the divine chicken piccata, not to be outdone by forgotten meatballs in tomato wine sauce sporting filmy green fungus. A color to die for in a nightgown. But the cookies won the day. With their decorations, they sported multi-colored millennium mold.

A gray sweat sock, once white, called out "remember when we laughed when Suzie said that?" a forgotten bathing suit reminded me of sitting at the pool with a daughter sharing confidences. A picture of blue hair made me smile at his adolescent fancy while he programmed our computer. The empty room where Kristina, our family Massotherapist, gave everyone massages on her professional table lugged from Arizona, complete with sheets, called out "Parents you really need a healing massage now." Amen.

When they all left our souls were empty. The silence was eerie. We searched each other's faces, stunned. "We were enough for each other once a long time ago and we are enough once again." Yet, we couldn't help but have that old missing kitten feeling. The most profound awareness of this Millennium Gathering was the song in our hearts that our love for each other has poured as surely as a waterfall down through three generations and now through the fourth. We hope our footsteps define wise paths.

Betts & Jack

The Magic Cord

The year two thousand blessed us with magic cords that stretched across the continent and ocean.

It brought us all together for the unforgettable Florida millennium gathering.

The magic cord also stretches between our two homesteads. It drew us back to Ohio and our peaceful lake in May so I could plant new gardens after leaving the Florida gardens waning. The umbilical gives us two tidal basins for homing nests.

Cope's magic cord draws him to sculpture in stone, discovering another nascent talent. It reaches easily to the golf course.

My cord draws me back to the student life to indulge my love of learning. Taking fascinating courses at the Longboat Education Center. It draws me to the Women's Resource Center where I facilitate women on the growing edge and allows the continuation of my love of working with people in therapy.

The magic cord draws us to the resident theatres of Sarasota and indulges our longtime interest in theatre.

The cord stretched our posterity with the birth of Eva Hanna, thanks to her creators T and Cait, and conferred upon us the title of Great Grandparents.

In August that remarkable cord drew all the family back to our Ohio Homestead to celebrate Jack's eightieth birthday in a deeply moving manner.

Old friends pulled our cord and September found us in Utah absorbing the most stunning scenery in the world.

Bella Italia wafted out her siren song once more and the magic cord drew us back to Italy. We ladies, Susan, Deborah, Kristina and I flew off on Friday, October thirteenth. Yes, it was propitious. It was a marvelous adventure from Roman ruins and *Vivaldi* to market days.

While ladies indulged their pleasure, Jack and Mike had a driving golfing adventure from Ohio to Longboat Key. Playing at all famous courses.

Now we find that we Florida incompetents are in charge of the presidency. We thought we had our feet in the sand. The ballot vote was rigged. We got Bush again and gasped, as we had no voice.

The year two thousand has gone faster than Superman. The older we get the more we want to savor each moment, the quicker it escapes.

A Poem To My Handsome Husband

To my Handsome Husband
my love, my life, my everything

Many words have been written
about Love

But when I look at you words don't
seem enough
to tell you how much
I love you

My love reaches from Forever
to Forever plus

My love for you is growing
richer with the knowledge
that you love me
deeply
unconditionally

My man who makes
the Bells Ring
"for me and my gal!"

Elizabeth, your sweetheart
2-6-01

Descent Into Hell

One morning Jack woke up in dire pain. His left shoulder and chest looked like raw hamburger! So off we went to the specialist who left a lot to be desired. He said, "People who contract shingles in their seventies rarely recover and many commit suicide." We walked out with a prescription and this cheery news, staring at each other, thinking of the years ahead. He was in his seventies.

True enough Jack never recovered. The severe pain never ceased, but he didn't commit suicide.

Mostly I hovered as he was in bed twenty-two hours of the day swathed in cold wet towels. I cooked and planted and checked his breathing - didn't want to leave him alone - except to buy more plants - use my excess energy. Now my energy is all gone and I have to water hundreds of plants every day!

So - the thumbnail of it. He was treated with three stellate blocks, thoracic epidural and another at Cleveland Clinic. But the first epidural was at another hospital while our primary physician was away and Jack was saying, "I don't think I can stand another twenty-four hours of this pain." So I rushed to the rescue and we were referred to, "the most "innovative" physician specializing in PHN,"- well, he almost killed him. Jack's blood pressure stayed at 67/33 for three hours while I watched over him in recovery and couldn't find the nurse (Jack was her only patient in his huge recovery room) when the monitor kept registering a red alert. He had a general anesthesia, which I'm told was all wrong and then the thoracic epidural was done too low to help the effected area. We were pretty concerned when his right arm was paralyzed, but it wore off with the anesthesia.

We both struggled and survived many serious and incurable illnesses. They have shortened our pleasant security and brought our mean genes to the surface, taking our lives' woes out on each other. Often too fatigued to care for the other. When Jack lay dying with oxygen mask and tubes, the doctor said, "two more days to live," and Jack said, "Honey, I know you are tired of taking care of me." I protested, "Please live and come home with me!" "Hush," he said, "and I was tired of taking care of you." This was a killer, but my therapist said "Don't you realize that he gave you a treasure."

So there it was. "Just keep the family together with love," were his final words to me. As the remaining matriarch I find this tough going often-times and sometimes wish I had died and he had lived.

Despair And Epiphany
Accepting My Cronehood

"There are only two ways to live your life.
One is though nothing is a miracle. The other is as though everything is a miracle."
Albert Einstein (1879 – 1955)

One twilight summer day I wandered the shores of our lake, exhausted from the trauma of events which had gathered like a storm around me.

The lake was a silent mirror of muted sunset. The wake of two geese was the only movement in the water as they swam to the lily bed.

As the sirens called the sailors in the "Odyssey," the lake called me. But I was not lashed to the mast. I pulled off my terry gown and naked, dove into the water. I didn't know whether this was an ancient unconscious cleansing rite or an intent to drown. But I went with it and swam and swam as though in a trance. It was a lovely freedom swim. My mind was uncluttered, my pace slow and meditative.

Suddenly I realized that I was out of breath and energy. I was sinking. It was dark and no one knew where I was. I had lost track of time.

In a state of panic, I realized only my nose and mouth were above water. Weakly, I called, "Help, help." My husband was in bed. The house was dark; I couldn't locate it.

So I gave myself to the deep, cold water. This was finally it. I started to sink into the ooze. In that moment a quiet, resonant male voice came out of the tall pine trees that Jack had planted. "I AM HERE." I just learned that was what God said in the Ninety Third Psalm! Why is my belief in God so elusive? I can still hear it. My guardian angel my daughter assured me I had? The diva, Goddess of the Lake? My purposeful male animus? God himself?

It gave me life. With new energy I searched frantically for a beacon. I caught sight of a dim light from our bedroom. Aiming at the tiny glow, I struggled toward it. I tried scrambling up the jagged rocks, but I had no leverage. I was stuck up to my knees in the brown ooze.

Repeatedly, I threw myself up on the rocks only to be repelled back into the water, bruised and bleeding.

Finally, I gave what my body told me was my last effort and threw myself backwards over the rocks and onto the ground.

I don't know how I made my way to the house, painfully, stumbling, falling, crawling.

When I pulled myself up the two flights of stairs to our deck I had only enough energy to scratch feebly at the door. Incredibly, there was Jack. He said, "I don't know what made me get out of bed and come to this door."

Three days later I was in relentless pain. I asked Jack to take me to St. Luke's Hospital Emergency Clinic in Solon to get some medication to temper my misery.

My body was bruised and bleeding with multiple sprains, neck, shoulder, and pelvis. No broken bones, said my doctor after many x-rays the next day. "You don't know how lucky you are to be alive," he lectured me, "You could have broken your neck or back and been paralyzed."

What followed I could never in my wildest imaginations have predicted. I told my story to the kindly Indian physician. He ordered an injection, talking gently as he examined my tormented body. Whatever the drug was, it made me crazy. I had recited my list of allergies: morphine, codeine and on. But this was a new one to add to my list. My poor husband was in tears. What a birthday celebration I had delivered to him! Neither of us understood what was happening until much later, I remember trying to crawl off the gurney to talk with my doctor as I heard arrangements being made to take me to the hospital by ambulance. No one listened to my voice. It was frightening to be unwittingly propelled by medical machinery, unheard.

By the time I was hoisted into the ambulance, I was lucid once again and chatted with my attendant about his favorite activities, fishing and softball. At the hospital I was trundled by two men through the maze of halls. When they stopped at the double doors to press the admittance button, I looked at the sign on the wall with horror. "Lock Psych Ward!"

"What are we doing here?" I asked in disbelief. "We don't know either, "said my former comrades turned traitors. I have visited clients occasionally in Locked Psychiatric wards and always developed claustrophobia. They were dreadful places.

I knew I should not protest. Unknown staff could treat me like Napoleon summoning his armies. After a brief intake they took me to a small bare room. One light bulb in the ceiling. "Pit and the Pendulum," was all I could think of. The only thing to do was to go to bed and figure out what to do in the morning. I realized that the story of my savior branded me to incarceration. There was nothing more to say about it to the medical establishment blinded by their own discipline.

Sometime later I awoke needing the bathroom. I tried to walk and collapsed into unconsciousness. Each time I came to and crawled a few feet I fainted again. When I finally made my way to the door I couldn't stand, but called out and scratched weakly at the locked door. When I heard footsteps and voices I called out, "Careful opening the door, I am right here, but can't move."

Lifted back onto the bed, I heard more footsteps and voices, an EKG, an IV, a gurney, concern, an alarm sounded. I came to in the cardiac ward.

Next day, more tests, more white coats. The verdict, hypo-tension, dehydration, electrolyte imbalance, internal bleeding. The shock and the toxic painkiller had done their work. Explanations, apologies, three days of medical management. Home with my bewildered husband.

It took me a long time to recover from my anger and humiliation. The pain settled in for the long haul, reminding me not to be overcome by hopelessness ever again. I understood what my body was telling me. Remembering Ulysses, I will lash myself to the masthead, stuff my ears so I won't hear the siren's song another time.

I know I was saved for a reason. I wonder what my mission on earth is to be? I must trust the epiphany and remember, "We create how we experience the events in our lives." Treasure the days, the moments. Life can rob us anytime with its infinite trickery.

A self-professed agnostic, a spiritual seeker, if not a religionist, I will never forget the wonderment of hearing that steady voice beyond the pine trees.

It would be easy to dismiss this sort of experience, to deny possibility of something I don't understand. The willingness to consider possibility requires a shift in perception from the known to the unknown, a leap of faith to accept that I will never know what actually happened.

I don't know the profundities of life - why I was spared, why I am here on this earth - as a student, to plumb for knowledge? To love and be loved? To know that I live a life of connectedness to my roots and wings? To know that I matter in this life? I find an incredible new energy for the quest, and the patience to listen and wait and see. My newly claimed croneself is, "holding loosely, setting free, letting go…"

I know now that my mission is to record my life writing this book.

I Tried To Say Goodbye Again

I suppose I need to include two very serious almost irreparable experiences.

Cope's eight nerve blocks were supposed to end the pain came to no avail. It was hell from then on. The pain rendered him irascible. Me too. So that Christmas Eve I couldn't stand life anymore. I over-dosed with all the pills I had and went to bed hoping never to awake. But sometime during the long unconscious night I stumbled into the bathroom and fell flat on the marble floor with such a noise everyone woke up and took me to the hospital. I wavered between life and death. Bob and Kris hovered over me like forgiving angels, massaged me and sent love into my wayward body. The doctor thought I had had a stroke.

I survived only to be sent to a locked psych ward again. Grim, desolate, my best friend among all the derelicts was a burned-out schizophrenic black man. He laughed and laughed when I railed against the grim existence, the system that locked me away. The psychiatrist said I could be admitted to the step-up area when I became "socially adjusted." Is that possible in this setting, I wondered? I could neither sleep nor eat.

When I was finally deemed "adjustable" I "stepped-up." More cheerful setting in that prison (so called "hospital"). Sleepless, when I tried to walk the corridor the black hospital guard punished me severely and sent me back to my no-sleep bed with my snoring mountain of a woman roommate. I found a young black woman six months pregnant – alone in her world. I asked her if she liked to sing. Her face opened like Christmas morning. I found a small quiet room and brought in everyone I could find in wheel chairs and asked her to sing to us. She sang African songs. She was lovely. Never took her eyes off mine. Transcendent moment. The warden (cum social worker) found us and took her away. That's therapy in the psych ward.

How could I have known that the worst was yet to come? I had to go to criminal court. It's against the law to try to take your own life in Florida.

The cards were stacked against me. An awesome court wanted me committed for I don't know how long. Perhaps I was in a grateful blur.

The Public Defender protected me. Kristina, Bob and Jack had been summoned. Jack was the color of a worn out sweat sock.

I was silenced when I ventured to speak. Kris fastened her begging eyes on the Public Defender who was moved to let her speak on my behalf. Kris spoke and saved me. I was rescued.

I learned that in a psych ward people are not allowed to be happy.

I realized I had a loving family and at least one mission left in life. This book was born: a legacy to my descendants with all the joy and pain included.

So much for all that. Amen, I thought.

Cope's Memorials

Cope's death was peaceful. In full denial of his imminent demise, I took him to the Mayo Clinic to "cure" him. Mike and I drove him to Jacksonville. After one day of tests, he said "I can't breathe," even with his oxygen turned up high. It was a rush to the hospital for biopsy, etc. He was full of small cell cancer: unbeatable. I didn't know until I read his journal months later that he had known his diagnosis for several months. Cope never told me, nor his attorney, or our children.

I can only grieve deeply for him suffering his fate in silent loneliness. Suzie mustered all the clan, our children and grandchildren. They flew from everywhere; we gathered around his bed and sang hymns and finally his signature piece "When the Saints Go Marching In," Laurie opened a window and his soul flew out. The staff didn't intrude, left us in our final hours for each one to say final words to him alone.

After he had died, Kristina asked if she could cut a little lock of his curls to keep. The other daughters also took a curl. Suzie had a dream that he was peaceful but said, "I didn't much like the haircut you all gave me."

We worked like crazy to get everything ready for the service; reserved the Chapel, got a jazz band according to his wishes. The service was lovely. Kristina gave a long Native American chant and friends came forth with their memories of him. We had refreshments at the Chapel and visited with all of our friends. They cried and expressed their deep feelings for him and for me. I never saw them after all our closeness through the years. Widows are not people.

The band played Jack's signature song "The Saints come marching in" as we all filed out. That was February, 2002.

In June in Aurora we had another memorial for longtime friends in our homeplace. Twenty-four members of the clan gathered. We had lots of gaily colored tents – looked like an Arab encampment.

In the morning we gathered at the cemetery where we deposited one-third of his ashes for posterity. Each person threw something in the urn that they connected with Jack. It was nostalgic and humorous; a golf

*Our picture is framed and in the lobby of the
Aurora Community Theatre. The theatre has
been renovated from top to bottom and is
absolutely gorgeous. The lobby has been named
after me; a bronze plate "Elizabeth Poss Colebrook"
I want my father commemorated. His trust fund
for me makes it all possible.*

ball, some tees, a poem, a rose, three pieces of toilet paper from Suzie (he had repeatedly said when the daughters were little and wrapped a half a roll around their little wrists, "three pieces of toilet paper are enough."

I wondered how many of our other cautionary sayings had become imprinted in their minds. Important ones I hoped.

Then we went to the "Church in Aurora" where we grew up. It was a moveable feast or more aptly a smorgasbord. Kevin Horak presided and spoke affectionately and respectfully of Jack and all his devoted efforts with Dan Frenz, three years of work to design an addition to the church and get it passed by the board and the congregation. Jack contributed the seed money for the huge addition.

Kristina gave her Native American chant. Since a single rose was Jack's symbol of love each one of us rose to the nave and laid a single rose on the alter while Paula and John sang the lovely "The Rose." David had made a special CD of Jack singing two of his favorite songs; a surprise to me which completely undid me. I hired the "Eagle Street Band: a group of hefty steelworkers whom we had followed where ever they got together in Cleveland; mostly small dives. They played their great jazz in tee shirts, baseball hats on backwards! What a sight in our sedate church. We followed them out the front doors as they belted out "The Saints."

After the church reception we came home and I fell into bed for an hour then joined the party at the cabin. We had boat rides and a catered dinner. The following night the extended family gathered. Suzie had arranged for Lonnie to tie small festive handfuls of ashes to distribute on the lake in two boatloads as he had wished. She passed out rose candles for Jack. Each person lighted another's. The brave little roses floated down to the north end of the lake like a choir and kept their lights on until after one a.m. So touching I fell in bed for two days I think, knowing he was properly memorialized.

I still had one third of the damn ashes to disperse in the inland canal in front of our home in Longboat Key. "Mary Lou, we're just going to toss them, no tears what's done is done" Amen. I couldn't stand anymore.

Today would have been his ninetieth birthday.

After his memorial in the Longboat Island Chapel, and all the family went back to their homes, a period of numbness settled over me like a grey cloak. Then I went to work re-doing the whole house to make it my own. I love it dearly, of course, there are reminders of him in every corner: his sculptures, his carvings, as it should be. We created it together with love. Our southern paradise.

When we first saw it, I said, "Let's buy it, sweetheart, it's a happy healing house," not knowing what was to come.

After Jack Died

I have become a child of nature, up with the blazing sun, keeping my tryst with the moon, full in early December. In the silent mornings there is not a single ripple on the canal between our pool and the mangroves. A sheet of water. The bay beyond the mangroves is a placid mirror. The white pelicans still sleeping, my world is soundless. I am an isolate. Peace is elusive; I cannot yet face my friends.

At night I sit with the moon and the crickets. My moon rises low on the horizon and shines a golden ribbon on the bay and our pool. Gradually, it turns silver. I want to float on that diaphanous trail across the water and get lost in the firmament.

Peace sorely needed is elusive, like waiting for a silenced doorbell to ring.

Things Come Full Circle

Possibly the most ironic thing is that I met Carl at Cope's memorial on Longboat. He was visiting friends at the time. I didn't at that point pay much attention to him.

He had just moved back to Aurora where he had grown up: following his roots after living all over the world. We had not known each other as kids. He was younger. In time we got to know each other and, in time began to like each other and in time became sweethearts.

Like the Unicorn – when one of its horns falls off, it grows another one.

We like doing most of the same things: concerts, opera, playing bridge with friends.

It's quite amazing, yet one more miracle in my life to find someone at my age.

Steeple People
By Jill Wilson

One might accuse me of being nepotistic because Betts Colebrook (Dr. Elizabeth) is someone I've admired and loved for more than fifty years. Because she is a relatively new member of our Chapel, I want you readers to know her well.

Betts grew up in the small town of Aurora, Ohio where she maintains a home-place where her children, grandchildren, and great grandchildren can gather together in the summer. She has belonged to the Aurora Community Church all of her life.

Betts graduated from Vassar College in 1944 and immediately married her childhood sweetheart. Jack, her husband of sixty years, and Betts were always leaders in the Aurora community. She started the first kindergarten in Aurora, after which followed their four children. Along the way, Betts saw the need of stimulating activities for children in outlying areas and thus the birth of the Summer Recreation Program, which has since grown to a comprehensive year-round offering for children and adults. She planted the seeds for an adult education program. There was no town library so she started one. Perhaps her proudest achievement, and possibly the most controversial, was the outreach program and job corps she initiated in Cleveland when the inner cities were supposed to burn and were disrupted and decaying in the late sixties.

After years of dreams, she and Jack founded the Aurora Community Theatre, in which I, too, participated. We used to call ACT an "off-Broadway Theatre" (five hundred miles off Broadway!). This embryonic effort has become a professional theatre with a stunning show place. A few years ago, in her golden years, Betts made her final bow in "On Golden Pond."

As if her civic accomplishments were not enough, Betts was not completely fulfilled, so at forty-five years of age she went to graduate school. Instead of planning to be a college dean, she trained to be a clinical psychologist and then established a practice in Aurora which she named "The Center for Better Living." Betts delineated six stages of Anorexia Nervosa from her extended practice for her dissertation. She then went on to receive her Doctorate at age fifty-eight, the oldest student to matriculate, with husband, family, children, and grandchildren applauding her - no one without tears.

A resident of Longboat Key for thirteen years, she recently lost her husband, Jack. She feels this church is her spiritual home and family and is exceedingly happy to be here. She hopes to volunteer at the Chapel to aid people, families, and children with the loss of a loved one.

She says her greatest blessing is her family who have spent devoted time with her during hard times of grief. In her words, "Life continually replaces itself like the spring bulbs bursting into flowers through the fallen snow." Her favorite things are her friends, her garden, theatre, and reading.

Byron Katies' Encampment

When I was eighty I signed up for boot camp. It was in Joshua Tree National Park, a sparse and intriguing high desert with strange trees found no other place, in northern California.

I knew not what was ahead for me. But my three daughters and granddaughter, Laurie, had been to many of Byron Katie's workshops and thought she was unusually gifted.

Katie, after a prolonged period of psychosis had emerged from bed and spent every day alone in the desert thinking.

As Stephen Mitchell, the famous scholar, who became her admirer and afterward her husband, writes that somehow Katie had developed the wisdom of the ancients. He was constantly astonished.

So there I was plunked in the cold desert with clothes fit for the beach. I was the oldest deafest person there. Nevertheless, it was a life changing experience for me.

We rarely knew what was going to happen to us next. I realized that Katie's strategy was to unbalance us so that we had to find our own balance again.

My first unbalancing was the entrance of my housemate. She could barely get through the door – weighed four hundred seventy pounds and arrived with no suitcase; instead a laundry basket filled with all her family's clothes.

We were ordered to start walking through the desert alone for half an hour before breakfast not talking to anyone. Silence was the rule for the whole nine day workshop. Unfortunately I tore the bursa in my left knee in the first five minutes of my first desert walk.

I was painfully gimpy for the long desert walks ahead to add to my list of disqualifications, but I learned to live with it.

Our first assignment was to meet in triads. Only four questions were allowed:

"I resent………..
Are you absolutely sure?
How do you know that?
How would you be without the resentment?"

The person chosen to start said:
"I resent God.
Yes, because he killed my dog.
I know because he left a note saying He did.
I can't get over it."
The next day was undoing the projection.
"God didn't kill my dog…etc."

She was a little woman who looked like she was made of dough. She had come halfway around the world to work on this problem.

We worked all day with the rule of silence except for the therapy sessions. Evenings we had various adventures.

One morning we proceeded to the mess hall for breakfast and found only a glass of water and a slice of lemon at each place. At lunch a glass of water and a slice of lemon. Dinner the same. Silence. Hungry.

Breakfast for which we lined up eagerly the next day: a glass of water and slice of lemon. The same. Then all two hundred and fifty of us were loaded into three buses. We were a mixed bag from all over the world; psychiatrists, psychologist, social workers, physicians and psychotics. We weren't told where we were going and for how long.

Tiny slips of paper were handed out containing the only three things we were permitted to say; "may I join you?" "I am hungry will you feed me?" and "thanks but no thanks." I saw an austere British gentleman who looked like an aristocrat or a butler sitting alone. "May I join you?" an acceptance by wave of hand. He held my hand for the whole drive of two and a half hours to Santa Monica. I never saw him before or since. But I realized that my deepest, unspoken fear was unfounded: that I would always be alone after my husband died. Not so: I would never be alone.

We were dropped near a homeless park, told we could not talk to each other if we happened to meet. No ID was allowed, no money, watch or jewelry. I became the most pitiful beggar imaginable. "I am hungry will you feed me?" On my third visit to the senior center a woman gave me an orange, a man handed me a small bag or trail mix. Another breakthrough for me: I realized that what I wanted most I didn't really need. I gave them to a young Asian couple sitting forlornly on a bench overlooking the sea. Hunger is an apparition.

I approached a group of druggies sprawled out on the grass – all black. When I asked if I could join them they all sat up and said "we love you momma" and hugged me. Another lesson in how to interact with poor unfortunate homeless blacks. One woman with them whose name was Berta with one tooth, was white. She offered me a reefer. I wisely said "thanks, but no thanks" (though I could have used one.) Because a cop came along and took her away saying "I see you are up to your old tricks, Berta."

I wandered around the pier watching families having fun together, joined some folks making sand castles with their children until one of them said "she's nice, but kind of queer isn't she? Doesn't talk." Couldn't stop yearning for a cup of coffee as the fragrance permeating the air wafted calling me. No free coffee.

Finally at six thirty we were called to meet and talk about our experiences. They were generally profound; a lavish spread appeared from our buses for dinner. Afterwards everyone started streaming up a steep hill. Gimpy behind. A lovely man with a white goatee and mustache took my arm and walked slowly with me. We talked! He was a psychiatrist from the Netherlands on staff with Katie.

At the top of the hill we arrived at a magical world of Santa Monica the trees festooned with tiny white lights.

Civilization!

The kind woman at the senior center had taken me aside. "I will take you to a shelter tonight, honey. This is a very dangerous place at night." I found that some people are kind to the homeless. After that I have never passed a homeless person without chatting and give some money. Many "God bless yous."

My comrade and I saw a coffee house. He asked "would you like a cup of coffee?" "Would I, would I? A million thank yous." We were only served herbal tea at the retreat and I was experiencing coffee withdrawal. When I started to drink the coffee the same realization dawned. What we long for so deeply isn't really what it's cracked up to be.

There was the on-going nightly need to nurture my cabin-mate who was sorely teased and called names for her obesity unfortunately. I learned that I didn't need much sleep. I learned to care for someone scorned. I also learned that everyone liked me and wanted me for a surrogate mother. Except for one young woman whom I asked to dyad with me. She refused saying "You can't hear anyway." I was sadly crushed. In the following exercise Katie asked anyone to stand to tell their experiences. I related mine and said "It really hurts to be thus treated about an infirmity I can't help, but I can lip read." The young woman cried and offered to give me a haircut.

One morning we were sent out to walk in the scorching desert. A straggly group, we didn't know where we were going or for how long. Sometime in the afternoon we were told to stop in a deep canyon. Box lunches were passed around. Silently with only eye contact partners were chosen. A man chose me. We were strangers, but I was glad that a man chose me – there were many more women than men. Our boxes revealed not ham sandwiches and potato chips for our starving bodies, but raisins, berries and nuts. We were instructed to feed our partner with our fingers to their opening mouths. Novel! I don't recall ever being fed by fingers: a bonding experience to be sure. There was more lilt in our steps back to the encampment.

One night we were sent out to the dark freezing cold desert. Laurie, my granddaughter who was on staff, saved me. She went to a Wal-Mart and bought a long piece of vinyl with a soft lining, put it over me and cut a slit for my head. A black cap and purple gloves completed my glorious outfit. She knew I would be freezing. We walked forever until I dropped.

*This is my children's favorite picture of me.
They say it is the real me!*

*Byron Katie Workshop
I was a perfect Bag Lady*

I learned survival.

Sometimes we danced and sang in the evenings. One night we were told to dress as a person whom we were most intolerant of. I dressed as Saddam Hussein. We had just been told that we had invaded Iraq; most of us were is shock.

The final morning we were instructed to throw something we thought we could not live without into a huge barrel. One woman threw her house keys, another car keys. I threw my last pack of cigarettes. A final lesson.

We departed, I was never the same.

Dearest Family,

Suzie (the sparkplug). Thank you all, David, Kim, Wendy, Margie, Leslie, T, Eve, Michael, Anikka, eighty-five million times for the gorgeous eighty-five roses that filled my home and my heart with love and joy.

I felt so celebrated, more than ever before in my life!

I just am coming out of seven weeks of hibernation with an ugly bronchial infection. I must have sat near someone from Patagonia (on the plane) with a strange strain that is not submitting to all of our usual antibiotics. I thought I was headed down to the beautiful warmth and sun on the key. Not so - 'tis very cold here - some of my new plantings shivered to death already. Oh well, I get to plant again. My nurse's aide started planting. Hurray for versatility.

My love always,
Mother
Grandmother
Aunt
Great Gram

Hi Carol

*My Best Friend At College
And Through The Years*

Hi Carol,

Yes, I am passionate about politics and pretty disgusted at what's going on. Especially since both my states, Ohio and Florida screwed up in the past two elections and then we got Bush. Of course neither one of the candidates now can solve what Bush has done. Obama has been a hero to me - I hate to see him dragged into this catfight. I have been pretty passionate about politics since Wendell Willkie, remember marching for him at VC?

Mark thinks political beliefs may be biological. I don't know my father was an unreconstructed Republican and I have always been a Democrat much to his disgust.

I have become a bionic woman in the past three years- cochlear implant was tough, but the corneal transplant was even worse - no meds for after eye surgery. The past two summers I've had two surgeries each. Two more different, unpronounceable eye surgeries. Broken bones from falls due to my imbalance problem caused by the above issues. But I am out of a walker and use a cane. Then the worst blow, a broken hip. I wish I could say I got it bungee jumping, but it happened just getting into bed. The terrible part was that my friend, David, who was helping me into bed, tried to break my fall and broke his back. He died four weeks later, full of cancer.

However, the wonderful project I've been working on all summer is my book. I have been getting it in order for my publisher. The pinnacle of my life! I have been writing for fifteen years. Pretty good for eighty-seven! Yes? I've worked so hard on it; I'm bogged down. I discover in my musty piles that I started writing when I was six.

I have an artist friend who designed the front and back covers - very fanciful. It's called "Digging Up Grandpa." I have a mentor in Florida who will read it and assist me with any editing. Writing steadily is hard work, as you know. I have a lot of assistance - a helper who types for me and works it into the correct format and font and her professional photographer husband who does mystical things with my photos and puts all my writing onto discs. I don't understand this at all. But, Kim and Scott, my gratitude overfloweth.

I have someone come in the morning and fix me breakfast and coffee, then someone for lunch and dinner on the evenings when I do not go out. I have sworn off cooking after sixty some years.

Problem is some women they send me from the agency can't cook. So I teach them and then we eat and I am paying them for it.

But finally I'm getting good caregivers and they are devoted to me. Kim is my business manager and loving pal - she takes care of the multitude of details in running this estate.

Aside from the other medical maneuvers, I then had problems with my teeth- two extractions and two root canals. The worst of all was the emergency surgery in the middle of the night for an intestinal blockage. I was in the ICU for eleven days during which they administered heavy drugs that literally paralyzed me. They kept me in bed then for two more weeks. The net result was that I couldn't walk. So I was sent to a rehab hospital to learn how to walk again, use my hands and learn how to dress myself. I looked around at the other women and men who were older and like zombies and decided I didn't want to live that long. Amen. While I was in the ICU all my kids were called, I was supposed to die or live with brain damage.

Now I have two jewels in Florida to help me. Marina from Russia who is as sweet and thoughtful as an angel. Maria from Italy who is my loving buddy. We go to chapel, brunches, theatre, concerts and discussion groups together. She helps out at parties which I have started to give again. Knowing I would be alone for Thanksgiving she invited me into the welcoming bosom of her large Italian family. Joy!

As a good friend once said - I somehow have the ability to bounce back out of the worst situations.

Fondly,

Betts

Labor Day Weekend

Deborah and I put on our archeological outfits and dig through languishing piles of photographs to put in the book. My spirits are up but my body is crying. I wonder if my hip will ever heal? It's painful to do most anything. A doctor friend said in his long practice he has never seen anyone who broke a hip in their eighties recover: usually bedridden and die. I never considered that as an alternative.

The bladder affair is out of hand. Did the bank manager know that while I was smiling and talking to him, I was blissfully peeing in my Depends? It turns out the three surgeries I had in Sarasota with a well-known urologist were wrong. My new specialist here gave me pills. I didn't know what was in them, so I got a printout from my pharmacy. It assured me that it would help my prostate. Whew, I was so worried about my prostate! Continuing, it said that if I got a hard-on that lasted more than four hours, I should call my doctor, and that if I couldn't ejaculate I should call my doctor immediately!

It is truly a puzzling world!

The days go by fast, by the time I eat breakfast and come to, the days shrink. As I work on my proofing of the book and we find appropriate photographs, at least, it is an antidote for my loneliness. Then I am filled. Last night the harvest moon glowed bright orange and reflected its brilliant orb in the lake. Debby and I were transformed as we watched moon shadows through the trees.

These blessedly sunny warm days help my unceasing fibromyalgia after the cold glum rainy summer that wasn't summer at all. The vagaries of weather in Ohio depress my body and spirits.

However, the ecstasy of having daughter Deborah here is a balm in Gilead. She has learned through Peter's tough year of fighting aggressive cancer how to roll with scary disheartening punches. Peter emerged a hero, the Phoenix from the ashes. She was the heroine.

Deborah with her new grand-daughter, Avelyn.
Was there ever more love?

Last night as we were making a late dinner, her son, Christopher's wife, Annie called. She is due to give birth to Logan in two months, a joy we all share. Annie was panicked, crying hysterically. She was spotting a bit and didn't know what to do, since she has to have a caesarian section. Chris was in Alabama chosen by his company, General Dynamics, to give an important presentation. Turns out with his graduation from Full Sail, a technological institute, where he specialized in creating video games (which didn't seem like a big thing to me with the huge investment of his two year training program) that he is actually doing important government work. We can't know anything about it.

I watched Debby with the earpiece of her cell phone cooking away and guiding Annie tenderly through her terror. "Now, get pillows and lie down on the couch with a cup of tea. Put your feet up and watch a movie. Chris will be home in two hours and will be there for you."

Chris called later and all was well. "Whew."

The whole Labor Day weekend was a joyous affair. Finding pictures of the past showing the family at play and Cope and me so happy together displaced the hard times that creep over me and enfold me.

How I Became A Bionic Woman

About four years ago I awoke in the night alone in my house with unrelenting pain. All I remember is screaming, "I don't know what's happening to me" over and over. I called my faithful friend, Kim, who took me to E.R., ambulance to hospital, awakening a few days later – PAIN. I had an abdominal blockage removed. I was in ICU for eleven days anesthetized out of my mind. It appears that I was throwing myself around so much; the doctors thought I would injure myself. Vivid dreams or hallucinations stayed with me for weeks as reality. They were hard to shake.

Nine months after the hip department, I am still struggling with walking, dressing, etc. Balance problems. Then, my wonderful eye surgeon tells me I have to have the other eye done. I said, "Thanks, but no thanks." That was probably the worst. So, I trudge on trying to avoid the medical maze. I have macular degeneration and hope to die before I go blind. The other day I was referred to a gastro guy. After filling out ten pages of what felt like irrelevant questions, I was ushered into his office. I said, "I am so damn sick of seeing doctors." He replied, "I'm so damned sick of seeing patients." So, I said what seemed like the most logical response "Let's go out for a drink."

This year I had to have bladder surgery and now spend the rest of my life with an ubiquitous bag for urine collection. My lifetime companion.

Thus endeth (I hope) my medical marathon.

Moral of the story: Stay away from doctors. They can harm your health.

Out Of The Rabbit Hole

Only now, at age eighty-seven, I realize that all my years of desolation and search for solutions in my life were worthwhile. I had hundreds of rooms in my house, and I thought my partner had few. It was hard for him to let me in to explore them. What a waste: he had many, all unspoken.

Eckerd Tolle and Byron Katie write of their years of depression; Katie in the desert alone, he his searching the world for wise men who might know the mysterious secrets of the meaning of life. The struggleful times appear to be necessary for a questor like me.

I see that people who are "flat," with no tearing apart of the guts, rarely have the impetus for the search. Many of us sleepwalk through life and miss the contentment of living in the "now" with all its rich bounty: the sheer bliss of the present moments, the stillness of the soul.

So, the struggles of my questing nature have brought me here. I used to waste my life with the old refrain "Is this all there is?"

I know not how long I have. I shall try to extract every moment I have to be in the "now." I learned this many years ago in the three-year intensive post-doc program at the Gestalt Institute. But it didn't sink into my core. Guess I wasn't ready yet.

They, Eckerd and Katie, struggled their way out of depression and desolation through silence. The trouble is I love "to think." My colleague, Mark Brown, who has done neuro-bio-feed back on me, says "you have the busiest brain I've ever worked on." My most creative thoughts on writing and living come out of my "thinking." I won't give that process up. The part I want to give up is indulging in regrets. Life can be full of them because of our imperfections. But the Greek derivation of perfectionism is to live with a mission, a purpose in life and I have a firm grip on that: to finish this book and to heal my family; the irritations and misunderstandings that are bound to surface in a close extended clan. This healing is happening while the book is happening - serendipity.

Dreamland

I was drifting in a golden dream world all night. The fiftieth anniversary of our first show, conceived by Cope and me and our merry bunch of friends, done on a fling. David and Shirley Baylor, Dick and Jill Wilson, Dallas and Kent Allison, and my sister were the nucleus. We put on our productions on a stage in the Church In Aurora. One of the trustees was sent to oversee our lines. He took some risqué ones out. We added them back in when we went into production.

We persuaded David Baylor who had radio experience to be our director. We literally dragged people out of their homes to fill the roles. I auditioned for the starring female role and was chosen. Thus, the Aurora Community Theatre was born with the production of "The Tender Trap." We had such a good time we mounted "Second Best Sport" the following year. Later "Pillow Talk" I was selected for the lead in all three plays. Peter Kinsey became our professional director. My leading man was a tall, gorgeous Texan. When we were seated at a side café table off center stage, he asked "Betts, do you have any children?" "Rex, let's talk about that afterwards." What I knew and he didn't know was that he had a two year old and I had a two year old grandchild. We had a romantic role to play and I didn't want to mess it up. Guess I looked pretty young for my age.

Interesting happenings in the course of the theatre. Divorces, re-marriages, etc... "The show must go on."

Some years later we moved to the splendid new performing arts center built by George and Ann Chapman.

A loyal and talented crew of Auroraites put on productions of professional level through the years, expanding to three each year. I started the youth theatre for eager youngsters. Many years later I was chosen to play the lead in on "Golden Pond," my swan song. I loved that show. Cope got me a dozen American Beauty roses for each of the six performances.

One day while I was watching a rehearsal of "South Pacific" a little boy came up to me and knelt at my side, clasping my hand, "Mrs.

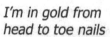
I'm in gold from head to toe nails

Dear friend Phyllis Grumney

Phyllis and Phil

Colebrook, I owe you my life." "Why sweetheart, what do you mean?"

"The theatre that you started is my life." I was stunned and fulfilled.

Fifty years after the first show the theatre held a golden gala ball for one hundred thirty people. It was a fairyland and I was the queen. Dressed in gold from head to toe with gold fingernails and toenails, I was celebrated. I was in a dream world. Kim came and showered me, anointed me with lavender lotion made from a nearby lavender farm and dressed me like royalty. I floated in to the gala attired in my beautiful gold dress, sandals and scarf.

I lay awake thinking about all this through the night, smiling. Some dreams come true if we dare to risk.

I found this poem and thought of you.
Love, Lang
(aka...Kim)

Because You're My Friend....

When you are sad,
I will dry your tears.
When you are scared,
I will comfort your fears.
When you are worried,
I will give you hope.
When you are confused,
I will help you cope.
And when you are lost,
And can't see the light.
I shall be your beacon
Shining ever so bright.
This is my oath.
I pledge till the end.
Why you may ask?
Because you're my friend.
Anonymous

And she has done that:

Kim is one of my dearest friends, staunch caregiver, nurse, typist, and business manager, overseeing the complicated affairs of a large home and property. She has been steadfast in her devotion for the past five years and has seen me through a lot of travail – there is no one like her – she is so special.

I christened her "Lang" which in Chinese means sweet potato. Sometimes I call her "Mei Lang" – beautiful sweet potato.

A Retrospective
Canaries In The Mines

We bought a house on Longboat Key, Florida while visiting friends for the weekend. We needed a new nest. But I was like an old crustacean moved to a new tidal basin. I had lived in my hometown of Aurora, Ohio, all my life.

Now, I know it was one of the best things we ever did. I take fascinating classes; we have great friends, (though, now I see that after old friends cried at Jack's memorial, I haven't seen any of them since.) I reinvent my life once again.

It wasn't until my forties that we progressed beyond "radio." No air-conditioning, T.V., videos, computers, Internet and no space travel. It is quite amazing to look back through my "over three quarters of a century life" and see the vast changes. I'm not sure we are any better off. It depends on what we do with it all and whether happiness becomes more elusive than it was when life was simpler. Relationships appear to be less sustaining and enduring.

At forty-five, I had reinvented my life by going to graduate school after raising four children and starting every community activity I could think of. I look back now and reflect how gutsy I was; I thought anything could be done. The power of a debilitative chronic disease, the aging process and displacement felled me for a while. We become dependent and depressed.

We lived through World War II, the Korean War and the Vietnam War when our son Michael was spared at the final hour, as his father had been by being rotated to Germany instead the night before he was supposed to ship out. The mass extermination of a people and nuclear energy let loose covertly and ineluctable, unquenchable affects were covered up. Our grandson, Michael Murray, was sent to the ill-conceived and devastating Gulf War and returned with so many experiences I can't know but with a GI Bill to help him through college. He is at Kent State University where I got my graduate degrees. We have also seen the flag of the United States planted on the far-away moon by our astronauts.

Now that the grip of a Bi-polar world is over and the Berlin Wall is down with communism collapsing in the Soviet Union, countries are dissolving their whimfully assigned boundaries; ethnic groups are destroying, raping, and starving each other in Africa. The cork is out of the bottle; the savage within ourselves has been unleashed. Uncontrollable tribal warfare is ensuing and the U.S. universal conscience tries to, "fight and kill for peace." We try to feed the hungry to make up, I suppose, for the massive arming of unstable countries in the covert, unwinnable, ill-conceived war in the mid-east we have irresponsibly created.

Hundreds of thousands of people are becoming nomads, fleeing their homelands. In our country social and educational programs have failed or been bungled. Unemployment is rife. We don't seem to use the sophisticated knowledge we social scientists know about, "conflict resolution." Instead, "Might is right."

So everyone is developing nuclear weapons, and our children have nightmares, while we destroy the only living planet we know about and our own earthlings. Now we rediscover the knowledge of extra-terrestrial beings, so many planets who have visited earth for thousands of years. Now what? We go about the business of everyday living as everyone else does and politely deny our vicious realities. Unbelievably, plans are in the works by serious scientists to populate the moon.

Cope and I have survived the lumps and bumps of marriage and children growing up in a vastly changing world. With our mutual adaptation to evolving roles we are more intimately involved with each other than ever. Like twins entwined in utero – but with our pursuits and personalities intact. We glided into our 50th anniversary and then our 60th when he died.

Out Of The Swamp

Ken preached a homily I use everyday now. He said "we've all been in swamps if we are human." There are three ways to deal with it: one is blame, next self-pity, and the third is to work our way out of it.

I know I have been a blameful old crone lately. Easily annoyed. Choosing a critical remark to my caregivers when they goof up or don't know how to do something. This attitude affects us both negatively: with a slight twist I could explain pleasantly.

How hard is that? Plenty hard.

I know we develop addictive brain passages with a thought. Hard to change those highly developed brain passages. All addictions are hard to change, i.e. eating disorders, anorexia, bulimia, overeating, judgementalism, angry responses, prejudices, etc.....

I worked with anorectic clients often, the hardest cases for a therapist to help because it becomes ultimately addictive. When I finally got around to writing my dissertation (which is a most daunting affair), I wrote three hundred and fifty pages entitled "Delineation Of The Six Phases Of Anorexia Nervosa," developed from work with my clients. Though it leads to brain damage and in the last phase cardiac and/or renal failure, they disregard any danger. How we risk our lives is an intractable mystery. Sadly, the disease has become worldwide, regardless of the culture and social class. They don't want to get "out of the swamp."

Writing this book has gotten me out of the swamp as I get in contact with all the joyous times in my life! I realize that too often I dwelled on negatives: sad painful times that are part of every life.

More and more I strive for the third way – and am happier, more content.

An Unexpected Blessing

I had a "Reading" that was astounding. Being a skeptic at heart, I didn't expect much. But Jan Assini solved a lifelong ever-plaguing problem for me – connecting me to the universe from whence my answers came.

She said "I see a jigsaw puzzle in your life. Do you like jigsaw puzzles?" I said "No I don't and never have. I consider them a waste of time." She said, as my medium. "I see you trying to fit a piece in that doesn't fit."

In bed that night I had one of those "Aha" experiences. Of course, I've spent my life trying to fix what has gone awry with family members and clients. I've wanted to fix the world.

Now I turn all difficult situations over to the universe where they belong. My shoulders don't hurt, my belly doesn't play discordant music and I am so at peace. Whatever comes up, as things do in daily life, I evaluate the problem to see if it's the piece that doesn't fit.

Whew! My gratitude to Jan is unbounded. She says she was just the medium: the universe supplies the information. So that's where I send problems back. That night when I went to bed I laid for hours just enjoying the greatest contentful peace I have ever experienced. And I find that the most difficult situations and relationships have righted themselves.

This awareness has been the greatest experience of my life. I pass it on to anyone who wants it. At age eighty-seven I find it a delight to learn something new every day!

A Happy Ending

After all these years I realize now as I write this piece that I did, indeed, find my replacement of my dear Grandpa whom I yearned for all through my youth after his death when I was ten. Jack has all of Grandpa's qualities that I loved and so sorely missed. He is nurturing and playful, resourceful and devoted to me and our family.

I guess our elopement wasn't so impetuous after all.

Ironically I appreciate him more now that he is gone. And so it goes.

Despite everything I can breathe, I can stand, walk with a cane or walker. Win at bridge and enjoy all my beautiful gardens that my daughters, my son and the marvelous landscaper planted and care for.

I am happily back at the home place in Aurora for the beautiful summer. I have family here and spread out across the country and I have Max who will do anything I need and I love him deeply.

And always Kim who makes my life possible.

Elizabeth Poss Colebrook graduated from Hathaway Brown Preparatory school with honors and then received her Bachelor's from Vassar College. Later in her life she went to graduate school at Kent State University where she received her Masters and Doctoral degrees in psychology. After the terrifying Kent State massacre, she was appointed Director of the Crisis Center. She established her therapy practice in Aurora and Chagrin Falls. Finally retiring after many years of practice.

Betts married her childhood sweetheart and has four wonderful children. Her abounding passion was the theatre; she founded a community theatre and various community organizations in her home town Aurora.

At eighty-eight she divides her time between a home in Longboat Key Florida; where she studies a multitude of subjects that fascinate her and her home place in Aurora Ohio, where she is surrounded by her lovely gardens, a large lake and acres of woodlands that provide a nature preserve for an abundance of wildlife.

Notes:

1. Thomas Moore, *Care of the Soul*, Harper Collins/NY 1992
   A guide for cultivating depth and sacredness in everyday life.

2. Jonathan Swift (1729), *A Modest Proposal*
   For preventing the children of poor people in Ireland
   from being a burden to their parents or country, and
   for making them beneficial to the public.

3. Wayne Muller, *How, Then, Shall We Live?* Bantam Books
   06/97 Four Simple Questions That Reveal the Beauty and Meaning
   of Our Lives

4. Judith Orloft, *Second Sight*. Warner Books 05/97
   A new book on intuition.